A

VIOLENT

HEART

A VIOLENT HEART

Understanding Aggressive Individuals

GREGORY K. MOFFATT

PRAEGER

Westport, Connecticut
London

Library of Congress Cataloging-in-Publication Data

Moffatt, Gregory K., 1961–
    A violent heart : understanding aggressive individuals / Gregory K. Moffatt.
      p. cm.
    Includes bibliographical references (p.) and index.
    ISBN 0–275–97336–0 (alk. paper)
    1. Violence. I. Title.
  HM1116.M65 2002
  303.6—dc21   2001054592

British Library Cataloguing in Publication Data is available.

Library of Congress Catalog Card Number: 2001054592
ISBN: 0–275–97336–0

First published in 2002

Praeger Publishers, 88 Post Road West, Westport, CT 06881
An imprint of Greenwood Publishing Group, Inc.
www.praeger.com

Printed in the United States of America

The paper used in this book complies with the
Permanent Paper Standard issued by the National
Information Standards Organization (Z39.48–1984).

10 9 8 7 6 5 4 3 2 1

CONTENTS

Preface		vii
Acknowledgments		xi
1	Introduction to Aggression	1
2	Teach Me to Fish: The Development of Aggression	19
3	*Doli Incapax*: Violence by Children	39
4	A Port in a Storm: Gang Violence	63
5	Till Death Do Us Part: Domestic Violence	79
6	Monsters among Us: Serial Killers	97
7	Balance Due: Mass Murder	121
8	Impulsive Murder: Air Rage, Road Rage, Sports Rage	141
9	Murder for Hire: Hired Assassins, Organized Crime	165
10	Instructions from God: Hate Crimes	187
11	Unwrapping the Enigma: Homicide Investigation	203
12	Past, Present, and Future: Conclusion	217
Bibliography		233
Index		239

PREFACE

Torey Hayden, a social worker and author, published a book in 1983 entitled *Murphy's Boy*. Written for therapists who worked with disturbed children, it was an agonizing portrayal of the difficulties of breaking through the thick shell of children who have been traumatized by abuse. Within the pages of this volume, Hayden related a short poem that was written by a child she once knew. It went like this:

> A parrot is a funny bird
> I wonder when it talks
> If it knows it speaks in human words
> But still has parrot thoughts.[1]

Each year when I teach counseling with children to future therapists, I point out the sagacity of these words to my students. We each speak the language that we know. When we try to speak in another language, as a parrot does when it speaks "human words," we still have our own thoughts—thoughts in our own language. This poem has helped me to remember that even when people appear to speak my language, they may not fully understand what they are communicating to me and, likewise, I may not fully understand what they are trying to say. After many years of studying aggression, I have learned to understand its language. All of our behaviors have meaning, and they express our thoughts and emotions. Our behavior betrays our thoughts even when we think we are good at hiding our feelings. In essence, our behaviors are representations of our thoughts, and aggression, like any other action, is a form of communication.

A few years ago I was demonstrating this principle for my counseling students. I gave one student play dough, another Legos, and another crayons and paper. I instructed them to create anything they wanted using the medium that I had provided for them and, based on what their creations communicated to me, I would tell each of them something about themselves. One student had been in several of my classes in previous semesters, and he decided he would try to manipulate my interpretation of his creation. He knew some of the things that I routinely looked for in drawings, so he made sure to include them. When he was done, I told him that his attempt to manipulate my impressions in itself was revealing. His need to or interest in manipulating my impressions and interpretations told me a great deal about his thoughts.

Sigmund Freud supposed that all of our behaviors said something about us. Slips of the tongue, called "parapraxis," for example, are, according to Freud, demonstrative of what is really on our minds. We can hide some, but not all, of our thoughts from one who is skilled at interpreting the language of behavior. After studying dozens of murders and other aggressive acts, I have concluded that Freud was at least partially correct.

Many people in our culture, if not all of us, speak the language of violence in one way or another. We may speak the language of violence in tantrums, foul language, sexual harassment, vandalism, throwing of objects, abuse of children or spouses, aggressive driving, or perhaps merely in aggressive thinking. We, therefore, understand some of the acts of violence and aggression that we see on the evening news and perhaps those that we witness firsthand. When a woman kills a husband who has been abusing her, we may not be able to fully relate to her circumstances, but we can understand, at some level, the pain and frustration that caused her to kill.

However, most of us are not fluent in the language of violence. Therefore, we do not always understand violence. My children and I were recently sitting at the drive-up window of a fast-food restaurant waiting for our order. In the parking lot of a gas station across a busy highway from where we sat, we could see several boys engaged in a confrontation. Even my seven-year-old daughter was able to recognize that these boys were about to fight, which they did. However, she asked a very difficult question: "*Why* are they fighting?" Of course, I could not know the reasons for the confrontation, and since I did not know the boys, I could only guess. However, regardless of who they were and why they were fighting, the reasons they chose hitting over other possible behaviors were certainly complex. Understanding the language of violence is difficult, even in this simple example. It is even more complicated in cases of extreme aggression, like the acts of serial killers and mass murderers.

The language of aggression is present in our vocabularies from our childhood, but we develop a social order that drowns the voice of violence and channels it into other behaviors that we regard as more acceptable. Like the fading of a foreign language skill that we have long since failed to practice, our primal aggressions are only distant relatives to the language of aggression that resides within normally functioning adults. Not only are all of us capable of aggression, but most of us exhibit aggression in one form or another throughout our lives. Our behaviors may be mild, such as temper tantrums, throwing golf clubs when angry, or other similar actions, but they are aggressive nonetheless. I believe that we are all capable of killing; the language is there, but the circumstances necessary to predicate murder will never present themselves for most of us to commit the act.

Understanding violent individuals requires one to recognize causes of violence, the different types of violence, and the different permutations of personal and environmental variables that precede violent behavior. Violence takes many forms, and this book will attempt to demonstrate those various forms, including what many of us consider the ultimate form of violence—murder. My goal is to provide a look at violent behavior that the reader may have never considered, without the burden of academic terminology and complicated research studies.

I watch the news with a heavy heart when a state prepares to execute a condemned criminal. Two groups of people are almost always present outside the prison—those who oppose the death penalty and those who are there to celebrate the execution of the condemned. It is my opinion that neither of these groups, by and large, understands the complexity of thought and action that leads one to kill. No two aggressive acts are the same. Some killers, like Jeffrey Dahmer, committed such gruesome acts that one is left wondering whether some component of humanness was missing in their cognition. Yet I understand someone even at this level of deprivation. Men who repeatedly batter their own children or spouses do not draw the attention of the media the way serial killers do, but, in my opinion, they can be equally as cold and heartless as men like Dahmer—perhaps even more so.

Understanding aggression requires learning to speak its language. When a parrot speaks, I wonder—does he think he is speaking our language, or does he simply think his parrot thoughts?

AUTHOR'S NOTE

In each of the cases I discuss in these pages, I made my best effort to properly present the facts. I have relied on police reports, press releases from law enforcement, personal interviews, and media accounts of the cases herein. In any reporting of incidents, whether by law enforcement, journalists, or eye-witnesses, the possibility of error may exist. I do not print a detail about a case unless two or more sources report the same detail.

Many of the cases that I address in the following chapters have not been fully adjudicated. Therefore, I have attempted to accurately indicate the presumption of innocence by those perpetrators whose trials have not yet been completed. Details of these cases may change somewhat as the evidence in the trial is presented. Even the cases where trials have been concluded may come before the courts again if and when new evidence becomes available.

I include all of this as a caveat. My intention is not to defame or malign, chastise, or belittle the victims or perpetrators named in these cases. Rather, my goal is to help the reader more fully understand the principles presented in the book by using illustrative cases. My overriding purpose in all of my books, articles, and lectures is that by learning from the past, I might provide information that may save lives and make our world a safer, more productive place to live.

NOTE

1. Torey Hayden. *Murphy's Boy* (New York: Avon Books, 1983), p. 106.

ACKNOWLEDGMENTS

I want to thank my many friends and partners, N.H., L.B., P.O., T.O., E.D., J.O., C.P., B.M., and D.G., who have encouraged me in my research, my writing, and my professional life, and motivated me to be better at what I do. To my friend and confidant, W.H., thank you for the many hours we have spent working through life's problems.

Thanks is due to the *Georgia Journal of Professional Counseling* for publishing my research version of a portion of Chapter 5 in the Spring 2002 edition of the journal.

I wish to thank my friend and fellow writer/researcher, Desiree Cooper, columnist for the *Detroit Free Press* and commentator for National Public Radio's *All Things Considered,* for the many conversations and documents she shared with me for the valuable guidance she provided, especially in my preparation for the case of Nathaniel Abraham.

I would also like to thank my children, Megan, Kara, and Benjamin, for their patience as I traveled, interviewed, researched, wrote, and edited this book. I also thank my wife, Stacey, for her endurance as I labor over projects such as this.

CHAPTER 1

INTRODUCTION TO AGGRESSION

> Anyone can become angry, that is easy . . . but to be angry with the right
> person, to the right degree, at the right time, for the right purpose, and in
> the right way . . . this is not easy.
>
> —Aristotle

Krystal Gayle Archer was a 17-year-old student working on her general equivalency diploma (GED) in northern Georgia. In the late summer of 1999, she and three of her friends went for a walk in the woods to look for hallucinogenic mushrooms. Among them were Danielle Hubbard, age 18, Michael Christopher Teal, age 19, and 21-year-old Timothy Curtis Cole. Hubbard and Teal reportedly were dating. Cole was married and he had a new baby. His wife had recently been released from juvenile detention where she had been incarcerated for a probation violation. During her detention, Archer had been having an affair with Cole.

The motive for what happened that day is unclear. While in the woods, Archer and Hubbard began to argue. In the course of the argument all three turned on Archer, stripping her naked, beating her with rocks and sticks, and forcing her to engage in sexual acts. Afterward, they threw her down a twenty-foot ravine into a small stream. As Archer tried to climb out, struggling to save herself and begging for them to leave her alone, they threw her down the ravine two more times and then lit her hair on fire. When Archer fell unconscious the perpetrators left.

The next day, however, all three returned and found that Archer was still alive. As Archer lay unconscious, the threesome covered her body with brush, hoping that she would not be found. They returned for a third time the next day and threw rocks at her trying to ensure she was dead. Miraculously, however, Archer survived, regained consciousness, dragged herself several yards along the creek, and pulled herself to a sitting position. By the next day, with broken bones, naked and exposed to insects and weather, she had spent three nights and parts of four days lying along the shallow stream. Her face was swollen and she had difficulty seeing when she heard someone coming. Thinking someone had arrived to help her, she tried to crawl toward the strangers and asked them, "How did you find me?"[1] But, to her horror, her attackers had returned once again. This time, one of the men had a butcher knife. He stabbed her several times in the neck and chest and then slit her throat.

Several days after the murder, Cole told his wife that he had cheated on her with another woman, but that the woman was dead. For several days, Cole's story about the dead woman waffled and changed, including a mystery man named "Lance" who had allegedly raped and killed the woman. Cole told his wife that Lance called him and told him about the murder and where the body was, but he could not explain to his wife how he knew Lance. Eventually, he and his wife talked about the crime with police, who referred them to a department in another county where the crime was supposed to have occurred. Cole drove to a building in a distant county. Leaving his wife waiting in the car for almost two hours outside an old building that she thought was a police station, he was inside supposedly explaining the story about Lance to the police.

The charade deteriorated and Cole once again found himself talking to investigators. When Archer's body was found, Cole's story quickly fell apart, and all three perpetrators were arrested and charged with the crime.

Crimes like the one I have just described almost defy the imagination. Many times I have told my students that Hollywood cannot produce make-believe monsters that are scarier than the ones that already exist. Fortunately, most of us will never cross paths with monsters like Jeffrey Dahmer, Edmund Kemper, or perpetrators like those in this crime.

I began writing this book while sitting on a quiet beachfront hotel balcony in St. Petersburg Beach, Florida. As I watched people hunting for shells, couples enjoying an evening stroll, and the rolling surf, the tragedies that I see month to month seemed very far away. And yet I could see the seeds of aggression right in front of me. Three children were arguing over a bucket and shovel they were using to build a sandcastle. Just a few yards away, several young men who appeared to be on the verge of intoxication made unappreciated comments to attractive women who passed by their cabana chairs. Children fighting over toys and college boys making sexual comments are behaviors that are quite distant from the heinous crimes you will read about in this book, but they are most definitely related—first cousins, you might say.

How can one human being participate in an act as vile as the one described at the beginning of this chapter? One would think that a person who had such potential would display a variety of warning signs before anything that extreme happened. Indeed, many times they do. However, we often fail to see these warning signs, and when we do, we do not always recognize them for what they are. For example, some environments accept a certain level of aggression that would not be acceptable in another environment. When I was an undergraduate student, I worked for a painting contractor. Our company held contracts with several coal mines in eastern Virginia. Coal miners, construction workers, painters, truck drivers, and all sorts of other workers crossed paths at these sites every day. Conflict was a part of our existence. It was not unusual for a man to threaten another man or even to engage in a brawl. Fights and arguments arose over money, women, gambling, or drugs, and sometimes simply over personality conflicts. To hear someone say, "I'll beat you to a pulp" to another worker was not unusual. Since we accepted aggression as a part of the world in which we lived, it would have been difficult to distinguish between the individual who would never do anything more than tussle with another worker and the one who had the potential to kill.

For the past twenty years I have worked in a white-collar profession, a quite different environment. Nearly everyone I work with in all of my interactions is an educated professional. Not once in all of those years have I heard one of my colleagues threaten another. One difference between these two environments, among others, is education, but I think the main difference is acceptability. Those of us in the college arena have the potential to threaten one another and even the potential to act on our aggressive words, just like those on a construction site or at a coal mine. Yet how long do you think I would keep my job as a professor if I threatened my students, my colleagues, or my bosses? In the blue-collar trades I was a part of, such behavior was not seen as unusual as long as it did not go "too far." As long as one got his work accomplished, it was a part of the accepted lifestyle. Therefore, the same behavior in one environment is accepted while in another environment it is totally unacceptable. I do not suppose that the businessman is in any way better than the factory worker. Their environments are simply different, and they live up to, or down to, the expectations of their respective environments. I am confident that if you displaced an individual from his white-collar environment and relocated him in a prison, he very quickly would take on a more aggressive personality.

In the following chapters I describe various types of violence and explain why these acts occur. In order to do so, it is necessary to have some understanding of the causes of aggression. This chapter provides an overview of those causes.

CAUSES OF AGGRESSIVE BEHAVIOR

The world would be much more orderly if I could conclusively explain the cause or causes of aggression, but human behavior is far too complex to be reduced to a single cause-effect relationship. The cause-effect relationship in the human animal can only be described, correlated, and hypothesized, and from these descriptions, correlations, and hypotheses theories are then developed. By addressing these theories we can begin to explain why people are aggressive. There are many helpful theories about human behavior, but unfortunately, there is no theory that fully answers every question. When I teach psychological theory to college students, I have a difficult time getting them to understand that theories are not facts. Therefore, when they identify a problem within a given theory they don't understand how I can concede that the problem exists and yet still adhere to the theory. A theory is merely a benchmark for answering questions—it is not the answer in and of itself.

Once I was being deposed for a court case on behalf of a child I was working with in my practice. I was convinced that a biological parent had seriously mistreated the child and that mistreatment would have significant long-term effects. When I finished my statement, the attorney for the biological parent said, "Well, that is all just theory, correct?" My response was, "Yes, it is theory, but nearly every area of our lives operates on theory. The way light travels, how time operates, how and why we age, and how we learn are all based on theory." What I was trying to impress upon the court was that we operate on theory all the time. Even though some theories may appear to be more functional than others, they are still theories.

Several things distinguish good theories from bad ones. Good theories are clear, consistent, testable, and practical. They are parsimonious, that is, concise, and they are not based on numerous unfounded assumptions. Useful theories accurately reflect what we already know, and through them we can make predictions about future events. Using this information about theory, you can evaluate the information in this chapter and decide for yourself which theories of the origins of aggression seem most reasonable to you. Theories concerning the causes of aggressive behavior can be grouped into three major categories—biological, sociological, and psychological.

Biological Theories

Theories on the biological causes of aggression posit that an organism is aggressive because of some factor beyond its control or perhaps even beyond its awareness. These theories suppose that our genetic makeup or our physical or chemical nature as individuals drives us to aggressive behavior. It is theoretically possible that some people are genetically preprogrammed to be aggressive. Our personalities are clearly and directly related to our genetic makeup. When they are only hours old, infants display distinct personality traits that can only be adequately explained by genetics. Our genetic heritage has been linked to behaviors such as alcoholism as well as to mental disorders. Therefore, some researchers argue that there is a genetic component to aggressiveness.

Nearly every species exhibits "fight-or-flight" behavior—a decision-making process that determines whether a threatened organism will run or stay and fight. One supposition is that this rule system is genetically determined for the species. Rattlesnakes, for example, despite their reputation, are very passive reptiles. They will look for a way out of a confrontation at almost all costs. A rattlesnake will only strike if it has no escape, if it is surprised, or if it is protecting a nest. Snakes do not have brains that allow for complex decision making. Their decision to strike, to hide, or to flee almost certainly is based on a very primitive process that has its basis in genetics.

There is variety in the way this rule system operates across the animal kingdom. Some species are more easily provoked than others. Wasps, ants, and spiders, for example, creatures whose brains are much too small to process information in any sort of logical way, appear to have a preprogrammed set of rules that determine when they will attack and when they will try to escape. When addressing audiences on the topic of aggressive behavior, I often ask how many of them believe that they could kill another human being. Usually, about half of the audience indicates that they have the potential. Then I ask, "Suppose your child is being threatened by someone and the only way to protect him or her is to kill the perpetrator. How many of you would do it then?" With this caveat, nearly every hand will go up. The variability within the human species in this nonscientific example is based on circumstances. Even though humans have the ability to analyze circumstances, one could argue that the decision to fight would be innate nonetheless.

Specific areas of the brain may be responsible for aggressive behavior in humans. When these areas are stimulated, the person becomes more aggressive. Other areas of the brain serve as a governor for one's behavior. When these areas are disrupted or damaged, the control over aggression is interrupted, therefore making the person more aggressive. For example, it is not unusual for stroke victims to lose social skills, saying things that are inappropriate or hurtful to others. The governing area that restrained such behavior prior to the stroke has been damaged; therefore words and actions are expressed unchecked.

Phineas Gage, one of the most famous patients in brain research, was a foreman for a railroad construction company in New England in the 1800s. He and his crew prepared the land for the construction of new track. In those days, explosives were tamped into the blasting hole using a steel rod about three and a half feet long, tapered to a point at one end. Occasionally, the dynamite in the hole would ignite and the resulting explosion would propel the tamping iron out of the hole in a way very similar to a bullet leaving a rifle. In 1848 this very thing happened to Phineas Gage. The rod was propelled out of the blasting hole and struck Phineas in the head just beneath his left cheek. The rod traveled through his brain and exited through the top of his head, landing 30 or so feet behind him. A huge piece of Gage's skull was displaced as the iron exited his head. A large portion of the left hemisphere of Gage's brain, the left frontal lobe, was either damaged or completely destroyed by this accident. After the explosion, his co-workers expected to find him dead, but to their surprise, he not only survived, but some reports suggest that he may never even have lost consciousness. Gage was treated by Dr. John Martin Harlow, who successfully replaced pieces of Gage's damaged skull bone, and to the amazement of everyone, Gage seemed to recover fully from the injury. By the middle of the following year, Gage reported that he felt good enough to return to work.

Before the accident Gage was known as a well-balanced gentleman. However, during the following weeks and months, Gage's wife noted distinct changes in his personality. He became irritable and aggressive, quickly losing his temper without apparent cause. One report summarized these changes, saying he was "fitful, irreverent, and grossly profane, showing little deference for his fellows. He was also impatient, obstinate, capricious, vacillating, and unable to settle on any of the plans he devised for future action."[2] Because of these personality changes, Gage's employers refused to allow him back on the job. The only long-term physical side effect Gage suffered that could be attributed to the accident was epileptic seizures that began a few years later, but the emotional changes were distinct and permanent. He died in May 1860, a dozen years after the incident. Gage's body was eventually exhumed, and his skull and the tamping iron are presently on display at the Warren Museum of the Medical School of Harvard University. The case of Phineas Gage was a precursor of brain surgery, and it demonstrated that the brain is responsible, at least in part, for aggression.

In the late 1800s, doctors began experimenting with brain surgeries to control or correct various mental disturbances, and by the 1930s physicians had begun separating a portion of the prefrontal lobe from the rest of the brain in a procedure that was called a *lobectomy* or *lobotomy*. By the 1950s this procedure became a common treatment for a host of mental disorders including depression and violent behavior. You may recall the end of the movie *One Flew Over the Cuckoo's Nest*, where Jack Nicholson's character was given a prefrontal lobotomy in order to eliminate his aggressive behavior. While the symptoms of mental illness in patients who received this barbaric procedure did abate, the damage to the brain robbed patients of their affect. In essence, like Phineas Gage, they lost their personalities.

In modern history, one can look to Charles Whitman as a possible example of someone whose violent behavior had a biological cause. Whitman, an ex-marine and sharpshooter, stabbed his mother with a butcher knife and then shot her in the head. He placed her body on her bed, cleaned her apartment, and then went home, where he also murdered his wife with the same butcher knife. He apparently killed his wife and mother to spare them the embarrassment of being associated with what he was planning to do. The next day, August 1, 1966, he entered the clock tower at the University of Texas. On the 27th floor, he hit 51-year-old Edna Townsley, the receptionist, in the head with a rifle, knocking her unconscious. He then carried his cache of weapons, food, and other provisions outside to the observation deck. As he was laying his materials out on the floor of the observation deck, he heard a group of tourists coming up the stairwell. He shot and killed two of the visitors and wounded two others. At this point, he reportedly returned to where Townsley lay and shot her. From the observation deck, 230 feet above the street, he shot and killed 13 more people, including a policeman.

Law enforcement officers tried in vain for 90 minutes to stop the killing, but they were unable to end his shooting spree. Finally, an Austin police officer named Ramiro Martinez, along with two temporarily deputized civilians, made their way into the clock tower and stormed the observation deck where they shot and killed Whitman.

In the end, Whitman killed eighteen people (including his mother and wife) and wounded thirty. He had complained of headaches and had exhibited uncontrolled rage for some time before his shooting spree. He left a note asking that an autopsy be performed to see if something was physically wrong with him that would explain his mental struggles. The autopsy revealed a small brain tumor in his hypothalamus, an area of the brain that is closely related to aggression. Some neuropathology experts have discounted the tumor as the cause of Whitman's violent behavior, but there is at least a possibility that it contributed to his dysfunction. To my knowledge, Whitman is the only mass murderer for whom a biological cause of this nature has been demonstrated. As a side note, the Whitman episode gave rise to the development of SWAT (Special Weapons and Tactics) teams around the country.

One final biological theory addresses our chemical makeup. Testosterone, the principal male hormone, appears to be directly linked to aggressive behavior. It is no accident that boys are more aggressive than girls. Even though our culture raises boys differently and accepts a level of aggression from boys that it does not accept from girls, there is still a distinct difference between the two genders in regard to aggression. Testosterone is the most likely cause for this difference. The use of steroids, made up largely of testosterone, by body builders to enhance their muscle bulk has been a common, albeit illegal, practice for many years. A side effect of steroid use is aggressive behavior. Clearly, testosterone contributes to the reason that men far outnumber women in incidents of violent crime.

Other naturally occurring chemicals in the human body, called neurotransmitters, have also been related to aggressive behavior. Even hypoglycemia, a sugar processing disorder that affects millions of people, has been linked to violent behavior.

Chemicals artificially introduced into one's system may cause aggressive behavior. Some chemicals, such as alcohol, decrease inhibitions. Other chemicals, including amphetamines and phencyclidine (PCP), heighten one's sensitivity or increase agitation. Some reports indicated that Charles Whitman had been under the influence of amphetamines at the time of his shooting rampage.[3] Despite the information available on the connection between biology and aggression, these theories leave many questions unanswered. Sociologists have attempted to fill the void.

Sociological Theories

Social learning theories suggest that people act the way they do because of what they have learned either directly or indirectly. One's culture teaches the individual something about how to behave by communicating mores and expectations. Parents and siblings teach manners and coping skills, and peers modify, confirm, or discount these expectations as well.

When I was in the third grade, a boy in my class made a habit of picking on me after school. Many times as I walked or rode my bicycle home from school this boy would corner me and force me into a physical confrontation. I later learned that his mother had repeatedly engaged in aggressive confrontations with neighbors, once being arrested for fighting, and his father had also been disciplined for fighting at work. It should be no surprise that this child learned that fighting was an acceptable means for dealing with his frustrations and desires.

It has been years since I have heard of anyone having a "nervous breakdown." This used to be a fairly common response to severe stress in one's life. However, whereas we used to internalize our failures and misfortunes in the form of nervous breakdowns, our culture has taught us to externalize them. We have become a culture of "victims" looking for blame beyond ourselves. One way we externalize our frustrations and failures is by suing those we perceive to be responsible for our misfortunes. Our legal system has made it commonplace to search externally for blame regardless of the irresponsibility of our own behavior. When we spill hot coffee on our laps, it is not our fault for trying to drive and eat at the same time, and it is not our fault for being clumsy (as we would probably have said to a child in our car who spilled a soft drink). Rather it is the fault of the restaurant for making the coffee too hot, the cup manufacturer for making a cup that allowed the coffee to spill, or the person who sold it to us for not warning us that the coffee was hot and might spill as we drove. Take a few minutes next time you are at the hardware store to look at the warning labels on ladders and power tools. One publication listed several of these product warnings: "On a chain saw: Do not attempt to stop chain with your hands. On a mirror for a bicycle helmet: Remember—objects in the mirror are behind you. On a steering wheel lock: Warning—remove lock before driving."[4] Each of these labels, as ridiculously obvious as some of them are, was undoubtedly the result of a lawsuit. The right to sue has been around for centuries and is a necessary part of the protection of our society; however, we as Americans have perfected the extreme use of this social tool.

We expect more responsibility from our children than from ourselves. If our children were to run down a city sidewalk and trip over a raised piece of concrete, we most likely would chastise them for running, not paying attention, or something of that sort. Yet if we are the ones who trip, we sue the owner of the property on which the sidewalk is found, the city, and the construction company who laid the concrete. We have become a culture that thinks society owes us something, rather than the grateful people we were not too many years ago simply to be living in a free land. This point couldn't have been clearer to me one morning as I read an article in the paper. A cereal company had included a free CD-ROM in some of its products. Among the games and other data on the disc was a Christian bible. The CD giveaway caused an uproar. I nearly spilled my coffee as I read the comments of a rabbi who was quoted as saying, "I don't think it is right for any American to pick up a box of cereal in the morning and feel excluded."[5] While cultural sensitivity is certainly appropriate, this statement demonstrated that this rabbi believed he should be protected from "feeling excluded" at his breakfast table. For some reason public social outrage was more reasonable to this person than simply throwing the free product in the trash.

Juvenile court laws were originally written to protect children who soaped windows, vandalized property, or broke into houses. Most juvenile crime involved behaviors like these. Today, teenagers are being tried under these laws when they have committed ruthless, cold-blooded assaults, rapes, tortures, and murders. People under the age of 21 account for the majority of violent crime in the United States, yet some pundits in our culture try to excuse these behaviors as the result of environment or a dysfunctional legal system. Prior to the

1960s or so, parents held their children accountable regardless of external factors. The parents of some of the children I have seen in my practice have tried to excuse their children's behavior by comparing it to what they consider worse behavior, rather than considering the behavior as inappropriate in and of itself.

This cultural aversion to responsibility creates a society of victims. When one perceives that he is a victim, he will then feel justified in seeking restitution or even retribution. Most people will not engage in violent behavior unless they can justify their actions. Normally passive individuals can justify shooting at other human beings if they are at war. In World War II, German officers who had been teachers, bankers and other ordinary citizens were able to justify their unconscionable treatment of the Jews and of prisoners of war because they were ordered to do it.

At Yale University in 1963, Stanley Milgram did a fascinating study that portrayed how far people would go, even harming another human being, if they felt justified in their actions.[6] In Milgram's study, subjects were told that they were a part of a research project studying the effects of punishment on learning. Subjects were supposedly given an electrical shock if they did not learn a set of facts properly. In this study, one group of subjects, known as "teachers," would read pairs of words over an intercom to another group, known as "learners" in an adjacent room. The "learners" would be shocked if they recalled the pairs incorrectly. In actuality, the subjects who were allegedly receiving shocks were cohorts with Milgram in the study. This type of participant is called a confederate in research terminology. Milgram's confederates were never actually shocked. The real purpose of the study was to see to what extent the "teachers" would obey Milgram and continue administering shocks to learners. Milgram had predicted that most subjects would refuse to harm other people, but what he found was quite the opposite.

The panel of 30 switches supposedly ranged from 15 to 450 volts, with each successive switch representing a more powerful shock. The higher voltages were clearly marked with danger warnings. In the adjacent room, the confederate would make sounds as if he or she was really being shocked when the "teacher" administered the punishment. As the study progressed, the confederate would complain about the pain, ask to be allowed to quit the study, and eventually stop responding all together, as if unconscious.

Some of Milgram's subjects refused to continue the experiment when they believed that they were hurting the "learner." However, most of the subjects continued to administer shocks even when the "learner" stopped responding. An astounding 65 percent of the subjects administered shocks all the way through the 450 volt level. Most of Milgram's subjects were visibly uncomfortable with the study. Some of them argued with him, complaining that the study was unethical, and yet they continued to participate. In follow-up interviews with subjects, Milgram asked them to explain why, despite their discomfort with the study, they continued to administer shocks. The most common answer was that they believed he knew what he was doing, so they continued. In other words, they justified their behavior and obeyed Milgram simply because he was in a position of authority.

Another aspect of the sociological causes of aggression is desensitization. In American culture, we are inundated by violent themes in music, movies, and television shows. Over time, we become desensitized to the violence we see. Behaviors that once were considered unthinkable are now readily embraced by our culture. In 1939 director Victor Fleming and actor Clark Gable stunned audiences when Rhett Butler said the word "damn" in *Gone with the Wind*. It was unheard of in those days for profanity to be used in film, radio, or newsreels. By the 1960s it was becoming commonplace to hear that particular word. By then, Americans had grown accustomed to hearing this word on television and in the movies. By the mid-1980s, one of the last forbidden words (f***), a word that still is unacceptable in a publication such as this book, found its way into the movies. Profanity is a form of aggression, and in the same way that we have become desensitized to profanity, as a culture we have also become desensitized to violence. There was a time in the movies when James Dean and Marlon Brando were considered rebels because they smoked cigarettes, rode motorcycles, and lived on the "edge" of life. Their version of rebellion is comical by today's standards. We have grown to accept their form of antisocial behavior as normal.

Movies and music do not *cause* us to act a certain way, but they influence our behavior. The media coverage of school shootings spawns a rash of threats or similar acts around the country. Of course newscasts do not cause these children to copy what they saw, but they give impressionable children ideas. One 1996 movie depicted teenagers playing a dangerous game of chicken by lying in the middle of a busy highway. Just after this movie was released, a series of accidents involving similar behavior were reported around the country. Likewise, a scene from the 1985 movie *Teen Wolf* depicted actor Michael J. Fox "surfing" on the top of a moving vehicle. After this movie aired, a number of accidents around the country occurred when young people emulated this behavior. These movies did not force these teenagers to copy the behaviors they saw on the screen, but they provided an idea, glamorized the activity, and disconnected the activity from its consequences.

On final social cause involves our culture and its approach to weapons. It is undoubtedly appalling to people from other countries where guns are strictly controlled to learn that in the United States almost any adult can walk into a K-Mart or Walmart and buy a variety of ammunition and firearms, not to mention a number of other types of weapons. In Scotland, for example, even the purchase

11

of ammunition is regulated, and in Japan firearms are strictly regulated. The availability of weapons in the United States sets the stage for violent behavior. Because of their availability and the glorification of weapons in movies like *The Terminator*, *Natural Born Killers*, and *Die Hard*, our culture has, in essence, put a stamp of approval on vengeance, aggression, and the use of weapons.

Despite these logical arguments, the astute reader would no doubt notice one glaring omission. How do we account for the fact that many of us have been exposed to the same chemicals, have similar brain compositions, and have been exposed to the same cultural issues that are linked to aggression, and yet have not engaged in violence? To account for such individual differences, we must also consider psychological theories.

Psychological Theories

There are individual issues that must be considered when studying the causes of violent behavior. Certainly, mental health is an issue. People who do not accurately perceive reality could easily either justify or perceive it to be necessary to behave in a violent manner. Individuals whose thinking is disrupted by disease, who have poor social or coping skills, or who suffer from dysfunctional thinking may behave aggressively as well. They may misinterpret the words or behaviors of others and believe they are being threatened and, in defense, they may behave aggressively. In its extreme, mental illness may cause a person not only to misinterpret the behaviors of others, but also to completely create events in his or her own mind, believing that those events are real. Russell Weston, Jr., who in 1998 killed two security officers at the United States Capitol building in Washington, D.C., believed that the government was housing a thing called the "ruby satellite" in the Capitol and was using this thing to turn people into cannibals. Because of his mental illness, Weston truly believed that this was really happening, and his delusions made it possible for him to justify his violent behavior within his own mind.

Patients in geriatric care facilities sometimes act aggressively toward their caretakers as a result of senility or dementia. Like schizophrenia, the disorder that affected Weston, patients suffering from these disorders misinterpret behavior. They may hear voices, and they may hallucinate. It is not uncommon for Alzheimer's patients to believe that the hospital staff is stealing from them or even threatening to harm them. Sadly for hospital administrators and patients alike, this form of abuse sometimes actually does occur, and it becomes a challenge for hospital staff to distinguish real events from the events fabricated in the minds of patients suffering from these diseases.

Another psychological cause of aggression is poor coping and social skills. Children will quickly resort to hitting when they run out of other ideas for dealing with their frustrations. The frustration-aggression hypothesis states that as a person's frustration builds, he will eventually resort to aggression. This is the proverbial straw that broke the camel's back. One's ability to cope plays a significant role in the prevention of aggression. The more effectively a person copes with frustration, the less likely he is to engage in aggressive behavior. Parents must teach their children how to cope with anger, resentment, and disappointment in ways that are acceptable within their culture, but there are several ways in which this educational process can fail. Children may be taught inappropriate coping and social skills, as was the case with the classmate I described above, or they may not be taught appropriate skills at all. It is also possible that even when a parent attempts to teach these skills the child may fail to learn effective coping and social skills. In all three of these circumstances, when these children are frustrated they may resort to aggression, continuing to use these unproductive strategies into adulthood. Their aggression is due not to mental illness or disease, but simply to the fact that they have not learned any better. Treating this type of patient is, in part, merely a matter of education (assuming willingness on the part of the patient).

Even when one has learned effective coping skills and is not suffering from the effects of mental illness, emotional and physical abuse can wear down one's resistance to aggressive behavior. In the 1980s when the post office was experiencing a rash of shootings, one theory as to the cause of this outbreak was that the postal environment was emotionally abusive. While this was never scientifically demonstrated, it made sense and the post office took steps to correct this perceived problem. Consequently, the 1990s saw fewer shootings in this environment.

One final psychological issue involves the psychological contract. At work, home, and play we engage in agreements with each other as to how we will relate and how our relationships will begin and end. Some of these agreements are formal contracts, such as the written contract you receive when you begin a job. Other agreements are less formal, but psychologically they are equally powerful. These psychological contracts are expectations that a person has with another person or group. For example, when one begins dating another person, it is understood in our culture that the dating relationship is a trial—a time to test the compatibility of the two individuals. Either person is free to disengage from the relationship if he or she decides that it is not what he or she is seeking. Stalkers, however, may believe that the other person does not have the right to end the relationship. They believe that the other person was committed to them simply because they dated—even if it was just one date. In essence, they incorrectly perceive a contract with the other, and they refuse to let it go.

The same kind of thing happens at businesses. We all know that there is a possibility that we could lose our jobs. We could be fired for failure to perform, but we could also be dismissed because of financial hardship within the company—something totally beyond our control. A person with healthy coping skills accepts, however reluctantly, a misfortune such as a layoff and moves on with his or her life. Some people, however, perceive that they have been wronged and personally attacked by the employer. They believe that the "understanding" between employer and employee was that the employee would keep his job as long as he performed properly. Even though this is sometimes a safe assumption, we know that this is not always true. Around the country, airlines, manufacturing plants, and other industries lay off employees simply for fiscal reasons. There is no promise that one will always have a job, but because of the psychological contract, one assumes that the job will always be there.

Psychological contracts operate in marriages as well. Most people who marry in this country do so in a religious ceremony of some sort. In that ceremony, each partner agrees to stay with the other permanently, and yet the obvious reality is that many marriages end in divorce. When one files for divorce, one is asking to break the legal contract of marriage. Perhaps even more significant than the legal contract of marriage, however, is the psychological contract. While we all know that many marriages fail, we do not think it will happen to us. I have spent hundreds of hours with engaged couples in premarital counseling and have yet to meet a couple who thinks they are going to divorce someday. When one partner finds out the other is having an affair, for example, it shakes his or her reality. Even though the victim may know that affairs happen, her belief system does not accept that behavior as a possibility in her own relationship. Hence, the underlying assumptions and agreement between the two are violated. This violation is deeply distressing. At its extreme, this violation predicates violent behavior.

PERSPECTIVE AND EXPECTATIONS

One final point is important to consider. On rare occasions, the way we interpret aggressive behavior is a matter of perspective. What one thinks to be true is, in fact, reality for that individual; therefore, an understanding of perspective and expectations is crucial.

In December 1995, three undercover Atlanta police officers were on patrol as a part of their precinct's Field Investigative Team (FIT). As Officers Willie Sauls, Waine Pickney, and Ivant Fields drove toward the International House of Pancakes, where they had planned to eat, they passed a Pontiac 6000 occupied by four young men. Ironically, the car was similar to the cars driven by Atlanta's undercover officers, and their first thought was that it contained colleagues who were also on duty. But as the officers passed the Pontiac, they did not recognize the men in the car.

The officers said that the vehicle's occupants avoided their gaze and behaved suspiciously, so they turned around to follow the vehicle, believing it may have been stolen. The occupants of the car later said they thought the three men in the unmarked car were looking at them because their vehicles were similar. The four young men turned abruptly into a parking lot next to a motorcycle shop, and by the time the officers arrived the car was empty. One officer checked on the tag number of the car while another looked through a nearby dumpster. Officer Sauls headed toward the front of the motorcycle shop.

The car was not stolen and, as police would later learn, the men had apparently been going to the shop to check on repairs that were being made on a motorcycle belonging to one of them. Inside the shop, the four men discussed motorcycles with four employees of the store while Sauls was on his way toward the shop entrance. By chance, an automobile accident nearby created a loud noise that aroused the attention of the men in the shop. Believing a car accident had occurred, they headed toward the door to see what was going on. The officers, however, heard the loud noise and, since they already suspected that the shop was being robbed, thought a robbery was in progress. As Sauls approached the entrance, he encountered what he thought were robbers leaving the scene. However, the men were only going to investigate the noise. Sauls, weapon drawn, ordered the men to the floor.

At this point, the patrons of the shop saw an individual with a weapon shouting orders. They claimed that the undercover officer never identified himself as a police officer and that his credentials were not in view. Therefore, as Sauls attempted to search one of the men, a mechanic in the shop believed they were being robbed. He pulled out his legally registered weapon and shot Officer Sauls twice. Sauls, in pain and yelling for help, unloaded his 9mm weapon into the store and then crawled for cover behind a car in front of the business. By this time, Officer Pickney rounded the corner and saw his colleague down and bleeding. His perception of the situation was that a robbery had gone bad and Sauls had been shot.

Some of the men inside the shop headed to the back for cover, while 24 year-old Danny Jackson, one of the occupants of the Pontiac, ran toward the front. As Officer Pickney approached he fired several times. Jackson fell to the ground, and bullet fragments glancing off the pavement sheared through his neck. He died as a result of these wounds.

As uniformed officers began to arrive, they found Sauls and a civilian in the shop wounded, and Jackson lying on the sidewalk with no pulse. He was later officially pronounced dead at the scene. This became a very complicated legal case in the city of Atlanta. Details of what happened varied depending on who was telling the story. It is quite plausible, however, that everyone was telling the truth even though their stories were incompatible. For example, the men in the shop said that Officer Sauls never identified himself as a police officer, and yet Sauls maintained that he did. One man in the shop said that he did not learn that the men were officers until much later that day. The men in the shop and the police officers alike believed a robbery was occurring, but the difference in perspective involved who was robbing whom. It is quite possible that Sauls did, in fact, identify himself as a police officer. However, in the fleeting first moments of an intense situation like a robbery, he may not have identified himself forcefully enough to override the first impression of those in the shop that they were being robbed. We have all experienced this in a lesser form. Have you ever thought someone was going to tell you one thing and yet, when they said something else, you responded to the expected statement rather than the actual one?

As we attempt to analyze aggressive behavior, we must keep in mind that our expectations and perceptions direct our minds as we seek meanings of the behaviors we see. The civilians in this story worked and lived in a neighborhood with a high rate of violent crime. The noise they heard outside the building was initially correctly interpreted as an automobile accident. Yet when they were surprised by a man with a weapon, they quickly changed their perspective to match the new information and assumed Officer Sauls was attacking them. We know that at least one member of the shop allowed for such expectancies because he chose to carry a firearm.

The officers were already under the impression that the four men were up to no good. When they heard the car accident, they interpreted the noise within their perceptual framework, and what appeared to be men "fleeing" the shop confirmed these expectancies. Giving even more credibility to Sauls' perception that a robbery was in progress was the fact that someone shot him. While I am not blaming these men for their expectations and perceptions, it is evident that if all of them had correctly interpreted the behavior of the others, there would have been no gunfire that day.

No charges were filed against the officers, but the city lost a lawsuit when a federal judge ruled that the officers had "no justifiable reason to make an investigatory stop."[7] Both sides of this confrontation believed that the other was acting offensively when it is theoretically possible that they were all being defensive. Perspective directed action, and from action, two men received injuries and one died. Adding even another twist to the perspective on this case, several witnesses in an adjacent building saw some of these events and believed that a drug deal had gone bad. Was it a drug deal, a robbery, or simply a terrible mistake in perception?

CONCLUDING REMARKS

In this chapter I have discussed the variety of theories that address aggressive behavior. The motives of individuals when they commit aggressive acts are complicated. Biological, sociological, and psychological theories can be used to hypothesize motives for violence and aggression.

The murder of Krystal Gayle Archer, described at the beginning of the chapter, can be addressed using any or all of these theories. It is possible that all three of these alleged perpetrators were biologically predisposed to behave aggressively and chance brought them together on this occasion. Perhaps the chemicals in their system, either synthetic or natural, goaded them toward aggression. Social factors may have been at the root of their behavior. Perhaps their parents or society taught them that aggression was the most efficient way to pursue their short- and long-term goals. I suppose it is possible that all three of these young adults suffered from mental disorder, dysfunctional thinking, or poor coping skills and that these deficits led to their actions. Most likely, however, no single cause can explain their behavior. I propose that a complex interaction of all three of these theories is at the heart of the answer. In the following chapters I will address a variety of forms of aggression and explain the forces that goaded these perpetrators to their actions. These three theories are bases for my explanations.

NOTES

1. Susan Gast, "Torture, murder mystify Madison," *Atlanta Journal/Constitution*, September 3, 1999, p. E6.

2. "Phineas Gage's Story," *www.hbs.deakin.edu.au/gagepage/PGSTORY.HTM*, August 29, 2001.

3. "Austin's darkest hour: August 1, 1966," *www.members.xoom.com/_XMCM/ towertragedy/index.html*, May 2001.

4. *Reader's Digest*, April 2000, p. 101.

5. "Cereal maker apologizes for CD-ROM Bible giveaway," *Atlanta Journal/ Constitution*, July 23, 2000, p. A16.

6. Stanley Milgram, "Behavioral study of obedience," *Journal of Abnormal and Social Psychology* 67 (1963): 371–378.

7. Bill Rankin, "Police faulted in fatal '95 shootout; three Atlanta cops violated the rights of four people before a deadly exchange at the Moto Cycles shop, judge rules," *Atlanta Journal/Constitution*, July 29, 1998, p. B1.

CHAPTER **2**

TEACH ME TO FISH: THE DEVELOPMENT OF AGGRESSION

All of us, to some degree, remain in the shadow of our own unsatisfied childhood.

—Carl Goldberg, *Speaking with the Devil*

Even though there are a few rare exceptions, violent individuals are not born that way. Instead, they become violent through the process of cultural and sociological interaction, individual physiology, and psychological development. There is an old saying that goes like this: "Catch me a fish and I'll eat for a day. Teach me to fish and I'll eat for a lifetime." The meaning of this saying is that you can do something for someone once, but they gain nothing beyond the moment. But if you teach a way of life, the learner's life is changed by that experience—perhaps permanently. We often fail to fully appreciate the significance of our impact as parents and as a culture on developing children. We are driven to discover our own identity and our place in society. We seek approval from people in our lives whom we care about and respect. Even though the culture has an effect on children, parents are usually the most significant people in the lives of young children. As they approach adolescence, their peers gain more power over them, providing interaction that teaches them their place in society. Throughout life, even adults have this psychosociological need to belong, self-evaluate, and have their thoughts and actions evaluated by others.

My children sit in my lap and look to me for identity and purpose. When they show me a story they have written or a drawing they have done, they are not only interested in the drawing. In fact, the drawing itself is only a tool for seeking the answer to a bigger question—"Am I OK?" When my children bring me a report card, something they have created, or something they have done during their playtime, they are quite ready to forget about its existence almost the moment that I comment on it. If I say, "I'm very impressed with your drawing," the child will return to some other activity and never ask about the picture again. What my child sought was not a compliment on the picture, but a comment on his or her identity. A parent's words, "I like your picture," are translated by the child as "I like you." By the same token, if a parent implies either directly or indirectly that the child's work is not good enough, the child translates those words to mean, "I'm not good enough."

Daily, we are teaching our children to "fish" through our words and by our behaviors, but our actions teach as much, if not more, than our words. For example, a father can say to his children, "I love you." But if he fails to spend time with his children, instead investing all of his energy in his personal and professional pursuits, his actions will more likely communicate exactly the opposite message—"You are not important to me."

Most of my adult clients over the years bore emotional scars from their pasts. The worldviews of these clients were based on a combination of things that their parents did or did not do, thoughtless things they said, and things they failed to say. The difficulties my clients had in their present lives were directly related to some of these events, and these were children of well-meaning parents. Imagine the complications that arise when parents are not well intentioned. For example, Ricardo Jose Davila and Josefa Davila were sentenced to 89 years in prison in 2001 for torturing their son. The couple forced the 12-year-old boy to eat his own vomit, locked him in a bathroom for days at a time, tied him up and blindfolded him, and duct-taped a bucket to his head. They also beat him with spoons and with a hammer. In court, the couple claimed that they were trying to bring the boy up right, but I believe that a reasonable adult could see that this was clearly abusive behavior. Unfortunately, there are many children living with parents just like this all over the country.

The culture at large is a part of this teaching process as well, through both words and action. Again, actions are usually clearer messages than words. For example, no matter how many public service messages air saying "Stop the violence," our children receive a louder message. Through movies, television, videos, music, advertisements, and athletics, our culture teaches that violence is acceptable or even expected. Whether we like it or not, our culture influences the way we think. I was very frustrated during the impeachment proceedings of the late 1990s. The president had lied under oath in a deposition, he had looked the American people in the face and lied, and he lied to his family, his closest friends, and his advisors. When the president was clearly caught in his deception, he aired a brief public apology, but then followed his words with a host of accusations against his political enemies, thus removing the focus from his behavior and directing it to others. Polls indicated that more than half of the American people accepted this as business as usual. Later, just as he was leaving office as president, he brokered a deal with the independent counsel to avoid prosecution. "I tried to walk a fine line between acting lawfully and testifying falsely, but I now recognize that I did not fully accomplish this goal and am certain my responses to questions about Ms. Lewinsky were false," Clinton said in a written statement.[1] Carefully wording his statement, he still would not say that he lied. Again, the public accepted this as a reasonable response. Regardless of one's political or religious bent, it is my opinion that this event sent a very disturbing message to us all about who we are and what we value.

Of course, the president's behavior does not cause violence in future generations. The focus of my comments is not the president, but rather the public's response to his situation. The majority of the people accepted his behavior, saying that he was doing a good job as president, so honesty was not that important. The cultural message is clear to me. We are willing to accept behavior from a professional that we probably would not accept from our children. Issues of character are secondary to our personal interests.

We can see similar behavior outside the political arena. At the end of the 1996 baseball season, Baltimore Oriole Roberto Alomar, after being thrown out of the game for arguing a called third strike by umpire John Hirschbeck, spit in Hirschbeck's face as the two argued at home plate. Commentators and the public at large condemned this deliberate and contemptuous behavior. However, the American League president merely slapped Alomar on the wrist, imposing a five-day suspension. That suspension, however, was to be served at the beginning of the next season, making it possible for Alomar to play in the playoff games that were just a few days away. The majority of the fans cheered as Alomar took the field a few days later for a game the Orioles went on to win. As the president would do three years later, Alomar apologized publicly, but then went on to provide excuses for his inexcusable behavior.

Much of what our children learn about our culture is gleaned through the media. Television, radio, movies, magazines, and other media teach our children how to behave. Aggression has been directly related to various media over the years. A study from Stanford University published in 2001 in the *Archives of Pediatrics and Adolescent Medicine* showed that the more television and video games grade school children were exposed to, the more physically and verbally aggressive they were. In turn, when children were exposed to less television and video games, their aggressive behavior decreased.[2] This may seem self-evident to you, but it is actually a new finding. It was once thought that television and video games detrimentally affected only children who were already aggressive, causing them to be more aggressive. Yet this new study presents the possibility that even nonaggressive children become more aggressive based on television and video game exposure, and that reducing exposure to these media can be a treatment for aggressive behavior in both types of children—those who are already aggressive and those who are not.

Another study, done at Penn State University, linked the amount of time children spent in day care and the level of aggressiveness in those children. This study demonstrated that children who spent 30 hours or more a week in day care were almost three times as likely to be considered aggressive by teachers, mothers, and caregivers.[3]

Other sociological processes are at work in our culture that predispose us to be aggressive. There are two general dichotomous cultural positions on opposite ends of a cultural continuum—individualism and collectivism. Collectivist cultures are group dependent and seek cooperation among their members. Collectivist cultures emphasize group cohesiveness—what is best for the group—rather than individual rights or choice. They base their emotional responses on how issues affect others; hence, the members of such cultures are more likely to take responsibility for their circumstances. When one takes responsibility for one's situation, and that situation is unpleasant, the resulting internalized emotion is shame. Asian cultures are more collectivist than otherwise. American culture is at the opposite end of the spectrum. Far from being collective, it is a culture that pursues individualism. Individualistic cultures seek individual self-reliance and foster competition among their members. Emphasis is placed on personal happiness, regardless of how it may affect the group or unit. We take little responsibility for our circumstances; therefore, our emotional responses to unpleasant outcomes are externalized, resulting in anger.

Suppose two men, one in Japan and one in America, both are fired on the same day. For the sake of argument, let's suppose their circumstances are nearly identical—they have similar jobs, similar financial needs/obligations, their family circumstances are the same, and so forth. The Japanese man, however, has been taught by his culture that he is responsible for his actions, that his behavior reflects on his family, and that one should never bring shame upon one's household. For this man, internalizing the event of losing his job causes regret, shame, and a sense of failure. The situation may seem irreparable and hopeless. An extreme reaction would be to destroy the one responsible for the shameful behavior (self) by killing oneself. It is for this reason that suicide is not uncommon in Japan.

The American, however, has been taught that you get what you go after and that the culture owes you a chance. He has learned that you don't have to take responsibility because you can sue for things that are your own fault. There-fore, in this individualistic culture, the loss of a job is seen as something done to the man, rather than a result of something the man has done. Hence, the ex-treme reaction here would be to externalize rage by destroying the cause (i.e., killing the boss who fired him).

Members of individualistic cultures expect things that are not expected in other cultures. For example, the Western culture in which we find ourselves is one of the most affluent in the history of the world. We have more leisure time and more expendable income than any people in history. What some American families spend on dog food in a year exceeds the entire annual income of many families in other countries around the world. Yet somehow, in all of this afflu-ence, we still find ourselves wanting more. In short, we have very little grati-tude for what we have. Our ungracious, individualistic nature has created a population of egocentric and hedonistic people. The less gracious we are, the more we believe that we are owed something. When we believe others owe us something, we feel self-justified in our anger when we do not get what we want. This issue is covered in more detail during the discussion of road rage and air rage in Chapter 8.

As you will see in the following case study, a person's behavior is the result of a number of variables. One must remember, however, that the most important variable is one of choice. People choose their behaviors based on their options, experience, and abilities. Choice is complicated in the case of children because of their cognitive limitations. As you will see in Chapter 3, children are incapa-ble of fully understanding the meanings of their choices—choices that sadly have led to the deaths of others. Therefore, individuals always have some level of responsibility for their circumstances, but that level of responsibility changes as one moves from childhood to adulthood.

Finally, let me summarize by saying that aggressive behavior develops over time. Psychologist Carl Goldberg writes in his book, *Speaking with the Devil: Exploring Senseless Acts of Evil*, that "evil" people go through six stages in the process of becoming thoughtless, emotionless, and mean.[4] These six stages, shame, contempt, rationalization, justification, inability or unwillingness to self-examine, and magical thinking, do not appear by themselves. Because ag-gressive behavior is developmental, it takes time and requires interaction be-tween the potentially malevolent person and others. For example, one cannot be "shamed," the first concept in the development of a malevolent person, by a dog, a piece of furniture, or an automobile. "According to German philoso-pher Georg Hegel, shame is anger about 'what ought not to be.' "[5] Shame re-quires an interaction between at least two people—the one with the power to shame and the one being shamed. This process takes time, and one can argue that, since it is developmental, the process can be interrupted. Ideally, interventions will not only stop the subject's digression toward violence, malevolence, or aggression, but will also reverse the process.

NATHANIEL JAMAR ABRAHAM

Perhaps no case could more poignantly portray the complex developmental interaction of familial, social, physiological, and psychological circumstances than that of 11-year-old Nathaniel Abraham. On October 31, 1997, the police liaison officer at Lincoln Middle School removed Nathaniel, his face painted for a Halloween party, from his classroom. Waiting in the hall was a Pontiac, Michigan, detective who was prepared to arrest Nathaniel, a tiny, 65-pound, four foot, nine inch boy, for first-degree murder, assault with intent to murder, and two counts of possession of a firearm in commission of a felony. Two nights before, 18-year-old Ronnie Greene, Jr., himself a young man to whom trouble had been no stranger, was shot to death outside a Pontiac convenience store. Nathaniel was accused of that murder.

Some said that Nathaniel was a child with a caring mother who chose a life of delinquency and that he elected to travel the path that led to the murder of Ronnie Greene, Jr. Others, however, insist that he was a victim of a society that failed to protect him and failed to provide resources to help him. They charge that the system failed to implement services on his behalf even when those services were directly sought, and that society failed to intervene during the numerous times opportunities arose. I aver that there is truth to both arguments. How could an 11-year-old commit first-degree murder? Analysis of this case reveals the complexity of that question.

Nathaniel's Background

Like that of many children in the United States, Nathaniel's family dynamic was complicated. His mother, Gloria, was a hard-working high school graduate. Her own mother died when she was nine years old, and her neighbors, Claudine and Tommy Williams, helped Gloria's father raise her and her five siblings. This same caring couple would later help raise Nathaniel. By 1986 Gloria had three children, Nathaniel being the youngest. Gloria never married Dennis Peoples, the father of these three children, and he abandoned his family just before Nathaniel's birth in 1986, leaving her alone to provide for her children. Having limited resources, she and her children moved in with her surrogate parents, Claudine and Tommy Williams. They remained in the Williams home for two years, at which time Gloria graduated from business college. By then, Gloria was financially prepared to move out on her own, but Nathaniel chose to stay with the Williamses. With some hesitation, his mother agreed, and Nathaniel stayed there for the next six years.

During his stay with the Williamses, Nathaniel seemed to be a normal child. They doted on him as an only child in their home. He engaged in normal school activities and had no trouble with the police. There is some evidence that Nathaniel was having behavioral problems during his stay with the Williamses, but they paid little attention to them, supposing them to be normal boyhood problems. His only recorded school problems related to his academic abilities. Even so, his teachers thought his problems were more far-reaching, even as early as kindergarten. On his kindergarten report card his teacher expressed concern about his self-control and his social-emotional development. Report cards from later classes indicated not only that his behavior was a concern, but that it was interrupting his learning.

In the meantime, his older brother was experiencing legal troubles, was skipping school, and had begun to affiliate with a local youth gang. He was eventually sent to live with his father in Minnesota. Also, during Nathaniel's stay with the Williamses, Gloria took up with a second man by the name of Robert Williams and gave birth to her fourth child. Williams, several years older than Gloria, asked her to marry him, but she declined his offer. Even after their relationship ended and he moved out of Gloria's home, he attempted to be a good father, spending time with not only his own child, but also with Gloria's other children. He stayed in Gloria's home, sometimes for several days at a time, and the children would also spend time in his home. Nathaniel looked up to him, but when Nathaniel was eight, about a year before he moved back home with his mother, Robert Williams died.

Five years after leaving Nathaniel with the Williamses, Gloria was prepared to move once again, this time into a larger home. Nathaniel, now eight years of age, made the decision to join his mother, his siblings, and his half-sibling in their new home. By this time, Gloria's sister, who suffered from schizophrenia, was living in the home as well. In 1995 Nathaniel's brother also moved back home from his father's house in Minnesota. By his tenth year, Nathaniel had experienced many difficult circumstances that most children do not have to endure. He had been born to an unwed mother, abandoned by his father, displaced from his home, separated from his mother and siblings, albeit by his own choice, and reunited with them. His quasi-stepfather, of whom he was very fond, died with little warning, leaving Nathaniel's delinquent brother as his primary male role model. Also complicating his home life, Gloria, in an effort to provide for her family, was working nights. She was excited about her job, and for the first time she had a job with benefits and set hours, as well as a chance for raises and promotion. Gloria was not out carousing or neglecting Nathaniel and his siblings, but nonetheless, her children had to care for themselves during her working hours. Given this unstable upbringing, it should be no surprise that Nathaniel began having problems. He began sneaking out of the house at night, following in his brother's delinquent footsteps.

Recognizing trouble, Gloria asked her sister, Doris, to pick Nathaniel up from school and to make sure he got home safely. Many days, Nathaniel was not where he was supposed to be when Doris arrived and she spent hours looking for him. Even when she did get him home safely, he would sneak out of the house as soon as he could, wandering the streets of his neighborhood where drugs were available and gangs and prostitutes felt at home. Despite a city-imposed curfew of 10:00 P.M. for children his age, Nathaniel was out on the street by himself at all hours of the night while his mother worked.

Neighbors and friends began to notice a digression in Nathaniel. According to some classmates, he could be nice at school, but mean in other places. His own mother even realized that Nathaniel was becoming a bully. It was the school system that made what was perhaps the most overt attempt to intervene and help Nathaniel. During his second grade year, the first attempt was made to identify Nathaniel's academic and emotional problems and to correct them. The school system tested him and found his IQ to be below average. Tests also identified him as emotionally impaired and showed that Nathaniel was "functioning three to four years below his age level."[6] He was taken out of the mainstream classroom and placed in a special education program for part of the day. By his sixth grade year, he was completely out of the mainstream classroom altogether. Between second and sixth grades, the school gradually changed his placement, even moving him to several different schools, in their attempt to improve his academic performance. Nathaniel's conduct both in and out of the classroom also began to digress. In 1996 he attended three or four sessions with a mental health counselor, but his mother noted that he did not respond well to the counselor. She asked to have a new community mental health counselor assigned to her son, specifically a black male counselor that she believed her son could most readily relate with, but her request was denied. Therefore, she stopped taking her son, and the counseling he received proved unhelpful. His aunt (Doris) told Gloria that Nathaniel would eventually either "kill someone or they'd kill him."[7]

It may have been inevitable that Nathaniel would eventually take a life, either intentionally or by accident. He was immature, he had no guidance, and he had a temper. Nathaniel was suspected by police of using a metal pipe to beat two different individuals. He also had developed an interest in guns. At least five or six times, Nathaniel allegedly either used a weapon to commit a crime or handled a weapon carelessly. His mother was opposed to having guns in the house, but this did not stop Nathaniel from bringing them home. Once he brought home a BB gun. When he could not find the gun, he became angry, accusing his aunt of hiding it. When he finally found the BB gun, he shot both his sister and his mentally disabled aunt with it.[8] Neither was seriously wounded, but this behavior demonstrated his willingness to fire a weapon at another human being. Even though police were called about this incident, they did not intervene.

In August 1996 he was the suspect in a street shooting, and he allegedly robbed a woman of her purse at gunpoint in the fall of 1997. Also in 1997, he allegedly pulled a gun on a nine-year-old, and one month after that he threatened to shoot a ten-year-old boy. On October 23, 1997, just six days before the killing, his mother found a stolen shotgun in her basement and turned it in to police, telling them that her son was a high risk. Again, Nathaniel was not held accountable for stealing the weapon or for possessing the weapon as a minor.

Police records indicate that Nathaniel began a digressive spiral that started in early 1997. Sometime in 1997 Nathaniel began spending a great deal of time with a street gang—the same gang his brother had joined some years before. Of his 22 contacts with police, which included assault, burglary, arson, and other crimes, 19 were between February and his arrest at the end of October. Eight of those contacts were between February and May 1997, and 11 of them were between late September and the end of October 1997. There is no question that Nathaniel was often in trouble. He allegedly committed assault, he misused firearms, and he allegedly was a thief and a burglar. But the grouping of these behaviors, February to May and September to October, leads me to believe that Nathaniel could have been helped even as late as October 1997, before the murder. In other words, if social services had intervened, even as late as the end of October, Nathaniel might be on a different course in his life and Ronnie Greene might still be alive. Finally, the night of the murder, he nearly shot a neighbor as he and a friend fired a stolen .22-caliber rifle in his backyard, the same .22 he used to kill Ronnie Greene. Given this history, it is somewhat amazing that he hadn't taken a life sooner. Although his police record shows that he was only charged with two crimes, the murder of Greene and one case of burglary, by the time he was arrested for Greene's murder, he had 22 contacts with police, and according to the prosecutor, 5 involved a firearm.[9]

Nathaniel's school behavior seriously digressed in the fall of 1997 as well. He was involved with using both drugs and alcohol, but the severity of this problem was not identified until several years after the shooting. He was in a new school and he apparently had difficulty adjusting. He was suspended from school four times in October, twice for aggression. In the first case he was suspended for fighting, and the second suspension, on October 14, was for attacking his girlfriend. The last two suspensions, October 24 and October 27, were for leaving class without permission and disregarding school rules. It was during the October 27 suspension that he broke into a home, stole the .22-caliber rifle, and killed Ronnie Greene. Given this chain of events, one has to wonder if sending a troubled boy like Nathaniel out on his own is an effective intervention.

During the two years that preceded the murder, except for the intervention by the school system, Nathaniel was ignored by the social systems that were put in place to intervene with children like him. It might not surprise us if his case got lost in an understaffed system, overloaded with paperwork. Yet several times his mother tried to make sure the system did not lose him—to make sure his paperwork did not get lost on some caseworker's desk. She took a proactive position to use the system to help her son. His mother asked Oakland County Children's Village, a facility for abused, neglected, and delinquent youth, to take her son, but they refused. She encouraged neighbors to call police when they complained about her son, hoping that his case would eventually be noticed and that some intervention would take place. "I was trying to build a case," his mother said.[10] Once, when police had detained Nathaniel, they called his mother and told her to come get him. When she said it would be good for Nathaniel to spend the night in jail to learn a lesson, they threatened to charge her with child abuse if she didn't come pick him up.[11] The system did not lose Nathaniel. It denied him.

Some people have criticized Gloria for not getting help for Nathaniel. Her older son had been through the system and eventually ended up at the Children's Village. She had worked through the criminal justice system before, allowing the legal system to work, which resulted in help for her older son. Perhaps she could have done more, but it would be easy to make such a judgment from the comfort of our offices and homes. Part of her may have given up on trying to change Nathaniel or to get help for him. Having worked with difficult children for more than 15 years, I know they can be exasperating and overwhelming. Perhaps she was not ready to fight the government gauntlet a second time. It is also possible she did the best she knew how.

Police claim to have referred Nathaniel to a youth assistance organization, but the youth assistance program argued that they never received the referral.[12] A county caseworker told reporters that some of the issues that appeared on Nathaniel's record were "automatic petitions" for interventions.[13] "If you don't send the kid through the system, it gives him the idea he can do what he wants without consequences."[14] That is, in fact, exactly what happened to Nathaniel. This was the child who killed Ronnie Greene, Jr.

The Day of the Shooting

The day of the shooting, Nathaniel and a friend went to another boy's home and retrieved .22-caliber rifle shells that belonged to the boy's father. The shells fit the .22 rifle that Nathaniel had stolen during the time he was suspended from school. The boys then went to Lincoln Middle School carrying the shells and the rifle. After shooting at street lights behind the school, they returned to Nathaniel's home. Just after 7 P.M., a 19-year-old neighbor heard the gunshots. The man was not concerned about the boys shooting the gun. He talked with them for a few minutes and then left them alone, thinking they would shoot the gun a few times and then go inside. Around that same time, another neighbor, Michael Hudack, also came outside to see what was going on. He saw Nathaniel in his own backyard and was about to intervene when a bullet whizzed past him, narrowly missing his head. Hudack went inside and called the police, but by the time they arrived, Nathaniel and his friend had gone to another boy's home, where they fired the rifle at balloons.

When they tired of shooting the rifle, Nathaniel wanted to leave the weapon under a porch at the friend's house, but the boy's mother refused to allow it, so Nathaniel left with the gun in tow. Later, around 9 P.M., he found himself on a hillside just beyond a small "mom and pop" convenience store where three friends, Ronnie Greene, Jr., Carlos Falu, and Cory Brock, had gone to buy beer. Ronnie was an 18-year-old who had experienced a life of drugs, alcoholism, and delinquency. His older sister had raised him after their parents divorced. Six months before the shooting, Ronnie's young niece died of meningitis. According to those who knew him, he was finally trying to get his life together and make something of himself.

Falu crossed the street ahead of his friends and waited for the other two to join him. As Falu looked back at his friends, Nathaniel fired two rounds from the rifle. Falu saw Greene fall face first onto the pavement. One round from the .22 had hit him in the forehead. Greene was taken to a hospital, where he died less than 48 hours later.

After shooting Greene, Nathaniel went home and hid the weapon. Around 10 P.M., he knocked on a neighbor's door, and she could tell by the look on his face that something was wrong. "Something terrible has happened," he told her.[15] His neighbor's roommate took him home, but his mother was still at work. Nathaniel then returned to the convenience store and watched events unfold as police investigated the crime scene.[16] But like so many children who commit crimes, Nathaniel could not keep his activities secret. The night of the shooting, he told his best friend that he had shot someone. The next day, October 30, Nathaniel's suspension was completed and he was back at school. There, he bragged to other friends that he had shot a man. "I got that nigga," he told his friend.[17]

When he returned home from school on the afternoon of October 30, Hudack confronted him about the weapon and told Nathaniel that he had almost shot him the night before. Hudack told Nathaniel to bring him the rifle, which he did. Since Hudack had called the police the night before and Nathaniel was still out walking around, Hudack did not think the police would be of any help, so he planned to talk to Gloria about the incident. Ronnie Greene died on the night of October 30, and the next morning the story was front-page news. Reading the story, Hudack realized the possibility that Nathaniel was the one who had committed the murder. Hudack called police and told them of his suspicions and also told them that he thought he was in possession of the murder weapon. Later that day, while Nathaniel celebrated Halloween with his classmates, he was arrested for the crime. Ironically, when he was sent to Children's Village where his mother had tried to get help for him, he was amid familiar faces. Both his cousin and his brother were also detainees.[18]

Prosecution of the Case

Nathaniel is one of the youngest defendants in the history of the United States to be tried for first-degree murder. Two years to the day after the shooting, on October 29, 1999, the case went to trial and lasted less than a month. The defense argued that Nathaniel had been shooting at trees, not the men. They also argued that the bullet that struck and killed Greene had ricocheted off a tree, proving, they said, that Nathaniel was not shooting at the men. Finally, the prosecution said that it was inappropriate to charge the child with first-degree murder. Since Nathaniel had never met Greene, they said, he could not have premeditated the killing. The majority of the defense, however, was centered on the ability of an 11-year-old (mentally impaired at that) to conceptualize, comprehend, and plan a murder.

Prosecutors, however, were convinced that Nathaniel had deliberately planned to take a life. Nathaniel had told a friend that he was going to kill someone. Lisa Halushka of the prosecutor's office said, "Nathaniel Abraham did exactly what he said he was going to do."[19] Even though it was true that Nathaniel and Greene did not know each other, first-degree murder has to do with the intent of the killer. Regardless of whether or not the perpetrator knows the victim, if the perpetrator planned the murder in advance, then it is considered murder in the first degree.

Regardless, the prosecution's case was solid. Nathaniel allegedly had told his girlfriend before the shooting that he was going to shoot someone, he had a history of aggressive behavior, and his record listed 22 interactions with law enforcement—several of those interactions involving weapons. Further, he had confessed. After his arrest Nathaniel waived his Miranda rights, and when his mother arrived at the police station after his arrest, she too waived Nathaniel's Miranda rights. The judge threw out the confession, but an appeals court reinstated it. In his confession, Abraham told police he was shooting at trees and said, "I guess I hit somebody."[20]

Reports on the shooting initially stated that Nathaniel was 100 yards away when he fired the .22 caliber rifle, but the actual distance was later adjusted to just under 70 yards. Either way, it was an incredible shot for even an experienced rifleman to hit anything at such a distance. Compounding this apparent fluke, the rifle was in terrible condition. There was no stock on the gun and the barrel was bent, making it difficult to use effectively. As if these two circumstances were not enough, Nathaniel was also shooting in the dark. For these reasons, despite any possible intent or lack thereof on Nathaniel's part, hitting Greene at such a distance had to be partially bad luck.

Unfortunately for Nathaniel, only ten months before the shooting the state of Michigan had passed a new law allowing children of any age to be charged as adults for serious crimes. If not for that law, Nathaniel would have been tried as a juvenile and the harshest sentence he could have received would have been confinement to a youth detention facility. At age 21, if not sooner, he would have been released. But since he was tried as an adult, the court had many more options. If the jury found him guilty, the judge could choose to sentence him as either an adult or a juvenile. If sentenced as an adult, Nathaniel could have received life in prison without any chance of parole. If he were sentenced as a juvenile, he could have been sent to a detention facility and held no longer than his 21st birthday. It was also within the rights of the court to impose a blended sentence where he would be held until age 21, at which time his case would be reviewed, and a decision would be made to continue his incarceration or to release him.

Little did the legislators know that their law would be tested by the case of a tiny 11-year-old boy. Critics of Michigan's new law argued that Nathaniel was the very exception to such a law that they had feared. Amnesty International protested, claiming that Nathaniel's case demonstrated how poorly children are treated by the justice system. The NAACP also voiced protest, and civil rights activists were present during the trial. The assistant prosecutor, however, discounted these protests, saying that Nathaniel was "exactly the kind of kid the new law is meant to address."[21]

On November 16, 1997, after four days of jury deliberation, Nathaniel was acquitted of first-degree murder charges. The jury questioned whether an 11-year-old could form the necessary criminal intent, but they did believe that he acted with reckless disregard for human life. Therefore, Nathaniel was found guilty of second-degree murder, but in a seeming contradiction, was acquitted of using a firearm during a felony. The defense interpreted this contradictory verdict as saying, in essence, that Nathaniel "shot someone without the possession of a gun."[22] Based on this apparent contradiction, Nathaniel's attorneys have suggested that they might seek a new trial.

Sentencing and Summary

There were numerous sociological variables operating in Nathaniel's life that set the stage for his dysfunctional behavior. Abraham's father had been absent his whole life. Fathers have many roles as they teach life skills to their sons. They teach them how to be husbands and fathers, and they teach their sons how to properly channel their natural aggression. Even though Tommy Williams, and then later Robert Williams, may have provided some fatherly guidance, their influence was temporary. In the absence of a father, Nathaniel found role models in his brother and in a street gang. His aggression went unchecked due to lack of supervision. He tried to prove himself a man by fighting, defying his guardians, disrupting school, roaming the dangerous streets of Pontiac at night, and collecting weapons.

The child's mother was not irresponsible, absent, a drug addict, or a prostitute. She was involved in the lives of her children and she worked hard to get help for the son she recognized was in trouble. Gloria was also a woman with a good heart who cared about those around her. She took in the 18-month-old child of a woman who was sentenced to prison and was raising the baby on the mother's behalf. "She [Gloria] was taking care of her mentally disabled sister. She's not collecting welfare. She's Newt Gingrich's dream," said the executive director of the Center on Juvenile and Criminal Justice in Washington, D.C.[23] Despite these facts, a good mother can not completely compensate for the lack of male leadership for a developing boy.

Psychological issues were also part of the Nathaniel who shot Ronnie Greene. Children need to affiliate with their peers. A peer group provides a sense of order and gives the child a place in society. When a child is left unsupervised, he is allowed to select his own peer group. In Nathaniel's case, he picked a dysfunctional one. Without supervision, without a father, and without effective intervention, he pursued gang affiliation where he chose a tough-guy role for himself.

Children need to feel empowered and important, and they need to see the world as a predictable and stable place. Nathaniel's background compromised this psychological need. He was born to an unmarried mother, abandoned by his father, moved several times, and lived with nonrelatives for several years. After moving back home, he shared a house with his siblings, half-siblings, and his mother's older sister who suffered from a mental illness. His relatively stable male role models were out of his daily life—Tommy Williams because Nathaniel no longer lived with him, and Robert Williams because he had died. The only male role model with whom Nathaniel had much of a history was his older brother, who taught him about gangs, skipping school, fighting, and drugs and alcohol. His well-meaning mother worked nights leaving him unsupervised.

Finally, there were also physiological issues that one must consider. Nathaniel was identified as having attention deficit hyperactivity disorder (ADHD), emotional impairment, depression, a below average IQ, and cognitive functioning several years below his chronological age. He was moved out of the mainstream into a special classroom, and he attended three schools in two years. Many of these issues could easily have their roots in his physiology.

Help that was sought for this boy was rejected, and the system that was in place to intervene in cases like Nathaniel's did not do its job. Given these three sets of variables and their interaction, one has to wonder if this boy ever really had a chance.

On January 11, 2000, Nathaniel was sentenced as a juvenile. The court sentenced him to juvenile detention until he turns 21, at which time he will be released. His attorney said he was pleased with the verdict and jabbed at the Michigan law that allowed Nathaniel to be tried as an adult. saying, "This is the exact outcome that would have resulted had the case gone to juvenile court."[24] As a footnote, the defense consistently maintained that Nathaniel was shooting at trees, but during a status hearing in December 2000, his psychiatrist testified that Nathaniel told him that he was, indeed, shooting at the men.

I have never met Nathaniel, but I have worked with children my entire professional life. Because of limits on cognitive development at his age, even among normally developing children, I am convinced that there is no way this young man was capable of understanding the broad implications of taking the life of another human being. Surely this boy could not be allowed to decide for himself to waive his Miranda rights. Even a very bright lad would not have been able to fully comprehend the meaning of a Miranda warning under the circumstances—being dragged from class in front of friends, and being hauled to the police station. This would be traumatic even for a mature, bright adult, making it difficult to make such a significant decision.

In these pages, I am neither trying to make excuses for Nathaniel nor to remove responsibility from him. Many social and familial factors contributed to Nathaniel's choices, but they do not excuse his behavior. Society is not to blame for the murder of Ronnie Greene—Nathaniel is. Nathaniel acquired the weapon, planned to shoot someone, put himself in the situation to do so, aimed the weapon at Ronnie Greene, and pulled the trigger. However, Nathaniel did not develop in a vacuum, and it would be reductionist to argue that he was just a "bad egg." To deny the social influences on any person's behavior is to omit a major part of their personal makeup. Nathaniel's family circumstances, his social network, his physiology, and his own psychological issues prepared him for that night on October 29 when he pointed a gun at Ronnie Greene and pulled the trigger.

Just as his culture had a role in creating him, it also should have had a role in intervention—intervention that was never adequately provided. I find it interesting that those who argue that culture doesn't "make" people act do not question the logic of a corporation paying millions of dollars for TV advertising time. Those TV minutes, they would agree, influence the buying behavior of the public. Yet if only minutes of commercial time can affect the behavior of consumers, how can we argue that a culture in which one operates every day could not affect the behavior of a child? Nathaniel's mother perhaps best summed up the social contribution to Nathaniel's circumstances when she said, "What does that say about the police if they've had 22 contacts with a child and they don't do anything?"[25] The county prosecutor agreed that the system had failed Abraham. "The state of Michigan 'owes Nate's mother an apology' for letting her son fall through the cracks," he said.[26] At his sentencing, Judge Eugene Moore placed blame on both the community and Nathaniel when he said, "We as a community have failed, but you have also failed us and yourself."[27]

Abraham's mother blamed herself as well as the system. "Maybe if I'd been more on top of things right when they happened," she said.[28] In retrospect, she may have been able to do some things differently, but I would argue that all of us could say the same thing about ourselves when we look at tragedies that have invaded our lives. However, the fault ultimately lies with Nathaniel.

Several reports indicate that Nathaniel's conduct has improved during the years following his arrest and subsequent conviction. Documents acquired by journalist Desiree Cooper of the *Detroit Free Press* indicate that Nathaniel has been doing well in the detention facility where he resides. These documents note that Nathaniel's diagnoses have been changed, as have his medications, and his attending psychiatrist reported that Nathaniel not only was not of marginal IQ, but was fairly bright. This psychiatrist argued that his apparent intellectual deficits were due to academic deprivation in his life, not cognitive limitations. However, it is too late to save his childhood and too late to save Ronnie Greene, Jr. In a few more years, when he turns 21, Nathaniel will get a second chance at life. He will have an opportunity to go to school, get a job, marry, have children, and many other opportunities that Ronnie Greene will never have. Whether Nathaniel begins his new life as a more productive citizen or as a hardened criminal will be determined by his treatment while he is incarcerated, his physical well-being, and his personal choices. Perhaps the hope from this situation lies in the words of Ronnie Greene's mother. When asked if she would take comfort in a life sentence for Nathaniel Abraham, she replied, "No. That child needs help. He needs rehabilitation. He needs somebody to stick close to him and listen to him."[29]

CONCLUDING REMARKS

The three areas of our lives, our physiology, our psychology, and our cultural interactions, set the stage for who we are to become. Dysfunctional behavior that has a physiological cause requires a physiological intervention. Likewise, dysfunctional learned behaviors, those that were taught us by our parents, can be unlearned with proper training. More difficult is dealing with the culture at large. There is little that individuals can do to change their culture. Yet identifying the problems in a culture that lead to dysfunctional behavior is the starting point in making changes. One's behavior is almost never reducible to a single factor of this triad. Rather, what we are as teenagers or adults is the aggregate of these combining factors. If our parents ignore us and if our culture teaches us that it is acceptable to be selfish, hedonistic, and egocentric, then chances are very good that this is what we will become. If our parents ignore us and if our culture demonstrates to us that dysfunctional behavior is acceptable, we should not be surprised when our behavior is directed exclusively toward our own interests. Identifying dysfunctional behavior is the starting point in making changes. Yet identifying the problems in culture that lead to dysfunctional behavior is not the only issue. Finally, even though this child was emotionally and cognitively impaired, and numerous other factors were operating that set the stage for his behavior, the ultimate responsibility for his behavior lies with Nathaniel. Even though the level of responsibility changes as we get older, we have individual choice despite our culture, upbringing, and physical makeup.

A reasonable response to the recognition of the role of these three variables is to take seriously our responsibility as parents. As a culture we must move away from our erroneous supposition that the U.S. Constitution grants us freedom to pursue our own personal happiness at the expense of others. We must realize that with freedom comes responsibility to consider how our actions affect others. We must accept the truth that some of our behaviors have physiological roots and may be very difficult to change without help. We must also be willing to accept responsibility for our own actions—something that requires us to say painful words like "I lied." Finally, those who are so ready to call for the firing squad when someone does something "evil" must be willing to recognize that the development of dysfunction is very complicated, and that terminating the evildoer does not remove the fertile soil that allowed that evildoer to grow.

NOTES

1. "Clinton admits misleading testimony, avoids charges in Lewinsky probe," *CNN Online*, *www.cnn.com/2001/ALLPOLITICS/stories/01/19/clinton.lewinsky/index.html*, January 19, 2001.

2. Thomas N. Robinson, Marta L. Wilde, Lisa C. Navrocruz, K. Farish Haydel, and Ann Varady, "Effects of reducing children's television and video game use on aggressive behavior," *Archives of Pediatrics and Adolescent Medicine*, 2001, 155, pp. 17–23.

3. "Study: Child aggression linked to hours in day care," *CNN OnLine*, *www.cnn.com/2001/fyi/teachers.ednews/04/19/daycare.aggression.ap/index.html*, April 19, 2001.

4. Carl Goldberg, *Speaking with the Devil: Exploring Senseless Acts of Evil.* (New York: Penguin Books, 1996).

5. Carl Goldberg, *Speaking with the Devil: Exploring Senseless Acts of Evil* (New York: Penguin Books, 1996), p. 53.

6. Desiree Cooper, "Childhood's end: How 12-year-old Nathaniel Abraham finds himself looking at a life sentence for murder," *www.metrotimes.com/news/stories/news/18/23/ChldMrdrer.html*, March 4, 1998.

7. Desiree Cooper, "Childhood's end: How 12-year-old Nathaniel Abraham finds himself looking at a life sentence for murder," *www.metrotimes.com/news/stories/news/18/23/ChldMrdrer.html*, March 4, 1998.

8. Desiree Cooper, "Childhood's end: How 12-year-old Nathaniel Abraham finds himself looking at a life sentence for murder," *www.metrotimes.com/news/stories/news/18/23/ChldMrdrer.html*, March 4, 1998.

9. "Prosecutor: boy, 11, bragged he'd kill, then did," *CNN Online*, *www.cnn.com/US/9910/29/young.murder.suspect.02/index.html*, October 29, 1999.

10. Desiree Cooper, "Faith, hope, tragedy: Mother of young slaying suspect relives her son's troubled past," *Detroit Free Press*, October 18, 1999, p. B1.

11. Desiree Cooper, "Faith, hope, tragedy: Mother of young slaying suspect relives her son's troubled past," *Detroit Free Press*, October 18, 1999, p. B1.

12. Ruby L. Bailey and Tamara Audi, "Troubled and alone, Abraham eluded help," *Detroit Free Press*, November 6, 1999, p. B1.

13. Jim Dyer, "Children accused of killing children," *Detroit News*, February 10, 1998, p. B1.

14. Jim Dyer, "Children accused of killing children," *Detroit News*, February 10, 1998, p. B1.

15. Bill Hewitt, Champ Clark, and Amy Mindell, "A life in the balance," *People*, November 22, 1999, p. 197.

16. Bill Hewitt, Champ Clark, and Amy Mindell, "A life in the balance," *People*, November 22, 1999, p. 197.

17. Ruby L. Bailey and Tamara Audi, "Troubled and alone, Abraham eluded help," *Detroit Free Press*, November 6, 1999, p. B1.

18. Desiree Cooper, "Childhood's end: How 12-year-old Nathaniel Abraham finds himself looking at a life sentence for murder," *www.metrotimes.com/news/stories/news/18/23/ChldMrdrer.html*, March 4, 1998.

19. Ruby L. Bailey and Tamara Audi, "Troubled and alone, Abraham eluded help," *Detroit Free Press*, November 6, 1999, p. B1.

20. Ruby L. Bailey and Tamara Audi, "Troubled and alone, Abraham eluded help," *Detroit Free Press*, November 6, 1999, p. B1.

21. Desiree Cooper, "Childhood's end: How 12-year-old Nathaniel Abraham finds himself looking at a life sentence for murder," *www.metrotimes.com/news/stories/news/18/23/ChldMrdrer.html*, March 4, 1998.

22. "Appeal grounds debated for boy, 13, convicted of murder," *CNN Online*, *www.cnn.com/US/9911/17/young.shooter.01/index.html*, November 17, 1999.

23. Desiree Cooper, "Faith, hope, tragedy: Mother of young slaying suspect relives her son's troubled past," *Detroit Free Press*, October 18, 1999, p. B1.

24. "Michigan judge sentences boy killer to juvenile detention," *CNN Online*, *www.cnn.com/2000/US/01/13/abraham.sentencing.03/index.html*, January 13, 2000.

25. Desiree Cooper, "Childhood's end: How 12-year-old Nathaniel Abraham finds himself looking at a life sentence for murder," *www.metrotimes.com/news/stories/news/18/23/ChldMrdrer.html*, March 4, 1998.

26. Bill Hewitt, Champ Clark, and Amy Mindell, "A life in the balance," *People*, November 22, 1999, p. 197.

27. "Judge spares 13-year-old murderer life prison term; sentences him to youth detention until age 21," *Jet* (Internet edition), January 31, 2000.

28. Desiree Cooper, "Childhood's end: How 12-year-old Nathaniel Abraham finds himself looking at a life sentence for murder," *www.metrotimes.com/news/stories/news/18/23/ChldMrdrer.html*, March 4, 1998.

29. Desiree Cooper, "Loved ones can only ask why," *Detroit Free Press*, October 29, 1999, p. B1.

CHAPTER 3

DOLI INCAPAX:
VIOLENCE BY CHILDREN

> His voice rose under the black smoke before the burning wreckage of the
> island; and infected by that emotion the other little boys began to shake
> and to sob too. And in the middle of them, with filthy body, matted hair,
> and unwiped nose, Ralph wept for the end of innocence, the darkness of
> man's heart . . .
>
> —William Golding, *Lord of the Flies*

The first time I read Golding's classic novel "The Lord of the Flies" I was in the
seventh grade. An avid reader, I bought the book from a catalog of recommended books for children my age. I opened the first page of the novel not
knowing the plot. Like everyone who has read this captivating book, I was
drawn into its pages not only by its story, but also by the frightening truth
about the aggressive nature of man. What Orwell does with *Animal Farm*,
portraying the complexity of politics through farm animals, Golding does with
Lord of the Flies, portraying the complexity of our aggressive nature through
little boys stranded on an island. In the story the boys eventually resort to barbaric and savage behaviors against each other. When I first read this book I was
only 12 years old, but even at that age, I wondered if I would have behaved any
differently.

The Latin phrase *doli incapax* means "incapable of wrong." It is used as a legal term that describes the assumption that prior to a certain age, children are
incapable of formulating wrongful intent. In Great Britain, as you will see, by

the age of ten the principle of *doli incapax* no longer applies. The law assumes that by this age a child has the capability to form wrongful intent. The contrast between the chapter title and the opening quote from *Lord of the Flies* is intentional. Golding's novel, in essence, suggests the concept of human depravity and that we have the potential for evil at our core. The principle of *doli incapax* supposes just the opposite. The issue, however, is much too complicated to reduce to either chronological age or human depravity. In the following pages, you will see why.

My daily life is filled with starkly contrasting worlds. As a therapist for children, I not only see the brilliant light of life in the eyes of my clients, but I have the tremendous honor of working with them, their parents, and sometimes the court system to make their lives better. On the other hand, my work with violence, homicide, and brutality sometimes leaves me feeling hopeless and powerless. Most of the time, I travel between these two realms with ease, leaving the cases of my living clients in my office as I submerge myself in the darker recesses of our world. This darker world is filled with hate, rage, cruelty, evil, mutilation, and death, one that most people are thankfully spared from even knowing exists. Usually, when I reenter the world of the living, I can leave the dead to themselves. I desensitize myself to the emotional and physical pains of the dead that I study through sterilizing academic logic and depersonalizing investigation.

I have a strong stomach when it comes to crime scenes, blood and body parts, autopsies, and the most gruesome side of our existence. What is most difficult for me is the emotional side of murder—what victims were feeling and thinking at the time of their abduction, torture, and deaths. I can usually avoid thinking much about it as I analyze a crime. It becomes especially difficult when I come face-to-face with relatives and friends of survivors. It is a rare case that is frighteningly real to me—where I hear the victim's thoughts and he or she invades my dreams.

The therapy that I provide to the living serves as a window of hope in what could otherwise be a cynical and hopeless existence. Figuratively speaking, I rarely carry homicide cases home with me. Yet the case I am about to share with you is the most heartbreaking I have ever studied. I debated whether or not to include it here because I feared readers would be so lost in the tragedy of the child I describe that they would miss the reason why I have included this case. It is interesting that the two most difficult cases that I have studied involved two male juvenile perpetrators as well as juvenile victims—the Columbine High School case, which I discussed in my first book, and the case you are about to read. This word of caution is to remind you that this case serves to present a tragic example of how cruel and violent children can be.

"COME ON, BABY"

Robert Thompson and Jon Venables, two ten-year-old boys growing up near Liverpool, England, had difficult family lives. Robert's mother and father were both alcoholics, his father abandoned the family in his early years, and his mother allegedly physically abused him. Jon's parents also had a very rocky marriage. The Venables' marriage went through many separations and re-unions; hence, Jon's father was in and out of his life several times. Both boys lived in families where siblings had overt difficulties as well. Robert was the fifth of seven children, and his older brothers were well known to both law en-forcement and social services. His brothers regularly abused him physically, and he, in turn, did the same to his younger brother. One or more of Robert's brothers were accused of arson, sexual assault, and theft. Jon's brother was so disruptive at home that he was eventually sent to foster care, and his sister had developmental difficulties that required a great deal of attention and place-ment in a special school.

Even though many children experience some of these same difficulties and still function fairly well, Robert and Jon did not. They both responded to their circumstances with clear indications of problems. Both boys had difficulties at school and were held back one year for poor grades. Thompson's aggressive-ness was so obvious and frightening that parents who knew him chose to keep their children away from him.[1] After Jon and Robert had become friends, Jon's father, at the urging of parents who knew Thompson, refused to allow his son to play with Thompson. He warned his son to stay away from Robert, but that warning went unheeded. Because of his reputation, Thompson had few friends and would not relinquish his friendship with Venables.

Jon had his own difficulties, even before he began his friendship with Thompson. His teachers perceived him as a boy crying for help even though they did not think of him as a bad kid. However, anyone who works with dis-turbed children could not help but see symptoms of a serious problem. Re-ports abound of his deliberate cruelty to others, destroying their work, knock-ing things off desks, and disrupting classes. Even more significant were his self-destructive behaviors—cutting himself and his clothing and banging his head on the floor, the walls, and furniture. One of his teachers described him as the strangest child she had ever had in class. His destructive behaviors were not limited to himself or property. On one occasion he nearly choked another stu-dent to death with a ruler. After that episode, he was suspended. His mother tried to intervene and address his aggressive behaviors, but she met with no success, finally choosing to send him to live with his father, where he entered a new school and eventually met Thompson. At his father's home, he frequently watched violent horror videos, which has led many to speculate that these videos contributed to his violent behavior. But while they may have contributed to his aggressiveness, they certainly were not the cause.

Both Robert and Jon exhibited violence before the day in February 1993 when they killed James Bulger. Even though Robert was sometimes perceived as feminine because he collected troll dolls, he abused his younger brother and was also perceived as a bully. Just to be cruel, he once abandoned his own younger brother at the very canal where he and Jon would take James Bulger before they killed him. I do not believe any of the reports from friends who said Jon and Robert showed no sign of their ability to commit murder. Their capacity for violence was well established.

February 12, 1993, was not so different from those days we all experience—a day at a shopping mall, taking care of life's necessities and window shopping. Denise Bulger and her two-year-old son spent the afternoon in the Bootle Strand shopping center in Bootle, a town just a few miles north of Liverpool. After several stops, Mrs. Bulger made one last visit to a store, leaving her son at the door as she hurriedly made a purchase from a butcher's shop. She thought it would only take a moment to pay for her meat, but some confusion with her order caused it to take longer than expected. When she turned around, the two-year-old was gone.

Jon Venables and Robert Thompson had cut classes in a practice called "sagging." They went to the Bootle Strand to shoplift. There, they pilfered various items, including candy, paint, pencils, and batteries. They tormented an old woman and were chased out of several stores for running amok and basically raising hell.

Getting bored with causing disruption for shopkeepers, the two boys decided it would be "fun" to find a child, lure him away from his parents, and get him lost. Their first attempt failed. They lured a two-year-old out of a store and into the hallway of the shopping mall, but when Thompson saw the boy's mother come out of the store looking for her son, he panicked and told the little boy to go back to her.

They were not defeated by this failed attempt. Minutes later, they saw James Bulger standing by the butcher shop door and urged him to follow, repeatedly saying, "Come on, baby." They led the child by the hand and within minutes they were outside the shopping mall and on the busy streets. It was 3:42 P.M. Only moments after taking her eyes off her son, Denise Bulger realized he was missing. She frantically began looking for the child and when she had no success finding him, she notified the security officers in the shopping center. A search of the mall was made, but there was no sign of the boy. At 4:15 P.M., approximately 30 minutes after Thompson and Venables led the boy away from the butcher shop, the police were summoned.

For the next two hours, Thompson and Venables would pull, carry, and walk with little James Bulger over two and a half miles, a journey that would end at a set of railroad tracks not far from a police station. Their first stop was at the canal where Thompson had abandoned his own younger brother some months before. Thompson and Venables later told police that they were going to push James into the canal. While they were there, they were unable to trick the toddler into leaning over the canal so that he could be pushed in. At this point, Robert picked James up and dropped him on his head. James cut his head in the fall and began crying. Jon and Robert started to run away and leave James there, but for some unknown reason they turned around and went back to the child. I believe that it may have been Robert's intention from the beginning to leave James at the canal; in essence finishing a job that he started with his younger brother, but that was not to be. After returning to the injured boy, they again urged James to go with them with the words, "Come on, baby."

During the two hours that they led James through town, nearly 40 people saw the two boys with their victim. Some saw James crying for his mother, others saw him laughing, and others said nothing looked out of the ordinary—just three boys walking down the street together. A few of these witnesses tried to intervene, but even when witnesses felt uncomfortable with what they saw, they did not take significant action to stop Venables and Thompson from leading the child on toward his death. Among these witnesses were people who saw blood on the tot's forehead and/or who saw the boys kick or hit young Bulger. One woman witnessed the boys hitting and violently shaking James, but she pulled her curtains closed and ignored the event. Some of these witnesses interpreted what they saw as brothers having a spat.

Even though most witnesses passed by, a few at least made an attempt to intervene. One woman who saw the toddler crying and bleeding talked to Venables and Thompson. The boys told this woman that they had found James the way he was. After she instructed them to take James to the police station, they left in the opposite direction. She shouted at them, but when they did not stop, she let them go. Later, a second woman questioned Venables and Thompson, but the boys told her they were taking James to the police station. She did not believe them, but she had her dog with her and decided to let the boys take care of James on their own. Along the way, they went into a store, ran into some acquaintances, and were seen by numerous passersby. Some witnesses paid little attention to the boys, and others spoke with them. Each time they were confronted, Jon said that James was his little brother. James apparently never corrected him.

By 5:30, it had gotten dark and the boys were near the railway tracks. They could have easily turned for home or dropped the child off at a nearby police station, but they did not. Instead, they squeezed through a hole in the fence near the tracks. Robert took a can of blue paint that they had stolen earlier in the afternoon from the shopping center and flung the paint at James' face. The paint stung his eyes and he began to cry. Then, Venables and Thompson stepped up their assault on the boy. They threw rocks at him, beat him with bricks, and finally struck him with a 22-pound metal bar. Thinking he was dead, they removed his pants and shoes, and one of the boys inserted a battery into the child's rectum. They then covered his head with bricks, leaving him on the tracks to die. After leaving the scene, Jon and Robert wandered around for a while and eventually ended up in a video store. A passing train later severed the lad's tiny body in two. The autopsy report showed that the child was not dead when they left him, but died before being struck by the train. The train conductor saw the body before hitting it, but thought it was a doll. Later, however, he called the police because he heard about the missing boy. James' body would be found later by some children who were playing along the tracks.

In the meantime, news of James' abduction was spreading throughout the community. Venables' mother had been searching for him because she had heard about the abduction from the shopping center. She was furious when she found Jon and Robert at a video store and yelled at and hit them both. She told Jon that he could have been the one abducted by the "maniac from the mall." She then took him to the nearby police station and asked the duty officer to lecture Jon.

Back at the shopping mall, the police were gathering leads, including suspicions about the child's parents as well as a man with a ponytail. It was after midnight by the time they watched the video from the mall security cameras. There on the screen was the clear image of James Bulger holding the hand of another child and a second fuzzy image of another child just in front of them. The quality of the video image was poor, and police were unable to identify the two boys with James, but the police were stunned. Their experience told them that they should be on the lookout for an adult, but the video clearly implied that James' abductors were but children themselves.

Police searched the canal, fearing that they might find the body beneath the muddy waters, but their search turned up nothing. Tragically, the fears of the community were realized when James' mutilated body was discovered along the railroad tracks.

Police released the mall security video to the press. Many parents feared that their own sons were possible perpetrators, and police received a number of telephone calls from people providing possible suspects. Thompson's own mother asked him if the image on the video was him, but he denied it. She still had her suspicions and told a friend that she might take him to the police anyway.[2] One suspect was questioned by police, but later released. Jon Venables' father noticed blue paint on his son's coat and questioned Jon about it. Jon told him that Robert had thrown it on him.

An anonymous tip provided police with Jon and Robert's names, though neither boy was originally considered a likely suspect. Little did investigators know, when they arrived at both boys' homes on Thursday, that there was a tremendous amount of evidence there, including bloody clothing and shoes and clothes with blue paint. Nor did they know that the boys had "sagged" school the day of the murder. During routine interviews with the boys, police began to suspect Jon and Robert had something to do with the murder because of inconsistencies in their statements. Robert began to implicate Jon, who in turn was implicating Robert.

Jon cried throughout his interview, even sitting on his mother's lap through part of the process, but Thompson remained fairly composed. Throughout the several hours of questioning, both boys continued to change their stories, providing more and more evidence that they had something to do with the murder. By the end of the interviews, both children admitted taking James from the shopping center, but only Jon would admit his role in the boy's death, saying, "I did kill him." Charges were filed Saturday night against both boys. They were also charged with attempted abduction of the other boy at the mall.

Venables and Thompson were tested extensively and found to be of sound mind, suffering no mental illnesses. Under British law, the principle of *doli incapax* applies to a child only until he turns ten years of age. If the boys had committed the crime six months earlier, the law would have supposed that they were incapable of formulating wrongful intent, but since both boys had passed their tenth birthday they were tried as adults. Court experts said that the boys fully understood the implications of their behavior prior to the crime, but I argue that this was impossible. Understanding the permanence of death is not an all-or-nothing issue; rather, it is progressive. Even a very young child of four or five years of age can understand some things about death. For example, if a child's pet fish dies, he or she can understand that the fish is never coming back, but the child cannot "fully" understand what death entails. It is not until around age 12 or 13 that most children are capable of a cognitive understanding of the abstract nature of death. The older we are, the more we understand. Even adults cannot "fully comprehend" death and its permanence. To suppose that these ten-year-old boys could fully understand the ramifications of their actions, especially under the intense emotional circumstances surrounding the abduction of James Bulger, is ridiculous. I certainly am not excusing their behavior, only questioning the finding of the court experts.

On May 14, 1993, both boys pleaded not guilty. Who was the leader of the two is still a mystery. In some ways Thompson was more dominant, was bigger, and seemed to have control over Venables, who apparently looked up to him.

However, much of the evidence suggests that Venables took the lead, literally, in the abduction and the death of James Bulger. The prosecution tried the boys together, stating that they were both equal participants in the murder of young James. Court documents from this case are surprisingly sterile and dehumanizing. The court referred to them as Child A and Child B throughout the trial, and the emotional impact of what Venables and Thompson did is sometimes lost in the legal jargon of the trial transcripts. Venables and Thompson almost seemed to be third parties to the trial that would decide their fates. They did not take the stand in their own defense, but over the three weeks of the trial, the prosecution called to the stand all 38 witnesses to the abduction, who were referred to in the press as the "Liverpool 38." During the trial, Venables appeared shamed, with his head slouched and his face to the floor. Thompson, however, presented an arrogance that astonished spectators, including his own lawyers.

On Wednesday, November 24, the jury went into deliberation. By the end of that day they returned their verdict, finding both boys guilty. They were 11 years old by the time of their sentencing. The court originally sentenced them to a minimum of eight years each. That sentence was later extended to 15 years by British Home Secretary Michael Howard; however, his ruling was overturned by England's House of Lords.

Each boy blamed the other for the idea of taking the child, saying they tried to stop the other from beating James, but it is clear both of them had a part in the crime. Jon admitted that he killed James, and at least once Robert kicked the boy in the side of the head—a kick that was hard enough to leave an imprint of his shoe and laces on the side of James' face. Regardless of who was to blame for the idea, their motive was the same. Their intention initially was to get the child lost. As the afternoon wore on, Venables and Thompson got deeper and deeper into an escapade that ended in the child's death. I think their defense attorney was correct when he said the boys did not plan to kill Bulger from the beginning. This is indicative of the way children think—minute to minute. They started with psychological cruelty, then escalated to physical cruelty. By the time they found themselves in the dark along the railroad tracks, James was bleeding, they knew they were in trouble, and I suspect that they were frustrated and angry with their predicament and took their confusion and anger out on the boy. For most of the day they had been desensitizing themselves to the feelings of others as they terrorized patrons and shopkeepers in the shopping mall. Then they tortured James psychologically by denying the crying child his mother. Robert noted that James spent most of the two hours crying for his mother. James' fear and hopelessness must have grown each time a passerby questioned his abductors, but then failed to help him. Next, Jon and Robert practiced being physically cruel to James. They poked, kicked, slapped, and hit the child, once deliberately dropping him on his head.

Their assault on the boy escalated when they threw paint in his face, and finally they threw bricks and rocks. Once they had hit him with the bricks and the iron bar, they had gone too far to turn back.

Perhaps they hoped to cover their crime by allowing the train to run over the boy. If they had been serial killers, their crime scene would have been classified as "disorganized" because there was minimal, if any, attempt to cover their tracks. But unlike serial killers, these boys were disorganized because they were ten and they had no plan. On the one hand, they may have tried to cover up the crime by making it look like a train caused the child's injuries, but on the other hand, they left many other clues at the scene. The hood from James' jacket had been discarded along the tracks. The blue paint on his face, the child's discarded pants and shoes, the batteries in his rectum, and the bloody iron bar were all found at the scene—clues that would obviously be inconsistent with a train accident.

There is little doubt in my mind that both boys felt at least some remorse for their actions, but Robert and Jon dealt with their guilt in different ways. Robert expressed fear about being haunted by the murdered baby. For a child, immediate experiences seem to have no end. For example, pain can be worse for a child than for an adult because the adult is capable of thinking about a time when the pain will be gone, but children cannot do that. Therefore, at 11 years of age, Robert could not imagine a time that he would feel differently. His fear of being haunted must have been oppressive.

Perhaps to relieve some of his guilt, Robert brought flowers to the crime scene. Unlike serial killers who return to the crime scene for the thrill of reliving their crimes, Robert returned because his conscience needed appeasing. Jon expressed concern for James' family to his mother. It could be that he was trying to formulate an alibi, but I believe that both of these boys were "undoing" the crime. Psychologically, when a person feels remorse or guilt, he tries to compensate for the wrong that he believes he committed by bringing gifts, apologizing, and showing concern. Where one is afraid to express direct remorse for the behavior, one channels that "undoing" into other behaviors. Perhaps the most explicit form of undoing was the insertion of the batteries into James' rectum. I do not believe that the boys sexually assaulted James, and it is my opinion that it was most likely Robert who inserted the batteries. Several writers have noted the tremendous symbolism in the abduction of the boy, providing evidence of Robert's attempt to "undo" the crime. Robert was obsessed with dolls, he said that he and Jon went to the mall to steal troll dolls, and batteries were inserted in the child's anus as if to restart a broken doll.[3]

Jon cried throughout his interview and the trial, seeking comfort in his mother's arms. He diminished his role as one who is lying tends to do, rationalizing his behavior by saying that he threw only "teeny, little stones" at

James and only at his limbs. He said that even though he kicked him, it was "only lightly." This description is indicative of rationalization of one's behavior. Even though it sounds odd that *any* stones were thrown at the toddler, to Jon it was a way to diminish his responsibility and lessen his guilt. Also, each boy was extremely angry with the other, displacing rage and guilt from his own behavior to the other boy. It is far easier for a child to be mad at another than to condemn himself.

At the trial, the defense argued that neither boy had done anything violent before the abduction of James, but that was clearly not true to those of us who understand the language of violence. They bullied other children physically and emotionally; Jon attacked another child, whom he nearly choked to death; they stole, "sagged" school, and destroyed property, pushing every boundary that was erected to protect them and others. Even though I do not believe that their intent at the time they abducted James was murder, picking on the lad was just one more way they pushed others around.

Their counselors in prison indicated that both boys, now men, showed remorse for their actions, although Venables reportedly has responded better to therapy than has Thompson. In 1995, two years after the murder, Robert finally admitted to participating in the killing. One official created a stir in the community when he "spoke of the 'considerable admiration' he had for the way Thompson had responded to his punishment and said he would not like to see him sent to prison."[4] In 2001 the boys were released from the juvenile facility where they lived for eight years. The decision for parole was followed by a storm of protest, and the British government was forced to take unprecedented action to protect the identity of the 18-year-olds at the time of their release. They were given new identities, and the government granted them the right of anonymity, making it illegal to publish their pictures, information about their appearance, or information about their whereabouts. Bulger's father reportedly vowed to try to hunt the two perpetrators down.[5] The sad conclusion of this episode is that the Bulgers had to bury their son's mangled body and will never realize the hopes and dreams that most parents have for their children. As for Jon and Robert, they will live the rest of their lives with a much fuller understanding of their actions, and I suppose they will, indeed, be haunted by James until the day they die.

TENUOUS REALITIES

Many factors contribute to aggression in children. One thing that could lead to aggressive behavior in children is something called *reactive attachment disorder* (RAD). In normal parent-child relationships, a newborn child is cuddled, fed, and nurtured. This interactive process between caregiver and child teaches the child that the world is predictable and safe. The child learns that when she cries, someone comes to her aid and resolves her discomfort. Experiencing this predictable part of life allows the child to learn to trust other people. When basic needs are not met, however, such as in cases of severe abuse or neglect, the child does not learn to trust other people, but instead learns that when she cries, no one will come. This is called "failure to bond" or attachment disorder. Even children as young as three or four years of age learn that they must rely on themselves for their needs to be met, becoming extremely self-seeking, far more so than most children. These children also learn to manipulate others. An RAD child can easily manipulate even therapists and psychologists who are not properly trained to understand this disorder.

These children resent the void they feel—the void of human emotion, caring, and reciprocation of affections. Therefore, they are driven to inflict pain on others. Simply put, they didn't get comfort, therefore they don't want anyone else to have it. They may set fires in order to destroy property or deliberately hurt both animals and people, taking pleasure in the pain they inflict. They will even prey upon younger siblings. They take advantage of the helplessness of infants and toddlers, children who cannot protect themselves or explain to an adult what is happening to them. As reactive attachment disorder children reach adolescence, they become extremely dangerous to adults as well.

Anytime I work with a child, I look for three symptons that suggest the possibility of reactive attachment disorder—setting of fires, cruelty to animals, and bed-wetting outside of the normal range for that behavior. I ask parents if their child resists cuddles, seems manipulative, or is a compulsive liar. RAD children may also demonstrate inappropriate attachments—what the *Diagnostic and Statistical Manual of Mental Disorders Fourth Edition Text Revision* (*DSM IV-TR*) calls "lack of selectivity in choice of attachment figures."[6] For example, a seven-year-old child I once worked with called every male "daddy" and every woman "mommy"—even at a first meeting. Children with this disorder may also appear to quickly become everyone's best friend, but these relationships are very shallow. Even though RAD most definitely contributes to aggression in children, it is a relatively rare diagnosis. Other factors are more likely causes of the violence committed by most children.

A child's perception of the world is very different from that of adults. Interpretation of behavior, coping with problems, problem-solving, and delaying gratification are things that children are incapable of understanding in the same way that adults do. This difference in perception is due to a number of developmental issues that can contribute to aggressive behavior in children. First of all, children perceive that the world revolves around them and their needs. Everything happens either to them or for them, or is caused by them. This is called "egocentrism." Children cannot easily demonstrate gratitude because of their egocentric worldview. Since egocentrism causes children to demand that their needs be met immediately, they cannot comprehend or recognize the graciousness of others. Egocentric children, in other words, expect people to do things for them that adults recognize as favors or graciousness. Egocentrism sometimes carries over into adulthood, but by late adolescence, most children are beginning to understand that the world does not revolve around them. Also, by this age they are capable of empathizing—understanding the perspective of another person. Before one has the ability to empathize, one is incapable of putting oneself in another person's shoes. Hence, a child who kills another person cannot fully comprehend the loss or pain the victim's survivors experience.

Second, children have fewer coping skills than adults. I dealt with this subject at length in my first book, but in brief, the more coping skills one has, the less likely one will be aggressive. Effective coping skills and strategies allow us to deal with our anger, frustrations, discomforts, and difficulties as well as help us to solve problems. If a three-year-old has to go to the bathroom, he or she will go to a parent and explain the problem or perhaps just stand in place and yell about it. The child might have an accident in his clothes while he waits for a parent to take him to the bathroom. It doesn't occur to him to go to the bathroom by himself. As children approach adolescence, they learn to handle some problems on their own, but effective problem-solving and coping with the many emotions and disappointments of life are still several years beyond their abilities. The coping skills that they do have are often ineffective or dysfunctional. For example, a child may have learned to deal with anger by hitting. Hitting is a coping skill, but it is a dysfunctional one. As with egocentrism, by late adolescence, most young adults should have developed many effective coping skills and problem-solving strategies.

Third, children live in the immediate present at the expense of the future. This is called "immediacy." For example, if you give a three-year-old the option of cleaning his room now and watching TV later or the other way around, he will always choose the pleasurable experience first—no matter what it is—because children do not know how to delay gratification. Immediacy makes it nearly impossible for a child to consider the future consequences of his behavior, and it also causes immediate circumstances to be more overwhelming than they should. For example, if a grade school child is teased by classmates at school, the child cannot imagine a time when he will not feel that humiliation or embarrassment. He cannot put the situation into the bigger context of life.

This is why children become so upset over seemingly insignificant issues. My three-year-old son, for example, once threw a tantrum because he did not like the way I put toothpaste on his toothbrush. Life for him was wrapped up in that moment and his immediate wishes. Seeing that event in the bigger picture of life never occurred to him, and at age three he would be incapable of doing so. Sometimes even adults have trouble putting events into proper perspective. Couples going through divorce may find it hard to imagine a time when they won't feel the heartache they currently feel. These feelings can be overwhelming and, as you will see in the case study of Nathaniel Brazill, can lead to extreme behaviors that would not have occurred if a child could have put the situation into a realistic context.

Fourth, children are incapable of abstract reasoning prior to adolescence. Abstract issues are those that cannot be perceived by one or more of the five senses. Concepts like faith, hope, and right and wrong are abstract issues that can be partially addressed in concrete terms, but their deeper meaning is abstract. For example, we can talk with children about something being "right" in the context of rules, but adults recognize that there is an abstract level in regard to what is "right." Determining right and wrong in a given situation involves more than just knowing the rules. Prior to age 12 or 13, children cannot fully understand abstract issues. In the case of Jon Venables and Robert Thompson, several psychologists testified that these two ten-year-old boys "fully understood" the nature of death. This is developmentally impossible. Prior to adolescence, a child is incapable of fully comprehending the significance of taking a life. The best that they could understand is the fact that they could get in really big trouble for hurting someone else.

The boys who have killed their classmates in the many school shootings of the past decade will come to realize the significance of their actions only in their mid- to late teens. Prior to late adolescence, the guilt and remorse that these boys may have experienced would have been almost exclusively related to being in trouble and having people angry with them. By late adolescence, however, they will be capable of understanding the permanence of their actions and the broad ramifications of the pain they have caused. Only then will they begin to empathize with their victims and their victims' families—and then experience much deeper remorse, regret, guilt, and pain than they were capable of in their younger years.

Finally, children operate in a magical world. Magical thinking involves confusion or misunderstanding of cause and effect relationships, leading children to link behaviors that are not necessarily related. Superstitious behavior is an example of magical thinking—linking, for example, a black cat with bad luck. Children see people die on video screens and in the movies, only to come back in the next film or game. At one level, they can understand the difference between real life and video games, but they cannot fully understand it. Because of magical thinking, children do not fully understand the laws of nature. They may hit another child with an object without realizing the severity of the damage they could cause. For example, I had a client once who hit a sibling with a hatchet. The child did not intend to kill or severely wound his brother. He was simply angry and struck out at him with the object he had access to. There was no evil intent on the part of the boy. Once he saw blood on his brother's head, he became very frightened, yet even then he did not realize what he had done. These five limitations—egocentrism, few coping strategies, immediacy, limited abstract reasoning, and magical thinking—can be seen in the case of Nathaniel Brazill, a 13-year-old boy from southern Florida.

NATHANIEL BRAZILL

Children spend a great deal of their lives in school buildings or at school functions. Tests, books, extracurricular activities at school, administrators, teachers, and friendships dominate their lives. It should be no surprise, therefore, that children act out their aggression at school just as adults act out their aggression at work. It is in these environments that they spend most of their time. The school shootings in Colorado, Oregon, Arkansas, and Georgia over the past few years are only a few of those that have occurred. With some regularity, children are wounded at school or school events as a result of arguments over girlfriends, drugs, misunderstandings, gang interactions, and other juvenile behaviors. Stories about these violent incidents do not always make national headlines. It is only when there is no clear reason for an episode of school violence that the story makes national headlines. One such incident occurred in May 2000, when an otherwise good child shot and killed one of his favorite teachers.

Unlike many of the perpetrators that I review in this book, by all appearances Nathaniel Brazill was an upstanding child. He had a limited history of aggression and minimal issues in his background that would have allowed one to see foresee the events of Friday, May 26, 2000. This was the last day of school at Lake Worth Community Middle School before summer vacation. Nathaniel, an honor student, had a perfect attendance record. One teacher said that he had begun to notice a lot of anger in Nathaniel, but otherwise Nathaniel had no behavioral problems. He had a good reputation at school, and he had been selected to be a peer mediator for the coming academic year. His reputation away from school appears to have been good as well. His parents said he was a good child who was no trouble, and neighbors echoed that perception. His grades had begun to slip as he approached the end of the year, but that is true for many children all across the country as the drudgery of the school year approaches its conclusion and their minds drift from their studies to summer vacation. Adolescent infatuation may have contributed to Nathaniel's slipping grades as well. He was deeply entranced by a 13-year-old classmate named Dinora.

As was true of my own middle school days, the last day of school at Lake Worth Community Middle School was one where pranks, water balloons, and squirt guns were routine. Just after lunch, school counselor Kevin Hinds saw Nathaniel and another student, Michele Cordovez, throwing water. After discussing the situation with Bob Hatcher, the assistant principal, the decision was made to dismiss the two students for the rest of the day. Hinds called Nathaniel's mother at work, and she told Hinds to allow Nathaniel to walk home alone.

As Nathaniel and Michele walked home, his anger rose. He let Michele in on a secret he had only shared with two other children. He had taken a gun from his grandfather's house and had hidden it in his dresser at home. He told Michele that he was going to go home, get the gun, and return to the school to shoot Mr. Hinds. Michele did not believe him, but Nathaniel said, "Just watch, I'll be all over the news."[7]

After parting paths with Michele, Nathaniel experienced a series of disappointments over the next two hours. He could not get into his house because his mother was working late and he did not have a key. He went to his grandmother's home a few blocks away, hoping she would go to the school and talk to the counselor for him, but her car was broken and she had no way to get there. He apparently got a house key from his grandmother and then went to his aunt's place of employment to see if she could go to the school to talk to the counselor. On the way to his aunt's workplace, he crossed paths with a friend. Still angry about his situation at school, he asked the boy if he had a gun. The boy said no and asked Nathaniel what he needed a gun for. Nathaniel said he was gonna "f*** up the teacher at school."[8]

When he arrived at the nursing home where his aunt worked, he discovered that she was not there. After that, he went home, where he watched TV, but then the television broke. One last time he tried to get help from an adult. Stuffing the pistol into his pants pocket, he rode his bicycle to his aunt's home, but she was not there. Defeated by his efforts, he rode his bicycle toward the school.

Back at school, the bell was about to ring signaling the end of the semester. Barry Grunow, a 35-year-old English teacher with seven years tenure at the school, was monitoring his class, signing yearbooks, and keeping an eye on the hallway as he waited for the beginning of his break as well. Dinora, Nathaniel's object of affection, was in Grunow's classroom. Nathaniel came up to the door of the classroom and asked Grunow if he could speak to Dinora and another girl in the room. He wanted to tell Dinora goodbye for the summer, knowing he would see little of her over the next three months. Grunow, not knowing that Nathaniel had been sent home earlier in the day, invited Nathaniel into the classroom, but Nathaniel said he wanted to talk to the girl privately in the hallway. Grunow said he could not allow Dinora to leave the room.

In the classroom, students noticed Nathaniel standing in the doorway talking to Grunow. Nathaniel saw Dinora and she saw him. Grunow gently pushed

Nathaniel out of the doorway as if to shoo him on his way. Nathaniel later stated that it was a gentle push and Mr. Grunow was not being aggressive toward him, but when that happened, Nathaniel pulled the weapon from his pocket. The tiny nickel-plated, .25-caliber pistol, holding only four rounds, was five inches long and looked like a toy. Grunow quite likely thought that it was a toy because many children had squirt guns on the last day of school. When Nathaniel pointed the gun at Mr. Grunow, the teacher told him to put it away. Nathaniel later recalled, "I smiled at Mr. Grunow and he smiled at me. He pushed the gun away like he thought it was fake. It was kind of like a joke."[9] Surveillance video footage showed Nathaniel about four feet from Mr. Grunow with the gun pointed at his head. At that moment the gun went off and Grunow fell to the floor convulsing. A single shot penetrated his face near the nose. For a moment, the students froze as they tried to comprehend what had happened. Then Nathaniel, realizing what he had done, ran away. The incident was captured on the school's security surveillance tape.

A geography teacher in the class next to Grunow's room heard the noise and went into the hallway to see what was going on. At first he did not realize that Grunow had been injured, thinking he was horsing around with his students, but then he saw the blood pooling around Grunow's head. He tried to stop the bleeding, but Grunow died minutes later. The 911 operator began to receive calls, and in less than two minutes from the time of the first call, an officer was on the scene.

As Nathaniel ran through the halls, another teacher tried to stop him, but Nathaniel pointed the gun at him and said, "Don't mess with me, Mr. James."[10] Nathaniel left the building and ran, with teachers, students, and others chasing him, about a quarter of a mile, at which point he saw a police car coming down the street. Nathaniel stepped into the middle of the street, fell to his knees, and put his hands on his head. He recognized the officer from a recreation center where he played. The officer stopped his vehicle and, recognizing Nathaniel, called him by name and asked him what he was doing. Nathaniel confessed to the shooting and surrendered his weapon. Within five minutes of the shooting, Nathaniel was in custody.

Nathaniel was detained at Palm Beach Juvenile Detention Center in West Palm Beach. If he had been tried as a minor, he would have been released no later than his 21st birthday. A grand jury, however, indicted Nathaniel as an adult on first-degree murder charges, which meant that if he was convicted he would receive a mandatory life sentence without the possibility of parole. Even if convicted, however, Nathaniel would be spared the death penalty because of his age. Yet, Nathaniel told a cellmate that he would prefer to get the death penalty. "If they give me life, I'll ask for the electric chair because I took somebody's life."[11]

The prosecution offered a plea bargain to Nathaniel's attorney that would have avoided a trial. The deal would have sent Nathaniel to prison for 25 years. His parents rejected the offer and the case went to trial in April 2001. While in prison awaiting trial, Nathaniel reportedly sent letters to his classmates asking them to testify in a favorable manner if they were called to trial. The prosecutor subsequently added witness tampering to his charges.

Toward the end of the trial, Nathaniel took the stand in his own defense. He said that he only pointed the gun at Mr. Grunow because he wanted the teacher to take him seriously. He told the court that before he shot Mr. Grunow, he was nervous and was afraid to drop the gun. Nathaniel claimed that he did not mean to pull the trigger, but the prosecutor made it clear to the court that he did not believe it was an accident at all. He forced Nathaniel to show the court how he cocked and then aimed the weapon. Then the prosecutor told Nathaniel to show the jury how he "shot Mr. Grunow between the eyes, unintentionally."[12] The prosecution argued that Nathaniel was not only angry about being sent home, but that he was also mad because Mr. Grunow had given him an F on a progress report.

After three days of deliberation, the jury returned a verdict of guilty of second-degree murder, meaning that they did not believe Nathaniel intended to kill Grunow. Nathaniel faced a minimum of 25 years in prison when he was sentenced in 2001, but he received a 28-year sentence. Nathaniel will be 40 years old before he is released.

All five limitations of thinking—egocentrism, minimal coping skills and problem-solving strategies, immediacy, limited abstract reasoning, and magical thinking—are evident in Nathaniel's case.

Egocentrism. Egocentric children want their desires to be met immediately, no matter what the cost to others or without considering the perspective of others. Demonstrative of Nathaniel's egocentric thinking was his inability to recognize that Mr. Grunow could not let Dinora and the other girl leave the classroom and join him in the hallway. Brazill was only thinking about his desire to say goodbye to Dinora, and he failed to account for Grunow's responsible decision to deny Nathaniel's request. (Egocentrism was also demonstrated in the case of Venables and Thompson. Robert Thompson reportedly was upset because his mother would be angry with him for getting blood on his clothes. In the context of killing another human being, his mother's upset over stained clothing should have been the least of his worries.)

Minimal coping skills and problem-solving strategies. Despite the decision to shoot Mr. Grunow, Nathaniel actually displayed a number of potentially effective problem-solving strategies. Unfortunately, each of his strategies failed him. All of us experience frustration when we run out of problem-solving strategies or when our coping skills fail us. For example, we get frustrated in heavy traffic because we are completely powerless to change our circumstances. Nathaniel first dealt with his frustration about his suspension by trying to go home, but his house was locked and he couldn't get in. Not to be defeated, he then went to his grandmother's home. In an attempt to resolve his concern about his school situation, he wanted an adult to help him. This was a reasonable plan, but his grandmother had no transportation because her car was broken. This second roadblock still did not defeat him. Next, he decided to try to contact his aunt with the same goal in mind. She was not at work as he had expected. Next he decided to entertain himself, taking his mind off his situation by watching cartoons. This strategy failed him as well when the TV quit working properly. Even then, he was not completely defeated. He tried one last time to contact an adult by going to his aunt's home, but she was not there.

Nathaniel took the gun to school, and in his frustration he may have contemplated living up to the threats he had made earlier against Mr. Hinds, but he did not go directly to Mr. Hinds' office. I can only speculate as to how events might have unfolded differently, but it is reasonable to suppose that if Nathaniel and Dinora had gotten together, he would have left the school and never fired the weapon. Nathaniel utilized at least five or six strategies before he shot Mr. Grunow, demonstrative of a child who is fairly bright and willing to seek alternative solutions when one or more strategies fail. Many children of his age would have given up after the first or second plan. We all have a breaking point, and Nathaniel reached his that day.

Barry Grunow was not responsible for the way Nathaniel dealt with his own problems, but by the time Nathaniel had returned to school and was confronted in the classroom by Grunow, Nathaniel was very frustrated. He had been sent home from school and had spent two hours trying to resolve his problem, but his efforts had been thwarted at each turn. Finally, Mr. Grunow denied (rightly so) Nathaniel privacy to say goodbye to his girlfriend, whom he believed he would not see for several weeks. When Mr. Grunow pushed him, even though it was a gentle push, Nathaniel knew that other children were watching, including Dinora. In light of his afternoon felt cornered and he felt the need to save face. He attempted to do so by pointing the gun at Grunow.

As Nathaniel made eye contact with the girl to whom he was attracted, he had to think of some way to look "big" in her eyes—he couldn't back down, even to a teacher whom he respected. Even when he withdrew the weapon, though, I seriously doubt that Nathaniel intended to use it. It is reasonable to believe the claim made by his defense attorney that the gun discharged by accident. The gun was a cheap model and the boy had no experience with weapons. In fact, I would not be surprised if Nathaniel was hoping that Grunow would think the gun was a toy, hence allowing Nathaniel to tell friends he pulled a real gun on a teacher, but not getting him in any trouble.

Immediacy. I doubt that Nathaniel even stopped to consider the fact that, even though Grunow would not let Dinora leave the room, in only minutes school would be out and she and her friend would have been in the hallway anyway. Nathaniel was deeply infatuated with her and wanted to talk to her at that moment. Earlier in the day, he had given her flowers and a card. On the card he wrote, "This school year with you has been the best school year of my life."[13] In his mind, if he didn't say goodbye right then, he would never have the chance again.

Immediacy can also be observed in Nathaniel's decision to run and his subsequent decision to surrender to the police. When he realized what he had done, he fled. With no plan, it took only a few minutes for him to realize that he had nowhere to run. When he saw the police, he stopped the officer and confessed. In his mind, he wanted the situation to be over. He could not have realized how he could have been complicating his future trial by admitting his crime to the officer.

Limited abstract reasoning. At 12 years of age, it is unlikely that Nathaniel could have understood the significance of taking the gun to school, nor could he have fully understood the implications of pointing the weapon at Grunow. Children do all kinds of things that adults recognize as risky. They climb trees, ride bicycles without helmets, and rush out into traffic without looking. Even when they are aware of some risk, they do not think anything bad will happen to them—bad things only happen to other people. Sadly, shortly before I wrote this chapter, a classmate of my daughter's drowned trying to cross a rain-swollen creek. My daughter's response was, "How could he drown in a creek?" Even at 12 years of age, my daughter failed to consider all of the difficulties involved with crossing a stream when the water was high. To her, swimming across the creek was like swimming across the pool. This may have been the logic that led to the death of her classmate. An adult recognizes that when the water is higher, the current is stronger than normal and that there may be potential snags and unseen hazards beneath the water, making a normally simple swim much more difficult.

Even if Nathaniel thought about the inappropriateness of taking the gun to school, which I doubt he did, I am confident he did not know what it would lead to. Unlike the boys at Columbine High School, whose behaviors were motivated by cruelty, Nathaniel's motive for taking the gun was desperation. He did not know what else to do.

Therefore, when Nathaniel pointed the gun at Mr. Grunow, he was not thinking beyond that moment and had no idea what he would do next. An adult with mature, abstract reasoning would not have brought the weapon at all, much less pointed it at another human being. I believe Nathaniel when he said he did not know why he shot Mr. Grunow.

Magical thinking. The depth of Nathaniel's infatuation as well as his magical thinking can be seen in an episode of jealousy. Nathaniel was once jealous of Dinora's interest in another boy and threatened to commit suicide by swallowing packs of gum.[14] Of course, there is little chance that swallowing chewing gum could cause death. In his mind, however, the cause-effect relationship between gum and suicide made great sense and seemed like a logical threat. In regard to the shooting, I believe that his decision to pull the weapon from his pocket and point it at Grunow is evidence not only of minimal abstract reasoning, poor problem-solving, and immediacy, but also of magical thinking. He believed that the gun would cause the desired effect—to allow him to speak with Dinora.

In my first book, I provided a system for assessing the risk of violence (i.e., history of aggression, threatening behaviors, antisocial behavior). By observing these risk factors one can then assess the likelihood that an individual might engage in violent behavior. There is evidence in Nathaniel's case that the rule system described in my first book could be used to prove that his intent was to harm others. For example, law enforcement discovered that Nathaniel had visited numerous Internet sites on his computer that had to do with firearms. Ordinarily, that would be potentially troubling, but Nathaniel aspired to be a Secret Service agent. According to his mother, Nathaniel had seen the movie *Air Force One*, which inspired him to consider a career in the Secret Service. Given his career interest and his age, some interest in guns is not unusual or troubling. He was not downloading bomb-making instructions, littering his room with firearm paraphernalia, or engaging in any other excessive behaviors. He simply visited a few Web sites.

Likewise, one could suggest that his interest in guns permeated his life beyond the Internet and that his aggression and premeditation were well established before the confrontation with Mr. Grunow. There is no question that he took the firearm from his grandfather. Further, three days before the shooting he showed the gun to two friends. On the way home from school the day he was suspended he told Michele Cordovez he was going to shoot Mr. Hinds and he later asked another boy for a gun, saying he was going to use it at school. He elected to take the pistol to school, he pointed it at Mr. Grunow, and he pulled the trigger.

Yet, considering his age, one could explain these behaviors from a different perspective—one that could suppose that the shooting was a terrible accident committed by a good child who made some very bad decisions. When asked why he had taken the gun from his grandfather, Nathaniel said that he wanted his uncle to teach him to use it. Nathaniel did not collect guns and had no history whatsoever of using guns. He did not try to purchase them either from friends or from other sources. Many children are fascinated with guns. The gun's shiny nickel-plated finish and its toylike appearance may have made it easier for him to rationalize taking it from his grandfather's house.

Concerning his comments to Michele Cordovez and the other boy, one could suppose he was trying to save face in his embarrassment for getting in trouble. Boys brag and make rash statements to others. His cultural context was one where violence was not uncommon. The school had twice the number of incidents of criminal behavior in 1999 than the national average.[15] Like Nathaniel Abraham, whose case was discussed in Chapter 2, he had been raised without strong male role models. Brazill's mother never married Nathaniel's father, but when Nathaniel was five, she married a man who was abusive to her. That marriage ended in divorce five years later. Then she married Nathaniel's stepfather, but he too had an aggressive history in the home. Therefore, one could discount Nathaniel's comments as coming from a young teen who had been embarrassed by a school administrator, and a child who had been exposed to a culture where men defended themselves when someone disrespected them. To the best of my knowledge, these threats were the only incidents of aggression that are recorded in Nathaniel's life. Most of the children and adults that I have evaluated or reviewed for my books and articles have numerous incidents over many months at home, school, and work. Despite existing in an aggressive culture, Nathaniel does not seem to have adopted aggression as a general lifestyle.

I do not believe that Nathaniel premeditated the shooting of Mr. Grunow. Grunow was a very popular teacher. He was known for his ability to relate to the diverse population he served, and he loved his job. Earlier on the day of the shooting, Nathaniel had asked Grunow and some other teachers to pose for a picture together. Nathaniel's parents said that he loved Grunow, and Nathaniel also described Grunow as "the best." I believe him.

CONCLUDING REMARKS

This chapter began with a consideration of the dichotomous views of the origin of aggression—is aggression caused by human depravity, or are children incapable of formulating evil intent prior to a certain age? The question is not easily answered. Children are incapable of fully understanding the impact of their behaviors because of their developmental limitations. But the case of Venables and Thompson also demonstrates that children can commit atrocities that cause even the most hardened investigators to shudder. I suggest that children's cognitive limitations, combined with innate human propensities, can cause them to act aggressively. Depending on how old they are, children can form only limited intent. Yet, as Golding suggests in his novel, there may be something aggressive at our core.

A VIOLENT HEART

Based on the case of Nathaniel Brazill as I understand it, I deeply believe that if he were released from prison tomorrow, he would pose no threat to anyone. Unfortunately, however, he will not see the outside of a juvenile detention facility for a very long time. While detained there he will need guidance, counsel, and training to ensure that if he is ever released from prison he will not make the same fatal mistakes again—something that I think is highly unlikely. The biggest risk with Nathaniel Brazill is that the system will fail to provide him with the guidance that he needs.

In the wake of their heinous behavior, Jon Venables and Robert Thompson left behind grieving parents as well as a stunned community. As a result of Nathaniel Brazill's actions, Barry Grunow left behind a widow as well as a five-year-old son and a nine-month-old daughter who will never know their father. Homicide is always tragic, but it is even more so when the perpetrators and victims are children.

NOTES

1. D'Arcy Jenish, "Unparalleled evil," *Maclean's* (Internet edition), December 6, 1993.

2. Shirley Lynn Scott, "Ten-year-old suspects," *www.crimelibrary.com/classics3/bulger/4.htm*, 2001.

3. Shirley Lynn Scott, "The death of James Bulger: Tragic child abduction caught on tape: Jon Venables," *www.crimelibrary.com/classics3/bulger/8.htm*, 2000.

4. "Toddler killers' sentence review due," *CNN Online*, *www.cnn.com/2000/WORLD/europe/UK/10/25/bulger/index.html*, October 25, 2000.

5. Amanda Ripley and Helen Gibson, "When killer boys grow up," *Time* (Internet edition), January 22, 2001.

6. American Psychiatric Association, *Diagnostic and Statistical Manual of Mental Disorders, Fourth Edition Text Revision* (Washington, DC: American Psychiatric Press, 2000).

7. "Police: student suspect boasted before killing teacher," *CNN Online*, *www.cnn.com/2000/US/06/01/fla.teacher.shooting/index.html*, May 30, 2000.

8. Jeff Goodell, "Nathaniel Brazill's last day of school," *Rolling Stone* (Online Edition), October 10, 2000.

9. "Boy charged in teacher fatal shooting 'wasn't thinking clearly, " *CNN Online*, *www.cnn.com/2000/LAW/09/11/teacherkilled.ap/index.html*, September 11, 2000.

10. Jeff Goodell, "Nathaniel Brazill's last day of school," *Rolling Stone* (On-line edition), October 10, 2000.

11. "Teen accused of killing teacher says he prefers death penalty," *CNN On-line*, *www.cnn.com/2000/LAW/08/11/bc.teacherkilled.ap/index.html*, August 11, 2000.

12. "Defense rests after teen shows how he shot teacher," *CNN Online*, *www.cnn.com/2001/LAW/05/09/teacher.shooting.04/index.html*, May 9, 2001.

13. Jeff Goodell, "Nathaniel Brazill's last day of school," *Rolling Stone* (On-line edition), October 10, 2000.

14. Jeff Goodell, "Nathaniel Brazill's last day of school," *Rolling Stone* (On-line edition), October 10, 2000.

15. Jeff Goodell, "Nathaniel Brazill's last day of school," *Rolling Stone* (On-line edition), October 10, 2000.

CHAPTER 4

A PORT IN A STORM: GANG VIOLENCE

The power of deep-set cultural assumptions is so overriding, the glorification of war so all-pervasive, that in spite of the fact that many more men than women commit acts of violence, thinkers such as Freud, Piaget, and Kohlberg can comfortably adhere to the view that it is women who are morally deficient.

—Myriam Miedzian, in *Boys Will Be Boys: Breaking the Link Between Masculinity and Violence*

Based on who I am and how I look, and no good background on my name, I guess I just have to settle for less.

—Gang member[1]

Gangs have been around for centuries. As the title of this chapter suggests, gangs provide refuge and predictability for those whose lives are often tumultuous, unpredictable, and hopeless. Gangs give an individual's life meaning, and the gang provides a hierarchy that defines the person and describes his place in its social structure.

The 1961 musical *West Side Story* portrayed not only the violence of street gangs, but also the senselessness of turf wars and macho behavior. Groups of aggressive, violent men and women, boys and girls, have grown in membership in recent years and have engaged in increasingly violent behavior. Their use of sophisticated weapons, engagement in turf wars, and involvement in illegal activities like the drug trade and robbery are condemned by most members of American society, but among their members, these notorious behaviors generate respect and prestige. Violent street gangs, however, are but one type of gang.

TYPES OF GANGS

Violent Gangs

When we hear the word "gang," it usually brings to mind one thing—the violent street gang. But according to Capozzoli and McVey, there are three types of gangs: social gangs, delinquent gangs, and violent gangs.[2] Social gangs and delinquent gangs are nonviolent, and social gangs can even have a benevolent purpose. Violent gangs glamorize violence, use violence to initiate and maintain membership, and use violence to move up in the ranks of the gang; hence, violence is self-perpetuating. Therefore, violent gangs could not exist without violence, and violence is perceived not only as desirable, but necessary. One mother, a former gang member herself, explained that it is through violence and being tough that members earn a "rep" for themselves.[3] This mother worried about her children, both of them in gangs, saying that "most of these kids don't have enough street knowledge, and they'll come up dead looking to make those reps. I don't worry so much about the penitentiary no more. I worry about the cemetery."[4] Gang membership provides a possibility of respect that these young people would not otherwise have. They don't get it from the culture at large, and they may not get it at home. However, if they are willing to endure beatings, protect gang members, and risk prison or death, they can earn respect from their peers.

Tagger Gangs

Tagger gangs are delinquent gangs because they break the law by defacing public property, but they are usually nonviolent. Their main activity is creating elaborate graffiti on bridges, overpasses, and buildings. They often wear baggy clothes in order to conceal cans of spray paint.

Racial Gangs

The function of racial gangs is to maintain ethnic identity, gain a sense of power, and provide an outlet for anger caused by racism. These gangs are often violent, and they provide hope to people who find themselves in hopeless situations. The Bloods and Crips are two gangs that are almost exclusively black in their racial makeup. Asian and Hispanic gangs are made up mostly of individuals from those two ethnic backgrounds. Racial gangs tend to attract membership among people in their very early teens into their mid- to late twenties. Some gangs, Hispanic gangs for instance, allow a sort of graduated membership for boys who are preadolescent and have a kind of "membership emeritus" for men who are in their mid-twenties and beyond. The younger members are called pee wees and range in age from 9 to 13. The hard-core members are 14 to 22, and the "veteranos" are men over age 23.[5] Especially among Hispanic gangs, a family may have gang members across generations. According to Capozzoli and McVey, "fathers take pride in seeing their sons initiated into the gang just as their fathers did."[6]

Skinheads and other white supremacist gangs or neo-Nazi gangs are also racial gangs. Their purpose is the same as that of other racial gangs: to maintain racial identity, gain a sense of power, and provide an outlet for anger caused by racism. Skinheads often shave their heads, hence the term, and they have identifiable tattoos, often Ku Klux Klan symbols, swastikas, or other Nazi symbols. These hate groups sometimes use colored shoelaces to identify themselves even within their own organization. White laces imply white power, red laces demonstrate that one is prepared to harm or kill, and green laces imply that one is a gay basher.[7]

Motorcycle Gangs

Like racial gangs, motorcycle gangs maintain identity, a love of motorcycles, by congregating. The Hell's Angels are one of the most well known motorcycle gangs, but there are many others. In fact, many motorcycle gangs, often called motorcycle clubs, are made up of elderly people who buy expensive touring motorcycles. They wear specialized clothing identifying themselves as members of a given club, they congregate on some cycle, and they provide a sense of identity for one another. The initiation rites for membership in motorcycle gangs or clubs vary, but may be passive and may only involve paying dues or owning a specific type of motorcycle, such as a Honda Goldwing.

Ethnically Diverse Gangs

While most gangs are homogeneous in racial makeup, some are not. Gangs such as Folk Nation and People Nation are ethnically diverse. They are violent gangs that have allowed membership across racial lines. This is unusual, since one of the functions racial gangs serve is to maintain ethnic identity.

Benevolent and Business Groups

Even though they are not ordinarily considered gangs, scouting groups like the Boy Scouts of America and the Girl Scouts meet the criteria for being gangs discussed later in the chapter. They have specific initiation activities, they iden-

tify with one another by how they dress and the activities in which they participate, and they provide meaning and purpose to each other through participation in the "gang." Likewise, trade unions also meet these three criteria. Unions have initiation rites that usually only involve payment of dues. Members
identify with each other through union cards, and they have uniformity of purpose in that they are interested in furthering their financial and workplace welfare. Both of these groups satisfy all three psychological needs, identification,
affiliation, and cohesion, as well.

It may seem unlikely to consider a trade union as a gang, but consider this
example. I have a dear friend who is a metal worker. His company employs
thousands of men and women around the world. I heard in the news about
some activities that his company's union had been engaged in and asked my
friend if he was a part of the union. He told me he was. I knew him well enough
to know that he would not have condoned the union's decisions on the issues
that had come to light, so I asked him if he was required to be a part of the union. He said that he was not technically required to be in the union, but prag-
matically, he had no choice. If he did not join the union, he would have no
support in any of his activities. He would be perceived as a traitor by his union-
ized co-workers and, therefore, expendable if a layoff became an issue. At the
very least, he would be ostracized by his co-workers, all of whom were union
members. It is interesting to note how similar some of my friend's reasons for
joining the union are to the reasons teenagers give for joining street gangs.
They say they don't have to join the gang, but many of their friends are in
gangs, no one will protect them if they are not in the gang, and they say they
will be ostracized by their neighborhoods if they don't join.

Female Gangs

Street gangs commonly develop along racial lines and are usually male, although there are racially mixed gangs as well as female gang members. A recent trend in gang development is the all-female gang. These groups are
rapidly increasing in membership as girls and young women seek equality with
their male counterparts. At one time female involvement in gangs was mostly
limited to their relationship as a girlfriend to a male gang member, driving a
getaway car, carrying a weapon for a male gang member, hiding weapons, selling drugs, and committing burglaries. This is changing and female participation in gangs is growing. In California in 2000, there were reportedly over
8,000 female gang members; 75 percent of them were in Los Angeles.[8]

The government reports in its annual publication, *Crime in the United
States*, that between 1990 and 1999 female juvenile crime increased in nearly
every category. Especially noteworthy were aggravated assault which increased 57 percent for females (but dropped 5 percent for males during the

same period) and simple assault, which increased 93 percent (but increased 35 percent for males during the same period).[9] The Office of Juvenile Justice and Delinquency Prevention reported in 1999 that arrests for females had increased 103 percent between 1981 and 1997.[10]

At one time, if a female wanted to become a member of a male gang, she was usually *sexed in* during an initiation. To *sex in* involves engaging in sexual activity with one or more gang members. However, as females have sought equality with males, they have begun to expect more traditional forms of initiation such as *beating in*, *slashing*, or committing a *drive-by*.

Sometimes called "gangsta-lettes," female gang members are less likely to use firearms, although they will. More common weapons for female gang members are knives or their fists.[11] It should be noted that even though females are becoming more represented in violent crimes, males are still five times more likely to commit violent crimes than females. Males even lead some female gangs.

GANG ACTIVITY AND PURPOSE

Regardless of the type or makeup of the gang, all gangs include three activities and serve three purposes. All gangs have initiation rites, a dress code or identifying characteristics, and uniformity of purpose. Initiation rites are behaviors that must be endured or performed that allow one admission into the gang or group. Dress codes may involve actual uniforms, but more likely involve specific types of clothing, tattoos, body piercing, or use of specific colors in clothing, jackets, hats, or shoes. Uniformity of purpose has to do with the reason the gang exists. This involves the activities that take up the majority of the group time of the gang. Their purpose might be to control a geographical section of a city, to create graffiti, or even to perform some benevolent purpose.

The three purposes a gang serves are identification, affiliation, and cohesion. *Identification* is the process of changing one's behavior in order to fit in with a group. This is a normal process that we all engage in. Fads can easily be explained by identification. People buy certain automobiles, wear certain clothing brand names, or read a specific author's books, not necessarily because they like these things so much, but because their friends find value in these behaviors. For example, I was a soccer coach for several years. One year my soccer players decided to shave their heads as a mark of solidarity. Their decision to shave their heads was not based on comfort or personal preference. It was exclusively based on the desire to conform and identify with the other players. Teenagers identify by the type of tennis shoes or hairstyles they have. These identifying symbols (clothing, jewelry, and so forth) are sometimes called peer trademarks and are to be expected, especially with teens and young adults.

In the same way, gangs will identify with each other. Gangs use tattoos, body piercing, professional or college sports team logos, hand signals, language, hairstyle, types and colors of clothing, graffiti, or even specific tennis shoes or shoelaces to identify themselves as part of a given gang.

Especially in prison settings, adult gang members have elaborate tattoos that distinctly identify them with one gang or another. These tattoos are cataloged and identified by law enforcement and other agencies that study gang behavior. Tattoos are usually clearly visible on the face, neck, arms, knuckles and hands, shoulder, back, or chest. Many of these tattoos are quite large, and some gang members have more tattooed skin than untattooed skin. Tattoos may be applied by a professional tattoo artist or they may be homemade. Homemade tattoos are constructed using ink from a pen and a sharp instrument like a straight pin or needle. The needle is dipped into the ink, and then the individual punctures his or her skin in a pattern of the desired tattoo. The ink is transferred to the subdermal tissue where a permanent stain is created.

A second sociological need that is met through gang association is *affiliation*. Human beings have a drive to socialize with others. We tend to group together with people who think and act like us, The need to affiliate is strong enough that people will sometimes change their behavior through identification in order to fit in. In other words, one might change one's preferences in order to identify, thus creating a greater likelihood of affiliating.

The third purpose of gang membership is *cohesion*. Once a group has formed, its members either cohere or they disengage association from each other. Cohesion develops through uniformity of purpose and similar likes and dislikes. For example, bigoted individuals who hate minorities or members of certain religious groups cohere through their mutual hate or bigotry. Psychologically, we like to be around people who think as we do and who agree with our opinions. When a gang forms and its members share thoughts, likes, and dislikes, they are more cohesive. Cohesion and affiliation, especially in the case of violent gangs, also provides security in a violent or dangerous environment.

HISTORY OF GANGS

In their book, *Kids Killing Kids: Managing Violence and Gangs in Schools*, Capozzoli and McVey provide a brief history of gang behavior.[12] They suggest that the first gangs were pirates who roamed the seas in the early days of ocean travel. According to these authors, gangs were first identified in the United States just after the Revolutionary War in 1783. The first criminal gangs did not appear until the 1800's in New York City and were made up of Irish immigrants. After the Civil War, Jewish, Italian, African American, and Irish gangs were found in New York City, and the Ku Klux Klan formed at this time as well. Asian gangs appeared in California in the mid-1800s, and Hispanic gangs appeared in Los Angeles in the 1920s and 1930s. Today, violent gangs are present in most major cities across the United States and are active in many suburbs and small towns across the country. Gangs are especially active in the cities of Detroit, Los Angeles, Chicago, Philadelphia, and New York, and they present an ongoing concern to the community.

Gangs operate in nice neighborhoods as well as in housing projects. In fact, many gangs have been selecting quieter suburban neighborhoods because there is less competition with other gangs, the communities are not prepared or aware of their existence, and the drug market is untapped.[13]

Some gangs have their own alphabet—such as Crips crossing out "o's" to avoid using a letter in the Blood name. Children of gang members grow up in a gang culture. It is normalized because it is what they know. Children as young as four or five flash gang hand signs because they have seen the behavior in their mothers and fathers, young people who are sometimes still children themselves.

In its most desperate form, gang behavior goes hand-in-hand with drug use, guns, and illegal activity. Gang members, often only in their early teens when they first have children, neglect their children, preferring to run with their friends rather than to bathe, play with, or care for their children. Loaded weapons, drug paraphernalia, and liquor bottles litter living rooms instead of strollers, games, and toys. In an interview with a reporter from *Rolling Stone*, one gang member noted that she had seen her friends leave their children with their parents, knowing that the parent was strung out on crack at the time and incapable of caring for the child.[14] In circumstances such as these, one could expect that the gang culture will be with us for a while.

VIOLENT GANG INITIATION

There are three general methods for initiation into violent gangs. Members can *sex in* by engaging in a sexual act with other gang members. Using sex as part of initiation is generally reserved for females who wish to initiate into male gangs, although both males and females can *sex in* to same-gender gangs. Gang members can voluntarily endure a beating by other gang members as a method of initiation. This method is called *beating in*. The third method of initiation involves committing some crime. There are many forms this method could take. A gang member may be required to select a victim at random, run past the person, and cut the person with a knife in a practice called *slashing*. Yet another method would involve the gang member breaking into a home where it was known that the residents were present. A gang member could also be required to commit a drive-by shooting. *Drive-by's* and *slashings* could be directed at specific targets, such as rival gang members, but the victims are often chosen at random—people who just happen to be in the wrong place at the wrong time.

EFFECT OF VIOLENT GANG BEHAVIOR

Violent gangs have a dramatic effect on the communities where they are active. Vandalism, crime, drug proliferation, and violence are everyday realities to men, women, and children who live in neighborhoods controlled by gangs. Law enforcement officers in these areas are at greater risk than in areas where gangs do not operate, because in addition to crime that is faced by many communities, these men and women are faced with combating a loosely organized force that perceives members of the law enforcement community as the enemy.

It is fairly clear that inner city children respond to the violence that surrounds their daily lives by exhibiting the symptoms of post–traumatic stress disorder (PTSD). Among many symptoms associated with PTSD, these children experience sleep disturbances, intrusive thoughts, emotional numbing, diminished expectations for the future, and impaired social and academic functioning.[15] A fascinating research study published in 1997 conducted by Garbarino and Kostelny demonstrated that children who grow up in areas controlled by gangs respond to their violent environment in a way that is very similar to that of children who grow up in war zones like Bosnia, Zaire, and Rwanda. In both cases there is a proliferation of weapons, and mothers bear much of the responsibility at home because men are either fighting, injured, fleeing, or killed. This creates a high level of stress in mothers. They are frequent victims of domestic violence, their stress leads to depression and neglect of their children, and they have few resources available to assist them in correcting their circumstances. Garbarino and Kostelny also note that in both situations, representatives of "mainstream" society have only partial control. Social workers in the housing projects and relief workers in refugee camps leave at night and gangs take over in both places.[16] Finally, they have found that diminished expectations for the future experienced by children in these two environments produce "depression, rage, and disregard for human life—their own and others."[17]

In another study published in 1997, researchers found that parents of children in housing developments where violent activity was commonplace had a diminished view of the significance of a child's exposure to violence compared to parents who were raising children in less violent areas. In this study, parents and police were asked a number of questions about the impact of violence on children. The sample was divided into parents living in or near housing developments, parents not living in or near housing developments, and police. Responses by all three groups were very similar, but one major difference was that over one-third of parents living in or near housing projects disagreed with the statement that children who witness violence will have more problems later in life than children who do not.[18] This was compared to only 14 percent of the other group of parents and the law enforcement group. In other words, exposure to violence appeared to have desensitized this group of parents to its importance in the development of their children.

Gang members are not particular about when and where they commit their violent activities. Schoolyards, hospitals, parks, city streets, and shopping centers are all equally likely scenes for gang-related shoot-outs and turf wars. Gang members are not likely to be marksmen, and in the case of drive-by shootings, they fire from a moving vehicle, spraying bullets in the general direction of their targets. Therefore, innocent bystanders are likely targets when these young men and women shoot rapid-fire assault rifles and handguns at each other.

The Santa Monica Pier, 16 miles west of Los Angeles, is a popular spot for moviemakers. *The Sting* and many other movies have been filmed there, but in the early morning hours of July 4, 2000, the shooting that occurred was real. Two gang members were wanted for questioning in connection with three separate gang-related slayings. Just a few days earlier, police also believed that the two men had been involved in a shoot-out with a police officer that fortunately had resulted in no injuries. In an attempt to locate the suspects, San Bernardino deputies called one of the men's pager. When the suspect answered, they traced the phone call and pinpointed his location at the Santa Monica Pier. Deputies then notified Santa Monica police, who had jurisdiction, that the two men were at the pier.

When police arrived at the pier, the two men were talking on a pay phone. As police moved in, one of the men attempted to draw a gun from his waist. He had two firearms in his possession, but officers, along with a police dog, quickly subdued him. The second suspect fled into a video arcade. As he tried to exit the rear of the arcade, he was confronted by police. As the 25-year-old suspect fired his weapon into the crowd, three officers and two bystanders were hit. The man withdrew into the arcade, and for the next five hours he held 15 innocent people hostage.

It was just after 1 A.M. when the shooting began and the hostages were taken. Throughout the night, the man allowed hostages to use cellular telephones to call relatives, and he periodically released hostages, including some children. Just after 6:30 A.M., negotiators finally convinced him to release his remaining two hostages. The suspect then crawled out a window from the arcade and surrendered to police. During the standoff, nearly 100 people were trapped in a restaurant at the end of the pier, unable to leave because of the hostage situation that lay between them and the parking lot.

One of the officers who was shot suffered two broken bones in her arm, and the other two officers were shot in the leg. The two civilians, a 35-year-old woman and a 17-year-old male, also suffered gunshot wounds to the leg. The gang member who was arrested first appeared in court with bruises and dog bites that resulted from the scuffle surrounding his arrest. The second suspect was uninjured. It is sad to think that men like these gain prestige from their peers for cowardly behavior such as shooting unarmed, innocent women and children at a video arcade.

ROBIN RAINEY

It is a common misperception that all gang members are poor, residents of housing projects, and minority. This is most definitely not the case. Robin Rainey was a teenaged Caucasian girl in an affluent suburb of Atlanta. The upscale suburban county she lived in only had 36 murders in 1999. While a middle school student, just 12 years old, she was recruited into a Latino gang. By the time she was 17 years old, her life was falling apart. Attempts to correct her life's path had come in the form of counselors, drug rehabilitation programs, probation officers, judges, social workers, and two incarcerations in boot camp, but she continued to pursue her life as a gang member.[19] In an attempt to fit in with her Latino gang, called Vatos Locos, she dyed her hair black, learned Spanish, and began speaking with a Spanish accent.[20] Vatos Locos means "crazy homeboys" in Spanish.

Rainey committed a serious offense against her gang when she was seen riding around with members of a rival gang called Sur 13. Sur 13 and Vatos Locos were in the midst of a feud, and Sur 13 had reportedly even sent for help from a Los Angeles division of the gang.[21] In an attempt to reconcile with her gang, Rainey planned to be re-initiated by enduring a beating by fellow gang members. On October 30, 2000, she ate dinner with six other gang members. She and her friend, Mechelle Marie Torres, 18, willingly went with the group to a soccer park where the beating was to take place. Torres was not a gang member, but was to be *beaten in* to the gang that night, along with Rainey. For some unknown reason, during the assault one of the five gang members, a female, decided to stab Torres in the abdomen. Then the 16-year-old assailant pointed a gun at Torres' head and pulled the trigger. She missed the first time and then tried to fire a second time, but the weapon jammed.[22] She then borrowed a gun from another gang member and shot Torres in the head. One last time, she put the gun to Torres' head and fired the weapon.

The gang members then turned their attention to Rainey and shot her in the throat. The bullet nicked her spinal cord and caused paralysis in her right arm. As Rainey pretended to be dead, she heard the members of her gang talking about cutting off her tattoo—a way of emphasizing the revocation of her affiliation with the gang, as well as a warning to others. However, they could not find a knife to do the job, so the five ran off. After she was certain she was alone, Rainey got up and stumbled along trying to find help. She began vomiting and fell, temporarily losing consciousness. Later she regained consciousness, made her way to a pay phone, and called 911. When the authorities arrived, she identified her assailants, one of whom was her own former boyfriend. Torres was dead at the scene.

Investigators learned that the "initiation" was actually a premeditated murder. Several male gang members had allegedly ordered that Rainey be executed for betraying the Vatos Locos gang. One of them was a 19-year-old man named Raul Garcia-Bonilla, Rainey's former boyfriend. Investigators said that he stood by and watched while the other members of the gang killed Torres and attempted to kill Rainey. Garcia-Bonilla had allegedly raped Torres the month before the killing, but she continued to associate with the gang.[23] Police also said that three months before the murder of Torres, Garcia-Bonilla had beaten Rainey for six hours, but Rainey, like Torres, continued to associate with the gang.[24]

Investigators have searched for a sixth female in connection with the killing of Mechelle Torres, but they believe that she has sought refuge in Mexico. The trial in this murder and attempted murder case is pending as of this writing.

The story of Robin Rainey does not have a happy ending. One might have expected that such a close brush with death would have proved to be a wake-up call, becoming a turning point in her life, but it was not. After leaving the hospital, Rainey took up with another Hispanic gang. Six months after the attempt was made on her life, a sixteen-year-old male was shot in the back and killed at a park in a north Atlanta metropolitan area. He was shot five times as he apparently tried to run for his life. The murder was thought to be related to gang activity, and soon five gang members were arrested and charged with first-degree murder. Among them was Robin Rainey.

INTERVENTION

It is easy for members of the middle class to criticize young boys and girls for joining gangs, but most such criticism shows a lack of understanding of the everyday world in which these children live. A child who wishes to focus on academics, mind his own business, and remain free from gang affiliation and activities may find such a lifestyle difficult. He may have to cross through many gang-controlled areas on his way to school, work, or social activities. Without gang affiliation, he is a sheep separated from the flock—easy prey. Any gang member can prey upon him without fear of retaliation from a rival gang, and even his friends who belong to gangs might pick on or bully him. Gang membership, however, provides safety through a kind of insurance-by-affiliation, at least in certain geographical regions. Likewise, this child's peers may see him as a traitor, an Uncle Tom, for trying to improve his circumstances. In their perception, he is choosing a "white man's" way, academics or work, rather than associating with members of his own race, class, and interest group. Yet if these children choose the gang lifestyle, their life expectancy is greatly reduced and their options for a future are diminished.

Well-intentioned community groups have attempted to curb gang activity by building youth centers and other places where young males can congregate, based on the assumption that the cause of gang activity is that young people do not have anything productive to do. They believe that providing something productive for these young people to do will eliminate the need for gang affiliation. This logic is based on a flawed assumption about the sociology and psychology of gang involvement. Building a youth center gives young people something to do and provides a place to congregate. However, gang members themselves may choose such a location to congregate, and it gives them turf to fight over. Hence, what is intended to curb gang activity may actually facilitate it. As a case in point, the park where Mechelle Torres was killed was supposed to be a safe place for children to congregate in one of metropolitan Atlanta's most affluent suburbs, with many activities and programs for children.[25]

Likewise, interventions that have attempted to find employment for potential gang members are well intentioned, but ignore the bigger issues. Many gang members are poor, minority, and have numerous disadvantages confronting them. Working 30 hours a week at minimum wage will earn them less than $200, not to mention the fact that within their culture, they would be seen as sell-outs or ostracized by their peers if they seek "legitimate" employment. Yet they can make $2,000 for just an hour's work selling drugs or stolen property. If they sold drugs, they would not only earn far more money and in less time, but they would also earn respect from their peers. Respect from peers, by itself, is an extremely powerful motivator to teenagers and young adults.

In order to be effective, intervention programs must include education on how to recognize a gang's existence. Recognizing the presence of gang members or gang activity is an important part of prevention. Some indicators of gang activity in school would include graffiti, clothing associated with gang "colors" or styles, an increase in vandalism and crime, weapons on campus, a decline in school attendance, tattoos (gang tattoos are visible), and the use of vocabulary and hand signs associated with gangs.[26]

Many inner-city children, especially males, have a limited life expectancy. Why should they spend time in school or training for a job if they believe that they will be dead or in prison by their early twenties. Intervention requires giving them hope—something to work toward. They believe they cannot get out of the circumstances in which they find themselves. While working for the Atlanta Project, I found that when I entered some neighborhoods, it was like driving into another country. It was as if there were invisible walls around neighborhoods. For many of these children and their families, their lives were exclusively restricted to the blocks around their homes. They lived there and they expected to die there. There was no hope, plan, or expectation for ever leaving those few square blocks that they called home.

Counselors who work with gang members or potential gang members cannot expect to use their regular tools, especially empathy, for they will not work. Empathy is perceived as a weakness. Strength is required for respect, not empathy, and strength demonstrates to the child that the counselor cannot be manipulated.

Intervention programs must provide a connection with one's culture. According to one probation officer, many Hispanic young people seek gang membership because it "helps them feel as if they have their own little culture away from their homelands."[27] Intervention programs need a component that focuses on cultural awareness, identity, and pride in one's heritage.

Any gang intervention or prevention program must address the three processes of gang development—identification, cohesion, and affiliation. As discussed in *Blind-Sided*, the HOME Safe Project focuses on the prevention of violence by providing hope, teaching observation, and providing mentoring and empowerment to high risk individuals.[28] An effective mentoring program will provide a healthy source with which young men and women can identify. It is imperative for athletes, actors, and other icons of our culture to take time out of their schedules to give young people something to aim for. Men like General Colin Powell, James Earl Jones, and others who have demonstrated in their writings and their speeches that they could rise to great heights can motivate those who come from similar backgrounds. The Big Brothers/Big Sisters of America (BBBSA) program organized by the Center for the Study and Prevention of Violence is an excellent model.[29] BBBSA programs require dedicated men and women who are willing to go above and beyond the minimum expectation of three to five hours per week, and these volunteers must plan to remain with their child for several years. Outcomes research on these programs has demonstrated their effectiveness. In one study in the early 1990s, it was demonstrated that after an 18-month period, youth involved in BBBSA were "less likely to have started using drugs or alcohol, were less likely to have hit someone, felt more competent about doing schoolwork, attended school more, got better grades, and had better relationships with their parents and peers than those who did not participate in the program."[30]

Programs focusing on intervention must do more than provide a place to congregate. The program must generate a sense of bonding, a unit, in order for its members to affiliate and eventually cohere with each other. Churches, clubs, and other such organizations can provide for these needs. Military programs like Reserve Officers Training Corps (ROTC) not only can provide for affiliation and cohesion needs, but can also provide a way for young men and women to earn respect in a productive way. ROTC members are validated by their uniforms, ribbons, medals, and honors associated with productive activity in the program. Especially for minorities, young men and women can become defeated in the culture at large, believing that there is nothing they can do to change their circumstances. Efficacy is the term for believing that you can succeed. Through programs like ROTC, these young people can gain a sense of efficacy, learning that effort can have its rewards. Many potential gang members, as the quote at the beginning of this chapter shows, believe that they have to settle for less. Intervention and prevention must include teaching them that they do not have to settle for less and that they can succeed through nonviolent and productive avenues.

CONCLUDING REMARKS

In May 2001 prosecutors in New York City announced the indictment of more than a dozen gang members associated with the Bloods and Bloodettes, the female counterpart to the Bloods. The indictment charged the members with varied crimes including murder, extortion, robbery, and conspiracy. A U.S. attorney familiar with the case said that the "indictment will go a long way toward eradicating the gang's influence in New York City."[31] I do not mean to disparage those who made the indictments, and I am hopeful that this attorney's prediction is correct. However, the arrest and conviction of some gang members, even leaders, will not quell the activities of the gang. Gang members, like members of the mob, can operate from within their prison confines, giving orders to associates on the outside. These arrests most likely will not stop gang activity. Gang activity may slow for a few days or weeks, but then it will pick up again. New gangs or gang members will take the place of those who are no longer present. Likewise, even if this gang were completely disbanded, another gang would take its place. Gang activity will not be eliminated by law enforcement and the district attorney's office. Law enforcement has a difficult time tracing crimes. Gang members are devoted to each other and extremely loyal. They will go to jail themselves before they would rat on a fellow member. In fact, sometimes gang members without records will voluntarily take responsibility for a crime committed by a gang member with a record.[32] This keeps the guilty member out of jail. To make a dent in gang activity, one must address the causes of its existence and provide for the needs of the gang member in a more productive way. As Cappozoli and McVey note, gangs develop as a response to "the needs of their members."[33] Meeting those needs is the key to prevention and eventual elimination of gang activity.

NOTES

1. Leon Bing, "Homegirls," *Rolling Stone*, April 12, 2001, p. 85.
2. Thomas K. Capozzoli and R. Steve McVey, *Kids Killing Kids: Managing Violence and Gangs in Schools* (New York: St. Lucie Press, 2000).
3. Leon Bing, "Homegirls," *Rolling Stone*, April 12, 2001, p. 78.

4. Leon Bing, "Homegirls," April 12, 2001, p. 78.

5. Thomas K. Capozzoli and R. Steve McVey, 2000, *Kids Killing Kids: Managing Violence and Gangs in Schools.* (New York: St. Lucie Press, 2000), p. 73.

6. Thomas K. Capozzoli and R. Steve McVey, *Kids Killing Kids: Managing Violence and Gangs in Schools* (New York: St. Lucie Press, 2000), p. 73.

7. Thomas K. Capozzoli and R. Steve McVey, *Kids Killing Kids: Managing Violence and Gangs in Schools* (New York: St. Lucie Press, 2000), p. 73.

8. Leon Bing, "Homegirls," *Rolling Stone*, April 12, 2001, p. 78.

9. National Institute of Justice, "Crime in the United States 1999" (Washington, DC: Government Printing Office, 1999).

10. "Investing in girls: A 21st century strategy," Office of Juvenile Justice and Prevention, *www.ncjrs.org/html/ojjdp/jjjournal1099/invest2.html*, October 1999.

11. Leon Bing, "Homegirls," *Rolling Stone*, April 12, 2001, p. 78.

12. Thomas K. Capozzoli and R. Steve McVey, *Kids Killing Kids: Managing Violence and Gangs in Schools* (New York: St. Lucie Press, 2000).

13. Kent Kimes, "Girls in the gang," *Creative Loafing* (On-line edition), *www.atlanta.creativeloafing.com/2000–11–18/cover2.html*, November 18, 2000.

14. Leon Bing, "Homegirls," *Rolling Stone*, April 12, 2001, p. 86.

15. James Garbarino and Kathleen Kostelny, "What children can tell us about living in a war zone," in *Children in a Violent Society*, ed. Joy D. Osofsky (New York: Guilford Press, 1997), p. 38.

16. James Garbarino and Kathleen Kostelny, "What children can tell us about living in a war zone," in *Children in a Violent Society*, ed. Joy D. Osofsky (New York: Guilford Press, 1997), p. 38.

17. James Garbarino and Kathleen Kostelny, "What children can tell us about living in a war zone," in *Children in a Violent Society*, ed. Joy D. Osofsky (New York: Guilford Press, 1997), p. 38.

18. Ana C. Fick, Joy D. Osofsky, and Marva L. Lewis, "Perceptions of violence: Children, parents, and police officers," in *Children in a Violent Society*, ed. Joy D. Osofsky (New York: Guilford Press, 1997), p. 272.

19. Beth Warren, "Once gang victim, teen now faces murder charge," *Atlanta Journal/Constitution*, April 10, 2001, p. A16.

20. Beth Warren, "Once gang victim, teen now faces murder charge," *Atlanta Journal/Constitution*, April 10, 2001, p. A16.

21. Beth Warren, "Once gang victim, teen now faces murder charge," *Atlanta Journal/Constitution*, April 10, 2001, p. A16.

22. Beth Warren, "Police: Murder suspect was persistent," *Atlanta Journal/Constitution*, November 10, 2000, p. D3.

23. "Gang members arrested in shooting," *Creative Loafing* (On-line edition), *www.creativeloafing.com/gwinnett/newsstand/current/n_report.htm*, November 11, 2000.

24. "Gang members arrested in shooting," *Creative Loafing* (On-line edition), *www.creativeloafing.com/gwinnett/newsstand/currentn_report.htm*, November 11, 2000.

25. Kent Kimes, "Girls in the gang," *Creative Loafing* (On-line edition), *www.atlanta.creativeloafing.com/2000–11–18/cover2.html*, November 18, 2000.

26. Thomas K. Capozzoli and R. Steve McVey, *Kids Killing Kids: Managing Violence and Gangs in Schools* (New York: St. Lucie Press, 2000), p. 82.

27. "County tries to head off gangs with early intervention," *The Telegraph* (On-line edition), *www.macontelegraph.com/content/mac . . . /GANGS_0402 HO.htm?template=aprint.html*, April 2, 2001.

28. Gregory K. Moffatt, *Blind-Sided: Homicide Where It Is Least Expected* (Westport, CT: Praeger, 2000), p. 186.

29. "Overview of Big Brothers, Big Sisters of America," Center for the Study of Violence Prevention, *www.colorado.edu/cspv/blueprints/model/ten_Big.htm*.

30. "History and description of Big Brothers, Big Sisters of America," Center for the Study of Violence Prevention, *www.colorado.edu/cspv/blueprints/model/chapt/ BBBSAExec.htm*.

31. "Sweeping indictment names alleged gang leaders," *CNN Online*, *www.cnn.com/2001/LAW/05/09/gang.indictment.ap/index.html*, May 9, 2001.

32. Leon Bing, "Homegirls," *Rolling Stone*, April 12, 2001, p. 86.

33. Thomas K. Capozzoli and R. Steve McVey, "Kids Killing Kids: Managing Violence and Gangs in Schools (New York: St. Lucie Press, 2000), p. 65.

CHAPTER 5

TILL DEATH DO US PART: DOMESTIC VIOLENCE

The most important thing a father can do for his children is to love their mother.

—Henry Ward Beecher

My client sat across from me in my office. Her gaze was distant as she recalled those many years ago, her father screaming at the top of his lungs at her mother, and her mother crying and sobbing for him to stop. The eldest of three children, my client felt responsible for taking care of her younger siblings, even though at the time she herself was only six years old. There in my office, more than 20 years later, she related to me how she gathered her siblings together and hid in a hallway closet. There she buried them in coats and hats and sang lullabies to them, soothing their fears. When the shouting and crying overwhelmed her singing, she pounded on the wall of the closet with a shoe, trying to drown out the cacophony in the adjacent rooms. It was clear to me as I evaluated this woman's situation that her early experiences had deeply scarred her worldview and had contributed heavily to the dysfunction that brought her to my office in the first place. One would not be surprised to know that her issues involved trust and control in relationships.

Another client of mine was a man in his late twenties. He described to me the abuse he had suffered at the hands of his domineering mother. She was often beaten by her live-in lover, a man who was not related to my client. In turn, she displaced her anger and aggression on my client in his younger years, before he became too big for her to manipulate. Once he had failed to finish his dinner in the amount of time his mother thought was appropriate. As a punishment, she took him to their fruit cellar. There she handed him a shovel and forced him to dig into the dirt floor. As he dug, she told him she was going to kill him and bury him in the hole. After many minutes of this torture she left, leaving him locked in the cellar with the lights out for the rest of the night. He slept in the hole. Two decades later, my client was not only afraid of the dark, but he distrusted both men and women and had noticed excessive controlling behaviors in both his professional and personal lifes, including abusive behaviors toward his wife and children.

These are only two of the hundreds of clients I have had over many years in therapy—some children and some adults—who lived in homes where chaos reigned. Many of the children in my practice went home from school every day to a tumultuous existence filled with nightly arguments, threats, and beatings. Their lives were overshadowed by secrets—the secrets of the activities within the walls of their homes. Many of them came to believe that the turmoil in their homes was normal and that everyone lived lives just like theirs. Some of them never even considered that things could be different.

Those of us who are married have little trouble remembering our wedding day. No matter how long ago it was, many things about that day remain clear in our minds—the candles, the guests, the gifts. Perhaps among the most vivid memories is the romantic love that we felt for our betrothed. We believed that our love would last forever and that there was nothing we could not overcome. Many of us stood before ministers, priests, or rabbis and vowed to remain beside our betrothed through both the good times and the bad, promising not to separate except by death. Those words were easy to agree to because we were so certain our love would never change. But time does change things. Even the best of marriages will occasionally go through rough periods when love is tested, yet most young couples are not prepared for these difficulties. I have yet to do premarital counseling with a couple who believed that they would end up in divorce court.

I have spent many hours over the years in family court, testifying on behalf of children I represented as a therapist. Many family courts take the easiest cases first, leaving the most difficult cases for later in the day. I am usually there for a complicated case, meaning I often sit through several cases before the court clerk calls my case. As I listen to men and women argue over children, household possessions, and visitation or even ask the judge for restraining orders, some so angry or hurt that they cannot even speak civilly to each other in the courtroom, I wonder how long it took for them to digress to that point and what led to the demise of their relationship. I have often told my students that I think everyone contemplating marriage should be required to spend a day as an observer in family court. The reality of the potential pain in relationships is eye-opening.

Marriages and relationships fail for many reasons. Some failures have to do with financial hardship, while others involve infidelity. Many marriages crumble after a serious illness or death of a child. In these circumstances, seeing the spouse only reminds the other of the pain and loss they feel in regard to the lost child, leaving an unbearable hollowness. Some relationships end because the couple drifts apart over the years—filling their lives with their own interests until they reach a point when staying together gives them no satisfaction.

Of course there are other reasons, among them abuse of the spouse, children, or both. Some relationships digress to abuse, either physical or emotional, and others start out that way. Having worked with college students for almost two decades, I have been in an advantageous position to see many relationships begin and eventually lead to marriage. I have performed premarital counseling for many of these couples, and at other times I have mediated their difficulties years later when their marriages began to crumble. In all of these experiences I have observed that even though people change as they age, many of the things that become a problem later in marriage were present in the relationship from the beginning. For example, a man who was possessive or jealous while he was courting his future spouse will probably continue to be possessive and jealous after they marry. Likewise, a man who is physically abusive to a woman he is dating will probably continue to be abusive to her after the wedding bells ring. There is no good reason to suppose that those behaviors will go away.

I have worked with young women who were dating abusive men. When I ask them why they put up with physical and psychological abuse from their partners, their responses are almost always the same. They seem surprised that I would ask, and they tell me that it "isn't that bad." They believe that their love will cause their boyfriend to eventually grow out of his abusiveness. They also frequently take the blame for "antagonizing" him. "What makes you think he will change?" I ask them. The responses range from an expectation of maturity to "I don't know" to blank stares.

What these women fail to see is the basic flaw in their logic. When people are dating, they are on their *best* behavior. This is the best they do. As people become comfortable in their relationships, either by marriage or when they feel sure that their mate will not leave them, they let down their walls and show the less desirable side of themselves. Therefore, in abusive relationships, we can expect that at the very least the situation won't get any better; more likely the abuse will get worse.

Some years ago I was working with one of my female clients on relationships. She had presented at our first meeting that she wanted to improve her relationships with men. Up to that point, she had found herself easily falling into bed with any man she dated, and she had also found that she was never emotionally able to go much deeper in the relationship even when she wanted to. She found it frustrating that most of the men she had dated were not interested in a deep relationship with her. Over time in our therapy sessions, she made great progress toward her goals, but during one of our last sessions she told me about two men that she was seeing at the time. One of them was overtly selfish, smoked cigarettes, drank alcohol to excess, and was very possessive—all traits that she disliked. These were also traits that he did not tolerate in my client. He dated other people, but was extremely jealous if she even looked at another man. The other man was very thoughtful and kind to her, but he was divorced, had a small child, and in her words was unbelievably insecure. She told me that she wasn't sure what to do with the two relationships.

I asked her if she was ready to be a mother. "No," she said. I asked her if she wanted a husband who would smother her with his insecurities. "Of course not," she said. I then asked her why she was dating the divorced man. She said she liked some things about him and she figured that he might grow out of his insecurities. I asked her about the other man, wondering aloud if she would be satisfied with a husband who would go out on her, drink to excess, and criticize her. Again, she said no.

"But I'm not marrying either of them now," she said.

"But why date them if that is not something that you are thinking about?" I asked. Of course, many people date for fun and company with no intentions of going deeper in the relationship, but I knew that she was thinking in terms of eventual marriage because of other things she had told me.

"They might change," she said.

"But what if they don't?" I asked.

"I guess I never thought of it that way," she conceded.

This pattern of thinking is typical of many people as they approach their marriages and other committed relationships. They marry or move in with people who are already doing things that they don't appreciate. These partners hit, verbally abuse, or are sexually unfaithful to them early in the development of their relationships. Yet when they marry, the victims seem surprised that their partners are engaging in the very behaviors that were present all along. Sadly, I have personally witnessed a number of relationships where the man was physically abusive to the woman while they were dating, and some of these relationships progressed to marriage. Of those that did, some ended in divorce, while others stood the test of time. In either case, though, the beatings continued. Once, a woman came to my office concerned that her boyfriend had a bad temper. As she told me about her concern that his temper was interrupting their social life with friends, she talked in passing about a time when he hit her. I told her that I was concerned not only about his temper, but also because she seemed to dismiss the significance of the fact that he had struck her. She acted surprised, as if she did not know why I was even addressing his abuse. She had normalized his abuse and accepted it as part of the relationship, never considering that it was abnormal. I expressed to her the meaning of this normalizing of abnormal behavior and told her that I feared for her future if she did not change her outlook on relationships. I was confident that if this woman did not change her perspective, she was in for a very frustrating, and perhaps dangerous, future.

Conjugal violence may continue for years as verbal and psychological abuse. In other cases, physical and sexual abuse is there from the beginning. Sometimes the abuse is kept secret and those outside the family never know, but at other times, abusive behaviors end in the death of the victim.

RICKY NOLEN McGINN

On May 22, 1993, in Texas, Janet Roberts left her home for the day, leaving her 12-year-old daughter, Stephanie Flanary, alone with her husband, 43-year-old Ricky McGinn, a mechanic with an 11th grade education and stepfather to Stephanie. After Roberts left, McGinn said that he and his stepdaughter drank beer together. He claimed that at some point she became sick to her stomach, vomited, and then lost consciousness.[1] Afterward, McGinn said that Stephanie woke up and went for a walk. That was the last time she was ever seen alive. Three days later, her body was discovered in a culvert not far from their home.

McGinn was arrested for the murder, and the case against him was strong. Blood was found on his shoes and clothing. The child had been killed by four blows to the head with an ax. An ax with blood on it was found under the seat of McGinn's truck. He claimed that the blood came from fish he had cleaned, but the blood on the ax, as well as the blood on his shoes and clothing and in his car, matched Stephanie's blood.[2] DNA tests on other trace evidence showed that he could not be ruled out as a suspect, but those tests were inconclusive.

In June 1995 a jury convicted him of the rape and murder of the young girl, and McGinn was sentenced to death. McGinn claimed that he had been framed and that the DNA evidence had been tampered with. He missed two dates with the executioner, the first time because his lawyer's office had been damaged by a tornado. The second time was in June 2000, when the governor, George W. Bush, who was at the time campaigning for the presidency, gave him a 30-day reprieve. The parole board had voted overwhelmingly to deny McGinn a stay of execution, but based on arguments from McGinn's attorney that the original DNA tests were inconclusive, Bush believed that more sophisticated tests available five years after his trial would either exonerate McGinn or confirm the jury's verdict. This reprieve came after McGinn had already eaten his last meal and just 18 minutes before his scheduled execution. It was Bush's first reprieve in five years, and the case became a political issue for him as he campaigned for the presidency. The new DNA tests on the pubic hair found in the child's vagina and on semen stains found on her shorts confirmed that the jury's decision to convict McGinn was the proper one, and McGinn was executed by lethal injection in September 2000. He denied his guilt even as he was being prepared for execution. Janet Roberts, Stephanie's mother, supported the execution.

Tragically for this child, evidence presented at McGinn's trial indicated that the murder of Stephanie Flanary was not his first aggressive act. McGinn was tried and acquitted of murder once before, and he was a suspect in two other murders, one in 1989 and one in 1992.[3] He was also accused of rape in yet another case, and a daughter from a previous marriage accused him of molesting her, although no charges were filed in either of these cases.[4]

My guess is that McGinn had mistreated his stepdaughter before the murder. Based on his own story, he apparently saw nothing wrong with letting a minor drink herself into a stupor and then was unconcerned when she lost consciousness, even letting her leave the house when she woke up. When alcohol is present in a home, the risk for child abuse and sexual abuse increases. I do not believe McGinn's argument that he did not rape and murder this child. It is also sad that despite her husband's history, Stephanie's mother felt comfortable placing her child in his care. Sexual and/or physical abuse is far more likely when a nonbiological relative is in a home. I shudder when a parent, usually a mother, calls my office with concerns about her daughter who "may have been sexually abused" and I find out that there is a stepfather, stepbrother, or live-in boyfriend in the home. Even though there are many possibilities, I am almost certain what I will find.

RONALD EUGENE SIMMONS

It was Christmas 1987 in Russellville, Arkansas, when 47-year-old retired air force sergeant Ronald Simmons shot and killed 14 of his relatives. Among the dead were his wife, seven children, four grandchildren, one of them only three years old, and the spouses of two of his children. A few days later, on December 28, Simmons quit his job at the convenience store where he worked. He returned later and shot two employees, killing one of them, a 24-year-old woman named Kathy Kendrick. Kendrick had repeatedly rebuffed Simmons' advances toward her.

After killing Kendrick, Simmons left the store and went to an oil company where he had once worked. There, he shot and killed his former boss.

Simmons made two more stops, one at another store and a final stop at a trucking company where he had once worked. He shot and wounded people in these locations as well. He was arrested at the trucking company. When police questioned him about his family, they became suspicious that something was not right. They went to his home and there they found the bodies of four of his family members. The next day they found seven bodies buried on the property and two more in abandoned vehicles. All had been shot to death.

One acquaintance of Simmons, the husband of one of the people wounded in his shooting spree in Russellville, told reporters that he was "a common Joe who came to work and went home. Then all of a sudden, crash, off the deep end. There was nothing to even indicate this would happen."[5] Those who read my first book, know that it is a common response to suppose that a spree killer is "a common Joe" and that there were no indications of his potential, but it is almost never true. Several people noted that Simmons had a surly attitude, and he had recently erected a cinderblock wall around his house, ringing the top with barbed wire. In New Mexico in 1982, he was indicted for incest with his daughter Sheila, but he fled the state and was never prosecuted.[6] One of his young murder victims was Sheila's child, who was allegedly fathered by Simmons. Simmons' sister-in-law accused him of abusing his wife.[7] He harassed a woman half his age even though he was married, and his behavior was overt enough that other employees noted his advances. The trigger for the murders may have been his wife's threat to divorce him. Simmons' potential was clear for many years before this event. If his wife were alive to confirm or deny my suspicions, I suspect that she would agree with me.

In its extreme, domestic violence leads to extreme behaviors in the children who experience it. John Wayne Gacy was a serial killer who murdered 33 young boys, burying many of them beneath his house after he tortured, raped, and sodomized them. In his childhood, Gacy was badgered by his father, who thought he was a sissy. He called Gacy names and cruelly accused him of homosexual tendencies and of being a "girl." It is no surprise that in interviews with Gacy in the years before his execution he voiced disdain for homosexual behavior even though he frequently engaged in it both with his victims and with others.

The father is not always the perpetrator of aggression in the home. Serial killer Henry Lee Lucas was tortured in many ways by his mother. She dressed him like a girl and once forced him to go to school in a dress. She beat him as well as his alcoholic father, and she forced them both to watch her having sex with a variety of different men. Once she hit Henry with a two-by-four and he lay in a semiconscious state for several days. His mother "destroyed anything that he liked or took pleasure in," including a mule that Henry was fond of, which she shot and killed.[8] She called him evil and verbally badgered him all of his life until the day he stabbed her to death with a knife. That was not the end of his mother's torment, though. After more than 20 years in prison for her murder, Lucas was paroled and almost immediately began his life as a serial killer during which time he murdered at least 11 women.

Edmund Kemper's mother despised him because he looked so much like his father, a man she had become estranged to. His domineering mother made him sleep in a dark basement, where she cruelly shut him in every night out of fear that he would molest his sister, even though he had never harmed her. According to John Douglas, who interviewed Kemper, Kemper's mother treated him as if he were a monster, and he chose to live down to her expectations.[9] Kemper became a serial killer. He decapitated one of his victims and carried her head around in a box before eventually burying it outside his bedroom window. His last victim was his own mother, whom he also decapitated. That, however, was not enough to silence her critical voice. He cut out her larynx and ran it down the garbage disposal and then threw darts at her head.[10]

These dramatic effects of child abuse and domestic violence do not excuse the behaviors of the perpetrators, but one hopes that they give insight into the significant responses that are possible in children who are victimized by cruel adults. Children do not even have to be the targets of violence. Simply being present where domestic violence occurs leads to a host of negative effects. There is a huge body of research that has addressed the responses of children who witness violence in their homes. When a relationship is in turmoil, the effects are not lost on children. Watching their parents assault each other presents a number of problems for children, including the possibility of violence in their own futures. Even though we all have the freedom to choose our behaviors, environmental conditions can predispose us to behave in certain ways. The presence of domestic violence predisposes children to behave in dysfunctional ways intrapsychically and in their relationships both in childhood and later in adulthood.

It is estimated that in the United States approximately 1.5 million women and 835,000 men are raped and/or physically assaulted by an intimate partner annually.[11] The Centers for Disease Control and Prevention (CDC) has reported that many homicide victims are killed by intimate partners. For example, in 1992 and 1993, 28 percent of all female homicide victims were killed by intimate partners.[12] In a study of 8,000 men and 8,000 women, the CDC demonstrated that for more than three-quarters of women 18 and older who were raped or assaulted, their attackers were intimate partners (former boyfriends, ex-husbands, current partners, etc.).[13] In Philadelphia alone in 1997, there were 200,000 domestic violence situations.[14] Altercations like these will expose over 3 million children every year to domestic violence.

The prevalence of domestic violence is frightening, but even more troubling is the fact that children are present more than half the time when domestic violence occurs between the adults in the home. At least a third of American children have witnessed violence between their parents, and most of these have witnessed multiple incidents. Several studies have shown that the majority of children who live in homes where there is domestic violence have observed the violence at least once (75 percent–87 percent, depending on the study).[15]

Perpetrators can be male or female, wealthy or poor, old or young, Caucasian or minority, and professional or blue collar. Domestic violence is an issue in both heterosexual and homosexual relationships. Most perpetrators of conjugal violence, however, are male and younger than 40 years of age, and many have previous convictions for violent offenses. While females are far less frequently the aggressor against males in domestic violence, they perpetrate violence against children. Research indicates that women who are abused are more likely to abuse their children.[16]

RESPONSES BY CHILDREN WHO WITNESS VIOLENCE

When domestic violence is present in the home, children must decide what to do both in the immediate situation and in regard to their long-term response to the violence. They are forced into loyalty problems, having to choose one parent or the other in the conflict. They will express affection for their father as well as resentment, pain, and disappointment because of his violence. Children who witness conjugal violence are often left not knowing what to do. Their confusion leads to a variety of responses. Case studies on domestic violence have shown many immediate reactions from children, including hiding, crying, ignoring it, running away, seeking help from neighbors, calling police, or trying to intervene. When children are present as their parents fight, they are jeopardized in three ways. First and most obvious is the risk of physical injury to the child. They may be physically injured either directly as the target of a violent parent's anger or indirectly during an attack on the adult victim. Children sometimes attempt to intervene in altercations between their parents and are inadvertently hit by flying objects, shot, or stabbed. Second, violence in the family may lead to neglect of the children because of the intensity of the parental relationship. Parents cannot effectively perform their parenting duties when they are either perpetrators or victims of aggression by their partners. Children who elect to flee the home during an altercation are left unsupervised; they may be injured or killed when they are exposed to the elements, potential perpetrators outside the home, or other risks that follow being outside the home without supervision. Of course, a spouse who is physically incapacitated (i.e., bound, severely injured, or unconscious) due to domestic violence is incapable of properly caring for children. Likewise, the poor coping skills or problem-solving abilities that lead to violence in the first place may also contribute to dysfunctional parenting. Finally, without intervention, the psychological and social ramifications of viewing domestic violence are long-term. The effects on a child of watching his or her parents out of control, or of watching one parent humiliate, beat, or even kill another are devastating and profound. Even when intervention is attempted, it may be ineffective as long as violence continues to be present in the home.

Dozens of studies have shown a series of problems exhibited by children who witness domestic violence. These problems include aggression, phobias, insomnia, conduct problems, depression, anxiety, lower levels of social competence, lower levels of self-esteem, poor academic performance, and symptoms consistent with post–traumatic stress disorder (PTSD). These effects can be categorized into five groups: externalized reactions, internalized reactions, intellectual and academic reactions, social developmental reactions, and physical reactions.

Externalized Reactions

Externalized reactions are those behaviors in which a child acts outwardly. These include aggressive behaviors, rage, conduct problems, temper tantrums, fighting, substance abuse, risk-taking behaviors, running away from home, aggressive language, and the perception that violence is an acceptable means for resolving conflicts. Many studies have shown that exposure to violence in the home was a significant factor in predicting a child's own violent behavior. Further, witnessing violence may generate an attitude in the observer that justifies his own use of violence or an attitude that acting aggressively enhances one's reputation or self-image.

Internalized Reactions

Internalized reactions include a variety of psychological disorders that sometimes are called "acting inward" reactions. Depression, anxiety, low self-esteem and low autonomy, phobias, insomnia, nightmares, self-blame, and bed-wetting have been shown to be related to viewing domestic violence. Anger, despair, grief, shame, distrust, powerlessness, guilt, intense fear of death, fear of losing a parent, and confusion are also included in this category.

Intellectual and Academic Reactions

Both internalized and externalized reactions lead to academic reactions. Children who are exposed to violence have lower scores on verbal and cognitive measures and are more likely to exhibit an inability to concentrate. Their minds are on their troubles at home; they worry, and they feel helpless. These emotions make it difficult to concentrate on studies or to remember to turn in their school work. In extreme reactions, children see no future for themselves and, therefore, see no point in even trying at school. I once worked as a volunteer counselor in a high school program where the truancy rate each day was 50 percent. The problem for these children was not that they were incapable of doing their academic work. They just didn't see the point. Many of them literally expected to be dead before they reached adulthood, and others saw no connection between success in life and academics. The principal told those of us who were counselors that our main job was to find a way to get the children on campus. If we could do that, he said, they could be taught. It was a tall order.

Social Developmental Reactions

Children raised in the presence of domestic violence have lower levels of empathy, poorer problem-solving skills (which are directly related to violence in adulthood), and lower competencies with peers and adults. These children have more difficulty making and maintaining friendships, and they have control issues in their relationships as well. Children feel caught in the middle between their parents and find it difficult to talk to either of them. They are more likely to have adjustment problems in young adulthood as well as difficulty in adult relationships later in life. Children who witness domestic violence are less willing to try new things, and their drive to explore the world is reduced. This problem leads to apathy, helplessness, and lack of motivation.

Men who witnessed their parents' domestic violence as children are three times more likely to abuse their own wives than children of nonviolent parents. The sons of the most violent parents have been shown to be 1,000 times more likely to become wife beaters.[17] These children are more likely to engage in delinquent behavior. They exhibit greater distress in life and greater levels of maladjustment, and generally function at a lower level of social competence.[18]

Physical Reactions

The most obvious physical risk is to children who are hurt trying to stop the violence or children who are targeted directly by an angry parent. They may be injured while intervening between their parents or by accidentally getting in the way of an altercation. Almost half of all children who are physically abused are injured when they are caught in the middle of an inter-parental attack.[19] Angry parents will sometimes attack the child in order to control or humiliate the spouse—their actual target.

Other physical responses to witnessing violence or being the target of domestic violence include mostly stress-related responses such as stomach cramps, headaches, sleeping and eating difficulties, and frequent illness. There is a positive correlation between witnessing domestic violence and the risk of teenage pregnancy, and children who are sexually abused are at risk for contracting sexually transmitted diseases.

DIFFERENTIAL RESPONSES BY AGE

Infants and Toddlers

Preschool children are more adversely affected by domestic violence than other age groups, perhaps because they are most dependent on their caregivers and have the fewest coping skills available to them of all age groups. Infants and toddlers respond to conjugal violence by failing to thrive, developing poor attachments, and experiencing developmental regression as well as sleep disturbances and nightmares. Psychologist and psychology professor Joy Osofsky has noted in her research that excessive irritability, immature behavior, emotional distress, fears of being alone, and regression in toileting and language are related to viewing domestic violence.[20] Osofsky has also noted that viewing violence in the home interferes with normal developmental exploratory behaviors and the development of autonomy and trust.[21] These skills are critical in the development of *efficacy*—the belief that one can succeed.

School Aged Children

Children of school age experience depression and anxiety, and exhibit violence toward their peers. They are less likely to play freely and explore their environment. They experience nightmares and fear of leaving home. They also experience PTSD symptoms, and they worry about being safe. These problems, no doubt, interfere with normal childhood social and intellectual development, hence contributing to the academic and social problems mentioned earlier.

Adolescents

Adolescents respond to viewing domestic violence by exhibiting school problems, emotional problems, sexual problems, and alcohol/substance abuse.[22] By adolescence, children also begin to exhibit symptoms of adulthood relational responses to violence, becoming more at risk for abusing a partner or falling into abusive relationships. They are also more at risk for running away from home and delinquency than are their peers who are not exposed to conjugal violence.

Adulthood

In adulthood, the negative effects of viewing domestic violence as children linger. Adults experience depression, low esteem, domestic violence in their own relationships, and increased levels of criminality as opposed to their age cohorts who were not exposed to domestic violence in childhood. Even though one experiences fewer adverse effects as the length of time since exposure to a viiolent event increases, children and adults do not forget what they have seen and learned from their parents, and the effects of witnessing violence are long-term.

DIFFERENTIAL RESPONSES BY RACE AND GENDER

Race

Few studies have found differences based on race and ethnicity, but where differing effects have been found, African Americans were more likely to exhibit externalized symptoms, while Hispanics have been reported to show more internalized symptoms, specifically phobias and anxiety. Gender differences, however, are more dramatic.

Gender

Boys are more likely to exhibit externalized problems such as hostility and aggression, while girls exhibit more internalized responses such as depression and somatic complaints. Some studies have shown that both boys and girls exhibit trauma-related symptoms (PTSD), but in addition to these symptoms, girls also exhibit low self-esteem where boys do not.

Boys who witness violence are more likely to approve of violence than girls. In other words, viewing domestic violence or being the victim of violence at home legitimizes violence in boys and gives them permission to include aggression in their behavioral repertoires. Research has clearly shown that boys are more likely to fight, to become bullies, and eventually to use violence in their own homes against their girlfriends, wives, and children. As mentioned above, they are also more likely to engage in criminal activities and to commit violent crimes. In their relationships with peers, boys function at a lower social level than girls who witness violence, and they have poorer self-control. In future relationships, while boys are more likely to be abusers, females are more likely to acquiesce to violence and accept it from their friends and partners.

RELATIONSHIP OF DOMESTIC VIOLENCE AND
CHILD SEXUAL/PHYSICAL ABUSE

There is a very close connection between spousal abuse and the existence of child sexual or physical abuse within the home. The U.S. Advisory Board on Child Abuse and Neglect suggests that domestic violence may be the *single major precursor* to child abuse and neglect in this country.[23] Research data consistently show that among families where children witness domestic violence, nearly half of them also report child abuse within the family. Consider these studies:

- In a 1993 study, the Oregon Department of Human Resources reported that domestic violence was present in 41 percent of the families experiencing critical injuries or deaths due to child abuse and neglect.[24]

- A number of studies have shown a higher incidence of sexual abuse among children in families where domestic violence existed.[25]

- A national survey of over 6,000 American families found that half of the men who frequently assaulted their wives also frequently abused their children.[26]

- A New Zealand study in 1991 suggested that in the families where children had witnessed violence, 50 percent of the children had also been physically abused.[27]

- In one review of 200 substantiated child abuse reports in Massachusetts, 48 percent mentioned adult domestic violence and of the 67 child fatalities in Massachusetts in 1992, 29 (43 percent) were in families where the mother identified herself as a victim of domestic violence.[28]

Risk for child abuse within the family increases the longer and more frequent the use of violence by one parent against the other. In short, as a therapist, if I know that there is domestic violence in the home, the chance of the child I'm seeing being a victim of physical or sexual abuse is almost doubled.

TREATMENT

The most significant challenge in regard to domestic violence involves finding solutions to the problem. As the previous discussion shows, children differ in their responses to violence in the home. Some children are quite resilient, while others, like the serial killers that I mentioned, exhibit extreme reactions to abuse. Osofsky has shown through her research that resilience among children is linked to intellectual development, attention, and interpersonal skills.[29] Yet these three variables are all compromised when the home is unstable, as is the case when domestic violence is present. Osofsky also notes that "the most important protective resource to enable a child to cope with exposure to violence is a strong relationship with a competent, caring, positive adult, most often a parent."[30] Yet again, when domestic violence is present, the child must look outside the home for this relationship—perhaps to a therapist, teacher, or minister. Connecting with an adult outside the home requires initiative on the part of the child, forced intervention by social agencies, or both.

I try to achieve four goals with the children in my practice who are exposed to domestic violence or who are victims of violence themselves. First and foremost, it is my responsibility to ensure that the environment is safe. This may involve calling Family and Children's Services or the police. Once I am certain that the child is in a safe environment, it is necessary to give the child permission to talk about the violence. Aggression in the home is a secret, and children are conditioned to keep family matters to themselves. Providing a therapeutic environment where children can discuss violence allows the therapist to help children understand their feelings and let them know that they are not alone. The next step is to help children learn to cope with their specific responses to the violence and to understand the fighting they have seen. Children often believe they are to blame for the violence that they experience, and it is my job to show them the flaw in their logic. Finally, as a therapist, I try to help the family resolve the issues that lead to violence, to teach them better strategies for dealing with their problems, and to help them focus on the needs of their children. Resolution may involve re-educating flawed thinking on the part of the mother, such as the errant view that "He hits me, but he is good to the children." Anger management for the abuser is also necessary. In family therapy it is important to note that self-reports from parents concerning the existence of domestic violence can be unreliable. In one study, for example, over one-third of children reported seeing violence used by fathers against mothers, yet their parents reported that no violence occurred within the family.[31]

Complicating treatment is comorbidity with poverty and substance abuse. Many families will experience difficulty pursuing treatment because of financial issues, often related to poverty and/or substance abuse, as well as the very dynamics that led to abuse in the first place. Therapists must also be aware of risks to children and women when the relationship between partners dissolves. The majority of assaults and murders of battered women occur after they have been separated or divorced from their abuser.

Other interventions involve social agencies, mandatory arrest policies, stalking laws, and civil orders. Change is difficult in our society, which seems to condone violence and which mistakenly believes that domestic violence is a "family matter" that is best handled within the family.

CONCLUDING REMARKS

I have not even begun to discuss other factors that contribute to violence in the home. For example, this discussion can be expanded to include violence on television and in other media as well. The typical American child watches 28 hours of television a week, and by the age of 18 will have seen 16,000 simulated murders and 200,000 acts of violence.[32] Commercial television for children is 50 to 60 times more violent than prime-time programs for adults, and some cartoons average more than 80 acts of violence per hour.[33] It is unquestioned that latent exposure to violence decreases sensitivity and increases aggression in children.

Denial within the family prevents parents from pursuing intervention. Many parents believe that their children are unaware of the level of stress in their homes, and that they can hide domestic violence from their children. The research on children living in these homes contradicts this belief. Between 80 and 90 percent of the children living in homes where conjugal violence exists are aware of the violence even when parents think they have kept it to themselves.[34]

Violence in the home has devastating effects on the victims, the witnesses, and even the perpetrators who many times find themselves in prison, lose custody of their children, or take their own lives. Exposure to family violence could lead to the extreme responses I have described in the serial killers in the preceding pages. More likely, however, children who are exposed to conjugal violence or who are abused themselves will have problems in their future relationships, issues of dependency and trust, and difficulty with intimacy—both sexual and psychological. Their selection of dating partners and future mates could be compromised, and some may even select abusive partners. Insecurities resulting in promiscuity during adolescence are also likely. Some victims of abuse, especially males, may become abusers themselves, thus perpetuating the cycle of violence.

NOTES

1. "Death row inmate gets reprieve from Bush," *CNN Online, www.cnn.com/2000/LAW/06/02/texas.execution/index.html*, June 2, 2000.

2. "Death row inmate gets reprieve from Bush," *CNN Online, www.cnn/2000/LAW/06/02/texas.execution/index.html*, June 2, 2000.

3. Jonathan Alter, John McCormick, Mark Miller, and Kevin Peraino, "The death penalty on trial," *Newsweek* (On-line edition), June 12, 2000.

4. Jonathan Alter, John McCormick, Mark Miller, and Kevin Peraino, "The death penalty on trial," *Newsweek* (On-line edition), June 12, 2000.

5. Nora Underwood, "Murder in America," *Maclean's*, January 11, 1988, p. 27.

6. Terry E. Johnson and Daniel Shapiro, "A mass murder in Arkansas," *Newsweek*, January 11, 1988, p. 20.

7. Terry E. Johnson and Daniel Shapiro, "A mass murder in Arkansas," *Newsweek*, January 11, 1988, p. 20.

8. Joel Norris, *Serial Killers* (New York: Anchor Books, 1988), p. 111.

9. John Douglas and Mark Olshaker, *Mindhunter*. (New York: Pocket Books, 1995), p. 105.

10. Robert Simon, *Bad Men Do What Good Men Dream*. (Washington, DC: American Psychiatric Press, 1996), p. 300.

11. John W. Fantuzzo and Wanda K. Mohr, "Prevalance and effects of child exposure to domestic violence," *The Future of Children Journal* 9, no. 3 (1999): 25.

12. "What Is Domestic Violence?," Centers for Disease Control and Prevention, *www.cdc.gov/ncipc/dvp/fivpt/spotlite/home.htm*, February 2001.

13. Patricia Tjaden and Nancy Thoennes, "Prevalence, incidence, and consequences of violence against women: Findings from the National Violence against Women Survey" (Washington, DC: U.S. Department of Justice, November 1998), p. 2.

14. John W. Fantuzzo and Wanda K. Mohr, "Prevelance and effects of child exposure to domestic violence," *The Future of Children Journal* 9, no. 3 (1999): 23.

15. "Facts and myths," Unite for Kids: Helping Kids and Teens Exposed to Violence, *www.bmcstage.tvisions.com/understand/facts.html*.

16. "Children and domestic violence," Family Violence Prevention Fund, *www.fvpf.org/kids/*, 2001.

17. "Domestic violence and children," Famvi.com, *www.famvi.com/othersts.htm*, 2001.

18. "Domestic violence and children," Famvi.com, *www.famvi.com/otherssts./htm*, 2001.

19. "Facts and myths," Unite for kids: Helping Kids and Teens Exposed to Violence, *www.bmcstage.tvisions.com/understand/facts.html*, 2001.

20. Joy D. Osofsky, "The impact of violence on children," *The Future of Children Journal*, 9, no. 3 (1999): 36.

21. Joy D. Osofsky, "The impact of violence on children," *The Future of Children Journal* 9, no. 3 (1999): 36.

22. Joy D. Osofsky, "The impact of violence on children," *The Future of Children Journal* 9, no. 3 (1999): 37.

23. "Children and domestic violence," Family Violence Prevention Fund, *www.fvpf.org/kids/*, 2001.

24. "Children and domestic violence," Family Violence Prevention Fund, *www.fvpf.org/kids/*, 2001.

25. John W. Fantuzzo and Wanda K. Mohr, "Prevalence and effects of child exposure to domestic violence," *The Future of Children Journal*, 9, no. 3 (1999): 27.

26. "Domestic violence and children," Famvi.com, *www.famvi.com/othersts.htm*, 2001.

27. "Children and family violence: The unnoticed victims," Minnesota Center Against Violence and Abuse, *www.minicava.umn.edu/papers/nzreport.htm*. May 1994.

28. "Children and domestic violence," Family Violence Prevention Fund, *www.fvpf.org/kids/*, 2000.

29. Joy D. Osofsky, "The impact of violence on children," *The Future of Children Journal* 9, no. 3 (1999): 39.

30. Joy D. Osofsky, "The impact of violence on children," *The Future of Children Journal* 9, no. 3 (1999): 38.

31. "Facts and myths," *Unite for Kids: Helping Kids and Teens Exposed to Violence*, *www.bmcstage.tvisions.com/understand/facts.html*, 2001.

32. "Psychiatric effects of media violence," American Psychiatric Association, *www.psych.org/public_info/media_violence.htm*, October 1998.

33. Joy D. Osofsky, "The impact of violence on children," *The Future of Children Journal* 9, no. 3 (1999): 34.

34. "Children and domestic violence," *Family Violence Prevention Fund*, *www.fvpf.org/kids/*, 2001.

CHAPTER 6

MONSTERS AMONG US:
SERIAL KILLERS

Abandon all hope, ye who enter here.
                                    —Dante *The Inferno*

A classic movie dialog comes from the 1986 James Cameron horror classic *Aliens*. In one scene, the heroine, played by Sigourney Weaver, was talking to a little girl, discussing the alien creatures that threatened their lives. The child said that her mother had always told her that there were no such things as monsters, "no real ones," she said. "But there are," she continued. "Why do grown-ups tell kids that?" "Because," Weaver replied, "most of the time it's true."

Like the characters in this fictitious thriller, we can take comfort in the fact that most of the time there are no such things as monsters, but they do exist. Most murder victims are not chosen at random. Murder victims often know their assailants, and we can usually find a cause-effect relationship, even if that relationship doesn't always satisfy us. Even in the case of workplace homicides, the mass killings that remind us of the postal shootings of the 1980s, there is often order and predictability. Whenever I address lay audiences on the subject, I always emphasize that statistics about homicide can be misleading. For example, according to the 1997 *Uniform Crime Reports* published by the U.S. Department of Justice, Federal Bureau of Investigation (FBI), approximately 7 in every 100,000 Americans in metropolitan areas were victims of homicide in 1997.[1] While that may be a statistical truth, one can reduce the likelihood of becoming a victim in a number of ways. For example, the rate of homicide for people who lived in metropolitan areas was 7 people per 100,000, but rural counties had a homicide rate of only 5 people per 100,000. Many homicides involve illegal activities such as prostitution, illicit drugs, and dealing in stolen property. Therefore, one can also reduce the probability of being a homicide victim by avoiding criminal behavior, drug activity, and geographic areas where one might be more likely to become a victim. I assure these audiences that the likelihood of becoming a victim of a serial killer is infinitesimal. Some serial killers, like Ted Bundy, have chosen their victims at random from shopping centers or other public places, but of all the homicides committed around the nation each year, the percentage committed by serial killers is very small.

Many acts of aggression are labeled "senseless" by the media, family members of victims, or law enforcement, but in fact most acts of aggression do make sense. That is, they make sense to those of us who study violent behavior because there is reasoning behind the act that can be identified, organized, and categorized. The reasons may not be satisfying to many of us, but there is order nonetheless. But this is not always true. There are occasions when there is seemingly no explanation whatsoever for the actions of a violent individual. For example, in September 2000 an 18-year-old man in Montpelier, Vermont, attacked a 37–year-old college student from Japan. As she rode her bicycle down the street, the man attacked her with an ax. The woman died as a result of blows to the head. The perpetrator's apparent motive was simply to kill "the first person he came across."[2]

Likewise, in August 2000, a man broke into the California home of John Carpenter. Carpenter and his wife were both out of the house at the time, leaving their five children home alone. While their parents were out, 27-year-old Jonathon David Bruce broke in, used furniture to block the exits from the residence, and began attacking the children with a pitchfork. The terrified children, ranging in age from 7 to 14 fought for their lives. While some tried to hide in a bedroom, one escaped through a window and ran to a neighbor's house, but when she found no one home, she returned home. As the man continued his attack, two of the children locked themselves in a laundry room. "Let me in and I'll be nice to you," the deranged man told 13-year-old Anna.[3] The man then turned his attention to 9-year-old Ashley who had demanded that the man leave her siblings alone. As he stabbed Ashley, Anna and her 14-year-old sister Jessica escaped through the laundry room window and ran to another neighbor's house.

"There's somebody in my house who I don't know. [He's] stabbing my brother and sister with a pitchfork," Jessica told the 911 dispatcher. When police arrived, they entered the residence through a window. When Bruce, who was still inside, lunged at them with the pitchfork, police shot and killed him. A subsequent search of the home led to the discovery of the two youngest children dead in their beds. No clear connection between the family and Bruce has been made, and the motive is a mystery to this day.

I closed my first book with several cases of murder that were so evil, so inexplicable, that, like the two cases above, even as one who makes a living making sense out of "senseless acts of violence," I had a hard time understanding how a human being could act in such a cruel fashion. No discussion of homicide would be complete without acknowledging that there are extreme cases that almost defy comprehension.

The names of many serial killers are familiar to the general public, and millions of dollars have been earned from books, movies, and other media focused on serial killers. We are drawn to this marginal section of our culture for three reasons. Part of what draws our attention to these monstrous individuals is the same thing that leads us to go to a horror movie or to ride a roller coaster. We have a need to confront our fears in an environment that is safe and predictable. Amusement park rides and scary movies allow us to face frightening stimuli in a way in which we are physically and psychologically at minimal risk. Thrill-seeking behaviors like skydiving, motorcycle racing, and bungee-jumping also test our fears, not our courage, but obviously with more risk of injury than sitting through a horror movie.

A second reason is that movies like *The Silence of the Lambs* and books by former FBI profilers have made sense out of a process many people did not understand. Knowing how the process works gives people a sense of control over their lives. Books and movies that focus on serial killers demonstrate how they function and how they are caught. Perpetrators like Jonathon David Bruce frighten us because there is no clear purpose or predictability to their actions. The profiling process has given the public the same sense of control that they receive from an amusement park ride—it has imposed order on activities that at one time seemed random and without purpose.

A third reason is that many of us have a perverse desire to observe the freakish side of life. From the two-headed calf in a carnival sideshow to *Guinness Book of Records* behaviors where participants thread needles through their skin, we feed a side of our minds that seeks the outrageous. How many times have you heard someone say, "That is disgusting. Look at that!?" Such a comment is rather ironic, isn't it? Why would you beckon someone to look at something that you find disgusting?

Unfortunately, marketing of the extreme can result in the glamorization of heinous behaviors. Several stalkers and serial killers have admittedly modeled their behaviors after their deranged predecessors. Through movies, books, and news profiles, serial killers, stalkers, and other criminals have been elevated to positions of celebrity rather than being shown for what they are. At the very best, they are mentally ill individuals who need a great deal of help. At their extreme, they are cruel bullies seeking opportunities to harm others for their own personal pleasure. The two demented perpetrators of the Columbine High School attack in 1999 were attempting to execute the "perfect attack" on a school, trying to outdo other school shootings that had occurred in the years preceding their assault. Fortunately for those on the scene that day, the ineptitude of the two adolescents led to the deaths of far fewer people than they had planned.

Dating back to the days of the Old West, the public has sanitized the criminal behavior of gunslingers like Jesse James and William H. Bonney ("Billy the Kid"). While the name Jesse James, for example, should bring to mind a deviant thief who took the lives of his innocent victims for his own hedonistic financial gain, we hold a general opinion of him as a celebrity from American history. Many of these men and women were mentally ill. Others were cruel for cruelty's sake. In either case, it is important that the reader understand that there is nothing glamorous about murder. As I said in my first book, I never want to be guilty of creating a window through which the voyeurs of our society can observe murderers merely for the pleasure of gawking. My goal, instead, is to provide information for those seeking to better understand the complex nature of aggression. From this understanding one might then gain information to predict such behavior in the future and to provide intervention that can save the lives of the innocent.

SERIAL KILLERS, MASS MURDERERS, AND SPREE KILLERS

Serial killers are defined by the FBI as those who commit three or more murders with a cooling-off period in between. A cooling-off period can be very brief, only days, or there could be many months or even years between murders. Ted Bundy, Ed Kemper, John Wayne Gacy, Jeffrey Dahmer, Leonard Lake, and Kenneth Bianchi were all considered serial killers. Serial killers, however, are only one type of multiple murderer. *Mass murderers* are those who kill four or more individuals at the same place and the same time. Thomas Hamilton, who shot and killed 16 children and one teacher at a Dunblane, Scotland, primary school in 1996, was a mass murderer. Workplace shootings such as those at post offices are also mass murders if four or more victims are killed, assuming the killer did not kill anyone else in another location first. If there were killings in other places prior to the workplace shooting, the killer would then be called a *spree killer*. Spree killers are those individuals who kill in two or more places, like serial killers, but there is no cooling-off period in between. Andrew Cunanan was a spree killer who operated across the eastern United States from April to July 1997. He is believed to have killed two men in Minnesota before he traveled to Chicago, where he killed again. Cunanan then killed a cemetery caretaker in Pennsylvania. Eventually, he traveled to Florida, where he allegedly killed designer Gianni Versace and later took his own life. Cunanan was a spree killer even though his crimes were committed over a period of several weeks. His crimes lacked the required cooling-off period necessary to be considered serial killings. Mark Barton, who killed his family and then killed several individuals at two separate day-trading offices in Atlanta in 1999, could also be classified as a spree killer.

Serial killers commit their murders for a variety of reasons. They may kill for money, sex, or some other obsession. Female serial killers more often than not kill for money. They often use poison as their weapon of choice (unless they team up with a male serial killer). They leave fewer clues and are harder to catch than male serial killers. Investigators and medical examiners may mistakenly attribute death to natural causes. Male serial killers may be *serial sexual killers*, like Ted Bundy, or they may kill for money with no sexual intent, robbing their victims, killing them in the process, and then moving on to another city or state where they rob and kill again.

Mass murderers and spree killers are very different than serial killers. Their motives, methods, and personalities are different. Mass murderers appear to "snap" even though they often have a history of aggressive behavior and/or mental illness. Serial sexual killers, on the other hand, are driven by deeply rooted disturbances. They may be classified by the *Diagnostic and Statistical Manual of Mental Disorders, Fourth Edition Text Revision (DSM IV-TR)* as having antisocial personality disorder.[4] This disorder is sometimes called "sociopathology," and these individuals are often generally described as people who have little or no conscience. While there is some truth to this perception, it is not exactly accurate. The novice investigator of serial sexual killers may believe that the killer has no conscience or remorse, but these killers often do feel guilt, especially with their first victims. The internal guiding voice that we call a conscience or guilt, is present, but much less audible in these killers. They kill their victims and then use sex, alcohol, or other drugs to drown out what little conscience they have. It isn't that they have no conscience at all; rather, their dysfunction overrides their conscience. In some extreme cases, or in cases where serial killers have killed many times, their conscience has been so silenced over time, desensitized by their brutality, that it is scarcely audible in their own minds. Some of these killers fear being caught, but their fear weakens as their list of victims gets longer. In the back of their mind, they know they may eventually get caught, but they begin to tell themselves that they are invincible. Therefore, they become very bold, even contacting police and talking to investigators working on their cases.

Serial killers can be very difficult to catch early in their careers because they may travel extensively, killing in one city or state, and then moving on to a new location. Unless investigators take advantage of national or global databases and killer profiles, they may never know that the murders committed in their jurisdictions were the work of a serial killer. Serial killers may work as day laborers, carpenters, or hired hands, jobs that traditionally have a high rate of turnover. Therefore, they can easily disappear without attracting attention.

Because they lead dysfunctional lifestyles, serial killers are often arrested for other crimes such as burglary, assault, rape, drunk driving, or possession of a controlled substance. Therefore, they may be in jail, thus out of action as serial predators for months or years, on charges that have nothing to do with their murders. These killers may be released after serving their sentences, their jailers being unaware all the while of the depth of the atrocities committed by these inmates.

All serial killers are hedonistic. They see their victims as objects that exist for their own personal pleasure. For example, serial sexual killers perceive their sexual behavior as a one-way activity, exclusively for the pleasure of the perpetrator, with no regard for the wishes, pleasure, or feelings of the victim. Many serial killers have abuse in their backgrounds, no father figure, and a mother who is cold or distant.[5] These deficits create a perception in the serial killer that the world is an untrustworthy place. Therefore, the person develops the attitude that one must take care of oneself, first and foremost, even at the expense of others.

Not all serial killers have abuse in their pasts, however. Ted Bundy has been described as a sociopath, but he had no known history of physical or sexual abuse in his past. At the time of his arrest, his friends adamantly stood by his side. arguing that he could not be the "Ted" killer. They found it impossible to imagine that someone who seemed so normal to them could also be a serial killer. Because Ted Bundy was relatively bright, he was able to effectively manipulate the perceptions of others. Even though he claimed to be well above average in intelligence, the truth is that Bundy was bright, but not brilliant. His intelligence made it easier for him to decide which part of his character he wished to display and in what environment. For example, when he wanted to appear normal, he could behave that way. If he wanted to accost or sexually violate a corpse, he would arrange that as well. In both circumstances, he was driven by his personal hedonistic desires. The following two case studies demonstrate the sociopathology and hedonistic lifestyles of serial killers.

ROBERT LEE YATES, JR.

The public was stunned in April 2000 when police arrested 48-year-old Robert Lee Yates, Jr. Yates was a family man, married for 23 years, a retired military helicopter pilot, and by all appearances a respectable member of the community. Yet this seemingly unassuming man led two distinct lives. Yates, the father of five children, admitted to the murders of 13 people over a 25-year period in what were called the "grocery bag murders" because many of the victims were found with plastic grocery bags over their heads. As was true when Ted Bundy was first charged with the "Ted" murders, upon his arrest, many of the people who knew Yates quickly came to his defense. There was no way, they claimed, that their friend could have committed such deliberate and terrible murders. "Bobby [Yates] is the type of person you would want to have as a friend," said a friend.[6] Yet just six months after his arrest, Yates confessed in court to the murders of 13 people as well as the attempted murder of the only known victim to escape from Yates with her life.

Yates was raised in a conservative Seventh-Day Adventist home in Washington State. He began his college career as a premed student, but then joined the army, where he spent almost 20 years as a pilot and flying instructor. Yates, however, led two separate lives. In his public life, Yates seemed no different than thousands of other husbands and fathers. After his retirement from the military, he continued to fly helicopters for the National Guard. An employee of Kaiser Aluminum Corporation in Spokane, he lived in a modest home with his children and his wife Linda. He appeared happily married and took good care of his children. Home videotapes show Yates pushing his children in a swing in the backyard. In his other life, though, he was well known to the prostitutes of Spokane, Washington. He reportedly frequented the drug-infested neighborhoods of Spokane where prostitution was commonplace. He was a regular customer, known to many of the prostitutes as a "good trick."[7] Even more secret was his life as a murderer.

Yates began his serial killing career in 1975. That year, two young hikers were found dead in a wooded area. Yates, who had been in the area at the time, was numbered among a long list of those that authorities had considered as suspects, but investigators never pursued this lead. Twenty-five years later, Yates admitted that he shot and killed the man and woman, but he provided no motive.

It appears that Yates waited fifteen years to kill again, this time in the Spokane area. It was 1990 when the first three dead prostitutes were found in a secluded area outside Spokane. Two years later, another prostitute was found, and then another in 1995. Between August and December 1997, seven more bodies were found around Spokane. Investigators recognized that they had a serial murderer on their hands, and a multijurisdictional task force was organized to investigate the murders. Profilers were brought in to give their opinions regarding the type of perpetrator that detectives should be looking for, but they proved to be of little help. As investigators would later discover, Yates did not match the profiles provided by the experts, nor did he match the profile of serial killers in general.

The routine investigative practice of combing through known rapists, killers, and ex-convicts produced no viable suspects, either. By the late 1990s, investigators were getting desperate. The rate of the killings had escalated and they seemed no closer to catching the murderer. By the end of 1998, costs for the investigation skyrocketed, reportedly to nearly $2.2 million, and the city police of Spokane were forced to withdraw from the investigation team.[8] That left six deputies from the county sheriff's department on their own to follow the hundreds of leads that remained in the case. Spokane County Sheriff Mark Sterk, in desperation, even sought financial and software help from the software giant Microsoft, but Microsoft declined to assist.[9] At one point some speculated that the person killing the prostitutes of the Spokane area may have been the Green River killer who terrorized Seattle in the 1980s, but this theory was dismissed. The Green River killer was responsible for the deaths of as many as 49 women, but was never apprehended.[10] A billboard in Spokane displayed pictures of 16 of the victims, mostly prostitutes, and pleaded, "Help us find our killer!" A total of 18 prostitutes would lose their lives before Yates was arrested.

In the meantime, Yates continued with his seemingly normal life, going to work at Kaiser Aluminum, playing with his children, and maintaining the appearance of a routine father and husband. In the dark of night, he pursued his other life as well. Once or twice his secret life was nearly exposed. Spokane police once stopped Yates with a known prostitute in his car, but he claimed he was only giving her a ride. The prostitute, however, told police she had agreed to "perform a sex act" on Yates for $20.[11]

For three years a special task force focused on these killings, but two huge leads eventually brought investigators to Yates' doorstep. The first lead came from a witness who had seen one of the victims, a 16-year-old runaway and prostitute named Jennifer Joseph, whose body was found in August 1997, in a white Corvette with a white, middle-aged man. Even though that sighting was nine days before she was found dead, it was the last time anyone saw her alive. Investigators developed a list of all registered owners of white Corvettes in several states. The name of Robert Yates, Jr., appeared on the list, but it would be more than two years before police questioned Yates. Investigators began methodically checking with all owners of white Corvettes. They had DNA from several victims and asked these car owners for a DNA sample. Case by case, they eliminated the Corvette owners as suspects when their DNA sample did not match the DNA found on the victims. It was not until September 1999 that investigators questioned Yates, but he refused to give a DNA sample. They noticed that Yates was very nervous during the interview and that he "sweated profusely."[12]

Investigators now considered Yates a serious suspect, but they discovered that he had sold his Corvette two years earlier. After tracking down the current owner of the car, they impounded the vehicle, hoping that precious evidence had not been lost. Fortunately, they discovered DNA evidence that belonged to Jennifer Joseph in the form of blood still in the stitching on the passenger's seat. Sealing the case in the minds of investigators was the discovery in the car of a mother-of-pearl button that matched one that was missing from Joseph's blouse. Unbelievably, for more than two years, the button had never been discovered by Yates or the new car owner during day-to-day driving or routine cleaning.

The second lead was not even known to investigators for more than a year. It was August 1998 when prostitute Christine Smith narrowly escaped with her life from a man who had hired her for sex. At 1 A.M. a Caucasian male in a van picked Smith up in Spokane. Wary because of the rash of murdered prostitutes, Smith asked her customer if he was the serial killer. He told her that he was a helicopter pilot for the National Guard and that he was not a murderer, "because he had five kids and 'wouldn't want to do that.' "[13] But when they were in the back of his van, parked in a secluded area, the man struck her in the head, so she thought, and then demanded her money. Dazed, Smith managed to escape from the van. She initially thought she had been hit over the head with a blunt object. She made her way to a hospital, where the medical staff said she had been stabbed in the back of the head. She received stitches for the wound and was sent on her way. However, almost a year and a half later, Christine Smith was in a car accident. As a result of the accident, her head was X-rayed at the hospital. It was only then that medical personnel discovered bullet fragments still lodged in her head.[14] Instead of being stabbed a year and a half earlier in 1998, she had, in fact, suffered a gunshot wound to the back of the head, just like the other victims of the serial killer.

On April 18, 2000, detectives, armed with an arrest warrant, stopped Yates in his Honda Civic while he was on his way to work. At his first court appearance after his arrest, Yates pleaded not guilty, but the case against him was convincing. Investigators had DNA and fingerprint evidence linking him to victims.[15] They had the missing button from Joseph's blouse found in a car he once owned as well as blood traces belonging to that same victim in the car. The surviving witness, Christine Smith, said she had been shot by a pilot, father, and husband, who had paid her for sex—descriptions that matched Yates to a T. Finally, they had carpet fibers from the Corvette that "closely matched fibers investigators found on [Jennifer] Joseph's shoes and on a towel near her body."[16] Also found on that towel was a hair belonging to a Caucasian male.

Yates realized that he faced the death penalty if convicted. In an agreement with prosecutors, he changed his plea to guilty, thus avoiding the death penalty. After his change of plea, his family received perhaps the greatest shock of all. Based on directions from Yates, one final search for bodies led investigators back to his own home. Just outside his own bedroom window, investigators unearthed the body of 43-year-old Melody Murfin, a drug addict and prostitute who was attempting to get her life back together just before her disappearance. Unbeknownst to his family, his wife had slept just feet from this body and his children had likely walked over Murfin's unmarked grave as they played in the side yard of their home.

"He looks like a little mouse," the mother of one of the victims said of Yates when she saw him in court.[17] But Yates was no mouse. Rather, he was a cold-blooded murderer. As I have almost always found to be true, even though many people were surprised at the revelation of Yates' involvement in these killings, his family had some suspicions that something was not quite right. Even though they never suspected that Yates was killing prostitutes, his behavior was far from ordinary. "My mom had her suspicions that he was sneaking around. He would stay out until 2 in the morning," his eldest daughter told reporters.[18] She didn't know even half of the story. Yates spent so much time with the prostitutes of Spokane that they immediately knew who he was when he was arrested. He had a good reputation among the prostitutes and some said that they were "happy to see him coming."[19] In June 1996 when he returned home after being out all night, the back of his van was covered in blood. He said he had hit an animal and that he had "transported the animal and its owner to a veterinarian."[20] His wife believed his story. One report stated that some of the victims may have been held captive for several days before their deaths.[21] One has to wonder how he explained his absence during this time to his family.

He also had been accused of abusing one of his children. One of his daughters had called the police in 1998, saying her father had abused her. Yates was charged with assault, but the charges were later dropped.[22] Yates was said to be "a loving, caring and sensitive son; a fun-loving and giving brother; and an understanding, generous and dedicated father who enjoys playing ball, fishing and camping with his kids."[23] But caring husbands and fathers do not frequent prostitutes, don't stay out all night long without explanation, do not lead two separate lives, and don't lie to their families.

Yates' attorney, public defender Richard Fasy, said that Yates was remorseful. Perhaps he was. Just prior to being sentenced to 408 years in prison, he turned to the friends and family members of his victims who filled the courtroom gallery and sobbed as he apologized for his actions. Yet I wonder how much of his remorse was for his victims and their families and how much was actually for his predicament. One could suppose that a man who could murder repeatedly and who could lie to his own family, could certainly find it easy to lie to the public. Perhaps his true identity and his contempt for the rest of the world are most accurately portrayed by the bumper sticker on his Honda Civic, the vehicle he was driving when he was arrested. It said, "Why Must I Be Surrounded by Frickin' Idiots?"[24]

"I still love you dad, even though you did this," were the tearful comments of Yates' 25-year-old daughter just prior to his sentencing.[25] Along with the 408-year sentence, the judge also imposed a fine of $620,000 on Yates.[26] He is considered a potential suspect in murders in 11 other states, and law enforcement officers in Germany investigated Yates to see if he may have committed any crimes during two tours of duty there while he was in the military.[27]

Yates was atypical of serial killers in many ways. He was at least ten years older than the age range of most serial killers, and he had a seemingly stable home life.[28] He also had a relatively stable life in work and recreation. Former FBI profiler Robert Ressler noted that it was unusual for a serial killer to use a firearm. "Most victims of serial killers are strangled, stabbed or beaten to death."[29]

Yates provided no motive for his actions. Money is an unlikely motive even though he apparently tried to rob Christine Smith after he shot her. Most of the victims were "found partially or completely undressed."[30] But sex could not have been the only motive because he frequently had sex with prostitutes whom he never harmed. As with most serial sexual killers, he most likely needed to control, dominate, and humiliate them. He preyed on prostitutes, as many serial killers do, because he supposed they would not be missed and that the public would not care. Law enforcement noted this apathy toward deceased prostitutes. "If they had been teachers," said one officer, "the dollars [for investigation] would have flowed."[31]

JEFFREY DAHMER

More than halfway across the country in the summer of 1991, not long after Yates had begun his attack on the prostitutes of Spokane, America discovered that its fear of monsters was justified. News from Milwaukee, Wisconsin, released the details of a killer who not only killed his victims, but sexually violated them postmortem, cannibalized them, and kept their dismembered body parts in the freezer in his apartment. For most Americans, Jeffrey Dahmer is one of the most notorious serial killers of all time. There have been many serial killers throughout history, but Dahmer's torturing of his victims, as well as his subsequent desecration and cannibalism of their bodies, is almost beyond comprehension. Dahmer was accused of killing 17 victims over a period of 13 years. More than once he changed his mind and allowed the victim to leave unharmed, and on at least two occasions, victims he intended to kill managed to escape. Once, however, a 14-year-old Asian boy, partially drugged by Dahmer as he was preparing to kill him, escaped and was intercepted by police. After discussing the situation with the officers, Dahmer convinced them that he and the boy were lovers and that the boy was drunk. He told the officers that they had had a quarrel, and the officers returned the boy to Dahmer's apartment and then left. Soon thereafter, Dahmer killed him.

Jeffrey was alone and isolated even in his very early years. Those who knew him as a child noted that he never seemed to fit in and exhibited feelings of isolation and abandonment. Dahmer's fascination with death dated back to his childhood, when he began collecting animals that had been killed along the road. Jeffrey collected parts from these dead animals, storing them in jars, impaling them on sticks, and nailing them to trees around his parents' property. He stripped the flesh from their bones and attempted to reconstruct their skeletons after dissolving their tissues with acid. When he was an adolescent, he began torturing and killing neighborhood animals.[32]

There is no evidence that Jeffrey Dahmer was abused, either sexually or physically, by his parents, but what seems clear to me is that they were disengaged from their son's life. Even as a very young child he was apparently free to pursue his fascination with death, dead animals, and so forth with little intervention by his parents. Although his father noted his son's unusual behavior, he did not know what to do with the boy to bring him out of his shell. By the time Jeffrey was a teenager, he was having trouble at school, he had very few friends, and he was abusing alcohol.

He committed his first homicide at his home in Bath, Ohio, in June 1978, when he was 18. His parents had fought that day and they both left the home. His mother took Jeffrey's younger brother with her and left Jeffrey to take care of himself. This departure of his parents and sibling solidified that fact that Jeffrey was in the world alone. Dahmer picked up a male hitchhiker and brought him home. His intention was to have sex with the man, a theme that would permeate all of his murders. When the man tried to leave, Dahmer struck him in the head with a barbell and then strangled him to death with it. He then dismembered the victim, masturbating in the process, and placed the body parts in bags. At 3 A.M. he was driving around looking for a place to dump the bags. On the way, his vehicle crossed the center line and he was pulled over by police, who thought he had been drinking. They asked about the bags, clearly visible in the back seat of Dahmer's car. Jeffrey calmly told them that the bags contained trash he had planned to take to a landfill. The police did not pursue the issue, missing an opportunity to catch a serial killer at the very beginning of his career. After this episode, Jeffrey returned home with the bags. He again masturbated while looking at the victim's head. Later, he stuffed the bags of body parts into a drainpipe on his parents' property. They would remain there for two years.

That fall, he briefly attended Ohio State University, but he flunked out because of excessive drinking.[33] He then joined the army and was stationed in Germany, but he was eventually discharged for alcoholism. After his discharge,

Jeffrey returned to his parents' property and removed the bags containing the victim's bones, crushed them into tiny fragments, and scattered the remains over the property.

In 1981 Dahmer picked up a young Laotian boy and offered him money to be photographed nude. The boy accepted, but when they returned to Dahmer's home, Dahmer drugged the boy and took two pictures of him. Sometime later, the young man regained consciousness long enough to escape. The boy led police to Dahmer's home and the police searched his residence, but failed to find a skull he had in a dresser drawer.[34] Police later arrested Dahmer and charged him with sexual exploitation of a child.

During his trial, Dahmer's attorney reportedly told the judge that Jeffrey was "not a multiple offender" and that he believed Jeffrey was "caught before it got to the point where it would have gotten worse."[35] Nothing could have been further from the truth, but the judge believed Dahmer's penitent pleas and Jeffrey was sentenced to prison release, where he worked during the day and stayed in prison at night. Eventually, he was released from prison and began serving probation. Rather than being caught before "it would have gotten worse," as claimed by his attorney, Jeffrey was just getting warmed up. After his arrest and conviction for child molestation, his parents made him move out. He moved in with his grandmother who lived in Wisconsin.

It was eight years after the killing of the hitchhiker before Dahmer would kill again. In 1986 he killed a man he met at a gay bar. Dahmer claimed that he did not remember the murder. He said he awakened with the dead man in a hotel room with him, but even though he had no memory of what happened, he said he had no doubt that he had committed the murder. He stuffed the dead body into a suitcase and called a taxi. The cab driver unknowingly helped him load the suitcase containing the body into the trunk of the taxicab. Returning to his grandmother's home in Wisconsin where he had been living, he stored the body in the fruit cellar. A week later he dismembered the body while his grandmother was gone and put all of the body parts, except the head, into the trash. He kept the head for several days and eventually threw that in the trash as well. This seemingly trivial behavior was in fact a symptom of his mental disturbance, common in many serial killers. A body part, piece of clothing, or other item belonging to the victim kept by the murderer is referred to as a totem. Perhaps as significant as his decision to keep the victim's head is the dehumanizing aspect of throwing the head in the trash. As noted previously, most serial killers perceive people as objects. Dahmer treated a human being's head as he would have an old candy wrapper or empty beer bottle. He simply tossed it in the garbage.

Dahmer was now in a routine that eventually led to the death of 17 victims. Dahmer picked up willing sexual partners at gay bars and nightclubs. When they returned home with him, he drugged them, took pictures of them, and eventually killed them. When they were dead, he kept parts of their bodies in his freezer, closets, and bathtub, just as he had done with dead animals in his youth. Dismembering them, he ate parts of their bodies, thinking that through this cannibalistic behavior he would gain supernatural powers. He planned to construct a temple that he called a "power center" using the body parts of victims. He believed that the "power center," made up of six skulls of his victims, two complete skeletons, and a variety of lights and other objects, would give him passage to a higher level of consciousness.[36]

Dahmer was not a true necrophile. His motive was to find a perfectly passive sexual partner who would never leave him. He told former FBI Special Agent Robert Ressler that once while viewing a dead body at a funeral home he became so aroused that he had to go to the bathroom and masturbate.[37] It was submissive passivity, not death, that motivated him. In his attempt to achieve his goal of a passive partner, at least three times, using an electric drill, Dahmer drilled holes into the heads of his victims while they were sedated. He poured boiling water or muriatic acid into their brains in a ghoulish attempt to permanently incapacitate them. All three victims eventually died, but not before regaining consciousness and complaining of pain.

One of these incidents occurred in 1991 as his reign of terror was nearing its conclusion. Dahmer met a 14-year-old Laotian boy at a shopping mall. In an incredible twist of fate, this boy was the brother of a boy that had escaped from Dahmer in 1988. Dahmer had injected him and then left the apartment to buy some beer. Like his brother, he was able to regain enough composure to escape. Several witnesses saw the boy running naked down the street and called the police. As Jeffrey was returning from the store, he saw the police talking to the boy. He showed them his ID and told them that the boy was 19-years-old and that the two of them had been arguing. He convinced them that the boy was drunk. The police helped the boy back to Dahmer's apartment. Sitting in the living room of the smelly apartment, officers were unaware of a dead body lying on a bed in the next room. In the apartment they found pictures Dahmer had taken of the boy in his underwear. Still only partially conscious, and unable to speak for himself, the boy remained silent on the sofa. The police left, certain that the two homosexual males had simply been quarreling. Tragically, after police left, Dahmer killed the boy and had sex with his corpse. If the police had checked, they would have found that Dahmer had been convicted of child molestation. If they had searched the small apartment, they would have found the dead body in the bedroom and would have saved the life of this victim. Once again, Jeffrey Dahmer narrowly escaped detection, solidifying his sense of invincibility.

Later that year, in July 1991, two police officers were on duty in Milwaukee when they noticed a naked man with handcuffs attached to his wrists running down the street. They stopped him, and the 32-year-old man led them to Dahmer's apartment, where the man said he had escaped from a "weird dude."[38] As before, Dahmer tried to assure the police that the two were quarreling lovers, but these officers elected to look through the apartment. What they found astonished them. They discovered photographs of body parts, and they found severed heads in the refrigerator. After a brief struggle, Jeffrey Dahmer was taken into custody. A detailed search of the apartment led to the discovery of vats of acid, containers of various chemicals Dahmer had used to preserve body parts, jars containing genitalia, and numerous Polaroid photographs of his victims, some in bondage before he killed them, as well as photographs of their severed body parts.

Dahmer was convicted on 15 counts of murder and was sentenced to 15 consecutive life terms, totaling almost 1,000 years in prison. Originally, Dahmer pleaded not guilty, but later changed his plea to guilty, but insane. The jury did not believe the defense's argument that Dahmer was insane, but the prosecution presented the fact that Dahmer did not commit any homicides while in the military and that he obviously had some control of himself during that time. He was able to deceive and manipulate for the purpose of concealing his crimes, they argued, so he must have had some idea that what he was doing was wrong.

Jeffrey Dahmer was desperately in need of comfort, company, and a sense of belonging. Instead of channeling these desires into normal relationships, his fear and desire fueled within him a need to totally dominate his sexual partners. But as horrifying as his behavior was, there are people who are even more frightening to me than Jeffrey Dahmer. They are equally dangerous, if not more so, but it is their motivation that separates them in my mind. Dahmer was motivated by mental disturbance. He was not malevolent in the sense that he deliberately sought to harm or torture others. He did harm and torture them, but it was for another end, rather than torture itself. Richard Allen Davis, on the other hand, was motivated not only by hedonism, as was Dahmer, but during his crime against Polly Klaas as well as throughout his subsequent trial, he demonstrated no remorse—in fact, just the opposite, thumbing his nose at the court, the media, and, most heartlessly, the grieving parents.

RICHARD ALLEN DAVIS

Richard Davis was not a serial killer. His list of murder victims includes only one, but Davis' crime shocked our country. I include him in this chapter because of the inexplicable evil of his actions. His behavior rivals the coldness of a more prolific killer, Jeffrey Dahmer. Davis shocked us with his crime not only because of its randomness, but also because he continued to torment the victim's parents and loved ones throughout his trial.

The night of October 1, 1993, was supposed to be a fun night with friends. Eve Nichol, the mother of 12-year-old Polly Hannah Klaas, had allowed her daughter to invite two friends, Kate McLean and Gillian Pelham, also 12 years old, to spend the night with her at her home in Petaluma, California. According to reports, after supper the girls walked to a nearby store for refreshments. As the evening wore on, they played in Polly's room, along with Polly's six-year-old sister.[39] Around 10 P.M., Mrs. Nichol told the girls to settle and to be in bed by 11.[40] She retired to her bedroom, taking the six-year-old with her. It was the last time she would ever see Polly.

At 10:30 P.M., as the girls prepared for bed, Polly opened her bedroom door and found herself standing face-to-face with a 6'3" man carrying a knife. At first, her friends thought that Polly had arranged some kind of prank to scare them.[41] However, they very quickly realized this was no prank. "Which one of you lives here?" the intruder asked the girls.[42] Davis tied up Polly's two girlfriends and then carried Polly out of the house. It was the last time anyone would see her alive.

Within 30 minutes, the girls were able to free themselves from their bonds. They awoke Eve Nichol and related the unbelievable story of the abduction to Polly's stunned mother. As she absorbed the reality of the event, Eve called police, beginning almost two months of hope and public support.

When news of the abduction became public, the community rallied. Hundreds of volunteers searched for the little girl, distributed flyers, and helped in a variety of ways to bring little Polly home. In the first two weeks, several million flyers were sent out across the country. Eventually, an estimated 2 billion images of Polly Klaas were distributed around the country and around the world.[43]

A key turning point in the search for Polly came almost two months after the abduction, on November 28, 1993, when a woman in Oakmont, California, found some cloth on her property. As police processed this information, they were reminded that they had received a call from the woman about a trespasser the night of the abduction. Investigating officers had questioned a man on the property that night, but had allowed him to leave. After referring to their records, police located and subsequently arrested 40-year-old Richard Allen Davis. Further investigation matched Davis' palm print to a print found in Polly's bedroom, and on November 30, Davis was arrested.

For several days investigators questioned Davis. He eventually confessed on videotape to Polly's murder, and 65 days after her disappearance, on December 4, 1993, Davis led police to a shallow grave at an abandoned lumber mill near Highway 101 near the town of Cloverdale, California. There, 50 miles from her home, all hopes of finding Polly ended with the discovery of her remains.

As they looked into the case, investigators discovered a series of problems that would embarrass police. First of all, Davis had been confronted by police just hours after he had abducted Polly. The Sonoma County sheriff's deputies who responded to the Oakmont woman's call about a trespasser found Davis standing beside his Ford Pinto. The car was in a ditch on Pythian Road, and the officers actually helped Davis push the car out of the ditch.[44] Following procedure, the officers checked for outstanding warrants on Davis, but there were none. Davis told them he was a "sightseer" and, after a cursory check of his vehicle, they let him go.[45]

Back in Petaluma, officers were already working on the case and had a description of the man, but they decided not to broadcast the description for fear the media might acquire the information.[46] If they had broadcast the description, the Sonoma deputies may have recognized Davis and detained him—perhaps saving Polly's life. After his arrest and the details of this incident were discussed, Davis told his attorney that Polly was alive when he was stopped by the Sonoma County deputies and that he was "amazed that [she] did not scream out."[47]

The California Highway Patrol also missed an opportunity to connect Davis with the kidnapping of Polly Klaas when, on October 19, 1993, they arrested him for drunken driving. This time, sketches of the suspect were posted in the Highway Patrol office, but officers did not connect the sketch with their DUI prisoner.[48]

Davis was no stranger to kidnapping. He had been convicted two different times, serving five years for a kidnapping in 1976 and then serving eight years for kidnapping and robbing a woman in 1984. He had been released from his second jail term in May 1993, just a few months before he kidnapped and killed Polly.

At his trial, Davis' attorney's claimed that Davis did not sexually molest Polly, but the prosecution argued that sex was the motive for the kidnapping, even though Davis was not charged with sexual assault. His attorney claimed that his motive was simply burglary, and Davis averred that he was "toasted on drugs and alcohol" at the time of the kidnapping.[49] Robbery, however, seems an unlikely motive, since he specifically asked for one of the chilren who lived in the home and nothing was taken from the Klaas home. Davis showed no remorse whatsoever for his actions. He calmly sat through each day of the trial as if he were watching a mildly amusing television program, even smiling as testimony was given.[50]

Davis continued to torture the Klaas family even during his trial. He displayed his overt disdain for their grief when in his statement to the court he accused Marc Klaas, Polly's father, of molesting his daughter. "The main reason I know I did not attempt any lewd act that night was because of a statement the young girl made to me while walking up the embankment [where she was killed]: 'Just don't do me like my Dad.' "[51] From the courtroom someone shouted "Burn in hell, Davis!" and Marc Klaas had to be restrained as he tried to charge Davis.[52]

Even though there was some speculation that a second suspect was involved, the court determined Davis was guilty of the crime. In June 1996, when the jury read their verdict of guilty, Davis turned to the cameras and made an obscene gesture with both hands. Even after he was sentenced to death, he turned to the cameras and smiled as he was led from the courthouse.

Marc Klaas once said that his daughter had expressed fear that a "bad man would come and take her in the dark."[53] He "assured her that everything would be all right [and] that he would always be there to protect her."[54] Most of the time, these comforting words from a father are true.

From this tragedy arose two positive outcomes. First was the organization of the Polly Klaas Foundation, which spreads the word of missing children around the country. Second, California later passed the "three strikes" law, which requires a life jail sentence for a third felony conviction. The kidnapping of Polly Klaas was largely responsible for the passing of this law.

Davis was motivated by hate, contempt, and hedonism. His malevolence was evident in his cruelty to Polly and his ruthless responses in court. A macabre irony links the cases of Dahmer and Davis. In both cases, the police missed several opportunities to arrest them and possibly save the lives of their victims, causing the media to call their behavior into question. In Dahmer's case, the police even brought an escaped victim back to his doorstep, and in Davis' case the police helped him move his vehicle out of a ditch even while his victim was in the car.

While I cannot excuse or condone the atrocities that were committed by Jeffrey Dahmer, I can understand them. When one is mentally ill, reasoning does not function in the normal linear fashion. Given our linear thinking, his behaviors were senseless. Yet Dahmer did not function on the same level on which the normal population functions. Therefore, what seems illogical to us appeared perfectly reasonable to him. For example, our lives are, in part, governed by conscience. This component of our personalities begins to develop when we are very small. It tells us what we can do, cannot do, should do, and should not do. When it functions properly, it restrains us when we feel the urge to perform a behavior that is illegal or immoral. "Morality" is influenced by the absence or presence of religious views, social convention, and mores within a culture, but even though there is tremendous variability from one person to another concerning morality, there are some behaviors we would largely agree across the culture that are taboo. Killing another human being or using another human being for one's personal pleasure, regardless of the cost to that person, is almost universally considered immoral.

But for Dahmer, this moral structure was either suppressed or absent. As with Ted Bundy, a clinical sociopath, Dahmer's governing structure or conscience had been so dulled by years of torturing animals, interaction with dead creatures, killing, and pursuing his own desires that he had no qualms about drilling holes in a live victim's head, or attempting to gain some "super power" by cannibalizing his victims. He had desensitized himself to the morbidity of his actions by repeated exposure to his self-created mayhem. His abuse of alcohol silenced whatever remnant of guilt may have remained, making it possible for him to kill a victim and then go to work and function in his seemingly normal routine.

In my first book, *Blind-Sided: Homicide Where It Is Least Expected*, I discussed the case of Russell Eugene Weston, Jr., who killed two security guards at the U.S. Capitol. Weston was schizophrenic and believed that the government was oppressing him. He also believed that housed in the U.S. Capitol building was a device that could reverse time. This "ruby satellite," as he called it, was also responsible for turning people into cannibals. He was trying to get to this device the day he killed the two guards and nearly lost his own life. I feel more pity than anger for Weston. His mind created a reality for him that made his actions seem reasonable. Likewise, Dahmer, although not schizophrenic or delusional, had created a reality for himself that made his pursuit of the perfect sexual partner, an automaton that would be completely and passively at his service, seem reasonable.

Jeffrey Dahmer was killed in prison in 1994, bludgeoned to death in a prison bathroom by another inmate. Some found this to be a just reward and a fitting end to a monster's life. I am deeply sympathetic to the trauma Dahmer inflicted on the families and loved ones of his victims, but at the risk of sounding compassionate for a man who committed such unthinkable atrocities, I must say that I cannot share that opinion. Dahmer would never have been rehabilitated, and had he survived his prison stay, he would always be a danger to society. But while he was not found by the court to be legally insane, he clearly was psychologically disturbed. His dysfunction was partially to blame for his circumstances. It is not compassion, necessarily, that I feel for Dahmer, but empathy for a man who was haunted, much like Russell Eugene Weston, Jr., by demons beyond his understanding.

There is a distinct difference between Richard Allen Davis and Jeffrey Dahmer. Davis was vicious, self-serving, contemptuous, and malevolent. His only goal was to feed his own personal desires, and he was well aware of the pain his behavior was causing others. I believe that Jeffrey Dahmer, while also narcissistic, was not motivated by cruelty or torture. Even though he knew that he was harming others, his intent was not destruction. His dysfunctional logic allowed for his hurtful behavior. In his own perverse way, he even attempted to alleviate the pain of his victims through their murders. Davis, on the other hand, will continue to attempt to intentionally inflict emotional pain on the loved ones of his victim as long as he breathes.

Jeffrey took full responsibility for his actions, saying that his parents were not to blame for his behavior. While the parents of many serial killers tortured and abused their children, this doesn't seem to have been the case with Lionel Dahmer and Joyce (Dahmer) Flint. Their home was not peaceful, and Lionel Dahmer was absent at work much of the time, but that can be said of many families. The turmoil and arguing between his parents did not create the monster that their son became, but it fostered his loneliness and allowed him to sink deeper into a dysfunction that eventually led him down the path he chose.

The final chapter of Jeffrey Dahmer's life followed his death. His wishes were that he be cremated, but a legal battle ensued between Joyce Flint, Jeffrey's mother, and Lionel Dahmer over what should become of his brain. Mrs. Flint wanted to allow forensic pathologists access to Jeffrey's brain in order to study it for abnormalities that could potentially shed light on the cause of his extremely dysfunctional behavior. Lionel Dahmer, however, desired to close the book on Jeffrey's life by having his body fully cremated. The court eventually sided with Lionel Dahmer.

CONCLUDING REMARKS

The reader may find it unusual that I can understand, organize, and classify a killer like Jeffrey Dahmer much more easily than I can someone like Richard Davis. Davis killed one child, 12-year-old Polly Klaas, while Dahmer not only killed 17 people, but also tortured them, sexually violated them postmortem, and even cannibalized some of them. While psychological dysfunction would seem to be apparent in both cases, it is easier to classify Dahmer than Davis because Dahmer was feeding his dysfunction, while Davis apparently was feeding his cruelty.

Serial killers, spree killers, and mass murderers terrify us because of the apparently random nature of their crimes. Most terrifying is a crime like Davis' where the perpetrator apparently not only picks a victim at random, but comes into one's house in the middle of the night, stealing an innocent young life. What leads these individuals to the life they choose? In some cases, clear dysfunction in one's upbringing can be linked to later behavior, as discussed in Chapter Five. In other cases, mental illness plays a significant role. I would most definitely classify Jeffrey Dahmer in this category. As Carl Goldberg supposes, there may also be a malevolent component, one that is too often overlooked or ignored by both the legal profession and those in the mental health profession. If such a component exists, Davis would no doubt qualify.

Robert Yates is harder to classify—a seemingly normal family man (and seemingly a normal customer to prostitutes, as well), yet all the while maintaining a secret life as a serial killer. As a researcher and psychologist, I like to organize and classify the behaviors I see. Sometimes, however, the circumstances do not allow that to be done. Life is sometimes too complicated to reduce to a tidy little package. It is possible that a combination of variables led Yates to develop into a serial killer. Then, again, we will never fully understand what motivated him.

NOTES

1. U.S. Department of Justice, *Uniform Crime Reports* (Washington, DC: U.S. Government Printing Office, 1997), p. 16.

2. "Vermont student killed in apparently random attack," *CNN Online, www.cnn.com/2000/US/09/29/vermonthomicide.ap/index.html*, September 29, 2000.

3. "Rural terror: California town baffled by stranger's pitchfork attack," *CNN Online, www.cnn.com/2000/US/08/25/pitchfork.killings.02.ap/*, August 25, 2000.

4. American Psychiatric Association, *Diagnostic and Statistical Manual of Mental Disorders, Fourth Edition Text Revision* (Washington, DC: American Psychiatric Press, 2000).

5. Robert K. Ressler and Tom Shachtman. *I Have Lived in the Monster: Inside the Minds of the World's Most Notorious Serial Killers* (New York: St. Martin's Press, 1997), p. 242.

6. Margot Hornblower, "The Spokane murders," *Time*, July 17, 2000, p. 43.

7. Margot Hornblower, "The Spokane Murders," *Times*, July 17, 2000, p. 42.

8. "Serial killer probe relies on old-fashioned police work, DNA technology," *CNN Online, www.cnn.com/2000/US/04/22/spokane.slayings.ap/*, April 22, 2000.

9. "Serial killer probe relies on old-fashioned police works, DNA technology," *CNN Online, www.cnn.com/2000/US/04/22/spokane.slayings.ap/*, April 22, 2000.

10. "Serial killer probe relies on old-fashioned police works, DNA technology," *CNN Online, www.cnn.com/2000/US/04/22/spokane.slayings.ap/*, April 22, 2000.

11. "Serial killer probe relies on old-fashioned police works, DNA technology," *CNN Online, www.cnn.com/2000/US/04/22/spokane.slayings.ap/*, April 22, 2000.

12. "Serial killer probe relies on old-fashioned police works, DNA technology," *CNN Online, www.cnn.com/2000/US/04/22/spokane.slayings.ap/*, April 22, 2000.

13. Margot Hornblower, "The Spokane murders," *Time*, July 17, 2000, p. 42.

14. Margot Hornblower, "The Spokane murders," *Time*, July 17, 2000, p. 43.

15. "Family describes suspected serial killer as caring man," *CNN Online, www.cnn.com/2000/LAW/10/19/spokaneslayings.ap/*, October 19, 2000.

16. "Serial killer probe relies on old-fashioned police work, DNA technology," *CNN Online, www.cnn.com/2000/US/04/22/spokane.slayings.ap/*, April 22, 2000.

17. Margot Hornblower, "The Spokane murders," *Time*, July 17, 2000, p. 43.

18. "Family describes suspected serial killer as caring man," *CNN Online*, *www.cnn.com/2000/LAW/10/19/spokaneslayings.ap/*, October 19, 2000.

19. Margot Hornblower, "The Spokane murders," *Time*, July 17, 2000, p. 42.

20. Margot Hornblower, "The Spokane murders," *Time*, July 17, 2000, p. 43.

21. "Suspect in Spokane serial killings doesn't quite fit the mold," *CNN Online*, *www.cnn.com/2000/US/04/28/spokane.slayings.ap/index.html*, April 28, 2000.

22. "Suspect in Spokane serial killings doesn't quite fit the mold," *CNN Online*, *www.cnn.com/2000/US/04/28/spokane.slayings.ap/index.html*, April 28, 2000.

23. "Suspect in Spokane serial killings doesn't quite fit the mold," *CNN Online*, *www.cnn.com/2000/US/04/28/spokane.slayings.ap/index.html*, April 28, 2000.

24. Margot Hornblower, "The Spokane murders," *Time*, July 17, 2000, p. 43.

25. "Admitted Washington serial killer is sentenced to 408 years," *CNN Online*, *www.cnn.com/2000/LAW/10/26/yates.sentencing.ap/index.html*, October 26, 2000.

26. "Admitted Washington serial killer is sentenced to 408 years," *CNN Online*, *www.cnn.com/2000/LAW/10/26/yates.sentencing.ap/index.html*, October 26, 2000.

27. "Charges loom in Washington killings," *CNN Online*, *www.cnn.com/2000/US/05/17/spokane.slayings.ap/index.html*, May 17, 2000.

28. "Suspect in Spokane serial killings doesn't quite fit the mold," *CNN Online*, *www.cnn.com/2000/US/04/28/spokane.slayings.ap/index.html*, April 28, 2000.

29. "Suspect in Spokane serial killings doesn't quite fit the mold," *CNN Online*, *www.cnn.com/2000/US/04/28/spokane.slayings.ap/index.html*, April 28, 2000.

30. "Suspect in Spokane serial killings doesn't quite fit the mold," *CNN Online*, *www.cnn.com/2000/US/04/28/spokane.slayings.ap/index.html*, April 28, 2000.

31. Margot Hornblower, "The Spokane murders," *Time*, July 17, 2000, p. 43.

32. Robert Keppel, *Signature Killers* (New York: Pocket Books, 1997), p. 303.

33. Marilyn Bardsley, "Jeffrey Dahmer: Why," *www.crimelibrary.com/dahmer/dahmerwhy.htm*, 2001.

34. Robert K. Ressler and Tom Shachtman, *I Have Lived in the Monster: Inside the Minds of the World's Most Notorious Killers* (New York: St. Martin's Press, 1997), p. 126.

35. Marilyn Bardsley, "Jeffrey Dahmer: Runaway trail," *www.crimelibrary.com/dahmer/dahmerevil.htm*, 2001.

36. Robert K. Ressler and Tom Shachtman, *I Have Lived in the Monster: Inside the Minds of the World's Most Notorious Serial Killers* (New York: St. Martin's Press, 1997), p. 128.

37. Robert K. Ressler and Tom Shachtman, *I Have Lived in the Monster: Inside the Minds of the World's Most Notorious Serial Killers* (New York: St. Martin's Press, 1997), p. 122.

38. Marilyn Bardsley, "Jeffrey Dahmer: Exposed," *www.crimelibrary.com/dahmer/dahmerexposed.htm*, 2001.

39. "Taken in the night," *People Weekly* (Internet edition), October 25, 1993.

40. "Taken in the night," *People Weekly* (Internet edition), October 25, 1993.

41. "Taken in the night," *People Weekly* (Internet edition), October 25, 1993.

42. "Taken in the night," *People Weekly* (Internet edition), October 25, 1993.

43. KlaasKids Foundation, "The Polly Klaas story," *www.klaaskids.org/pg-stry.htm*, 1996.

44. Don Knapp, "Richard Allen Davis gets charged in Polly Klaas murder," *CNN San Francisco* On-Line, *www.cnnsf.com/newsvault/output/pollykla.html*, December 1993.

45. Melinda Beck, "The sad case of Polly Klaas," *Newsweek*, December 13, 1993, p. 39.

46. "Police request may have aided kidnapper," *New York Times*, Current Events edition, December 9, 1993, p. B14.

47. Don Knapp, "Richard Allen Davis gets charged in Polly Klaas murder," *CNN San Francisco On-Line, www.cnnsf.com/newsvault/output/pollykla.html*, December 1993.

48. Melinda Beck, "The sad case of Polly Klaas," *Newsweek*, December 13, 1993, p. 39.

49. "Jury recommends death penalty in Klaas murder," *CNN On-Line*, *www.cnn.com/US/9608/05/klaas.sentence/index.html*, August 5, 1996.

50. Elaine Lafferty, "Final outrage," *Time*, October 7, 1996, p. 64.

51. "Killer of Polly Klaas sentenced to death," *CNN Online, www.cnn.com/US/9609/26/davis.klass/index.html*, September 26, 1996.

52. "Killer of Polly Klaass sentenced to death," *CNN Online, www.cnn.com/US/9609/26/davis.Klass/index/html*, September 26, 1996.

53. "Anguished dad says life 'in ruins' since klaas death," *CNN Online, www.cnn.com/US/9607/03/klaas/index.html*, July 3, 1996.

54. "Anguished dad says life 'in ruins' since Klaas death," *CNN Online, www.cnn.com/US/9607/03/klaas/index.html*, July 3, 1996.

CHAPTER 7

BALANCE DUE: MASS MURDER

An eye for an eye only ends up making the whole world blind.
—Mahatma Gandhi

My book *Blind-Sided: Homicide Where It Is Least Expected* dealt almost exclusively with mass murder; therefore, this chapter will just touch on the topic. I encourage those interested in this topic to consult my previous book. In this chapter I will briefly address some of the issues that contribute to a person's decision to commit mass murder. Many times these murders are committed in the workplace. In fact, workplace homicide gave me my start in the field of violence and violence risk assessment. In the 1980s and 1990s, post office shootings were becoming a regular topic on the evening news. Shootings in Edmond, Oklahoma, Dearborn, Michigan, East Palatine, Illinois, New Orleans, Louisiana, Dana Point, California, Royal Oak, Michigan, and Atlanta, Georgia, just to name a few, left almost 50 people dead or wounded. At the same time I was Vice President for Student Life at a private college in Atlanta. During this time I encountered students I believed to be a threat to our environment. It became apparent to me that there was no reason to suppose that our college was immune to attack by a disgruntled student any more than a business was immune to an attack by a disgruntled employee. My study of the subject led to several publications, my work at the FBI Academy, and my work as a consultant to businesses and law enforcement.

Mass murder is defined by the FBI as the killing of four or more individuals at the same place and the same time. They are differentiated from spree killers and serial killers (see Chapter 6). Mass murders can happen within families, in public places like shopping malls, parks, and courthouses, and in businesses. Perpetrators usually have some connection to the location where they commit their murders or to the victims. For example, Ronald Eugene Simmons, discussed in Chapter 5, was a mass murderer. Most of his murders were committed at home, where he killed 14 of his relatives. His relationship to the location and the victims is obvious. Timothy McVeigh, on the other hand, was also a mass murderer, but his connection with his victims and with the location was not as obvious. McVeigh detonated the bomb that killed 168 people at the Murrah Federal Building in Oklahoma City, Oklahoma, in 1995. He selected his target, both the location and the victims, because of what they represented. He had nothing personal against the physical structure of the Murrah Federal Building. Rather, he chose it because it was a federal building and it represented the government he sought to punish. Likewise, he had nothing personal against any of the occupants of that building. Rather, he choose them as victims because of what they represented—the government. I discuss McVeigh and reasoning that leads to behavior like his in Chapter 10. Mass murderers who have no connection to the location of their crimes or their victims, like McVeigh, are relatively rare.

Lethal employees or other mass murderers either cannot see reality the way the rest of the world does or they do not choose to see the truth as it is to the more objective observer. For example, a business once asked me to consider the case of one of their employees who was, among other things, propositioning customers, even calling them at home. The same man had a history of sexist behavior in the workplace and had also been disciplined on several occasions for a variety of infractions. Yet this man did not see anything wrong with his behavior. He was blinded not by mental illness, but by a decision to remain blind, for if he had opened his eyes to the inappropriateness of his behavior, he would have had to admit his wrongdoing. His perception of truth allowed him to justify and rationalize his behavior. These same defenses, rationalization and justification, made it likely that this employee was also stealing from the company, goofing off, faking illness, or engaging in other behaviors to get back at the company. These behaviors allow the employee to "balance the books" with their employers, a process that may go on for many years. This is why employees who have a history of grievances, workman's compensation claims, or other problems are at great risk to commit workplace homicide. These behaviors are symptomatic of someone who is trying to get back at the company. Shooting co-workers is the last in a series of steps, not the starting point.

One business asked me to review the case of a man who was being dismissed after being employed there for many years. During the last five years before his termination he had been reprimanded several times by his boss. The man was doing a number of things that his boss had forbidden him to do and was failing to do a number of things that were part of his job description. After numerous documented conversations with the man, his boss finally wrote a letter to the employee that contained a list of expectations. There were two very clear columns in the letter: one listed a number of things that the man was forbidden to do; the second listed a number of things that the man had not been doing, but was required to do. The letter clearly stated that this was the last attempt to save him as an employee, and it also clearly stated that failure to attend to any of the expectations contained in the letter would result in his termination. The boss discussed the letter with the employee in person, and the employee signed the letter, saying that he understood what was expected of him and that neither list involved anything that was outside of his job description. He also acknowledged that the items in the two lists were reasonable.

The employee was notified that in three months his performance would be reviewed. At that time a decision would be made whether to continue his contract or to terminate him as an employee. At the end of the three-month period the man had violated every item on both lists. He had failed to attend to the list of things that he was required to do, and he had done every behavior that he had been forbidden. He was summarily terminated. I interviewed the man as he was closing his work with the company. When I asked him what he thought about the situation he said, "I don't know why they are doing this to me." As I went through the list of things that he was accused of doing that he was forbidden to do, he provided an excuse for doing each one. The same thing happened when I asked him about each of the items he was required to do. Even though I could have provided a *DSM IV-TR* diagnosis on this man (*Diagnostic and Statistical Manual of Mental Disorders, Fourth Edition Text Revision,* is the manual most mental health professionals use for diagnosing mental illness), he was not mentally ill in the clinical sense of the term. He chose to ignore his misbehavior, to rationalize his activities, and in the end to blame his employer for his own choices. Notice also how, in reference to his dismissal, the man said that the company was "doing" it "to" him. In his view, the company was doing something to him personally, not reasonably conducting business.

Unstable people who believe that they have been wronged or cheated by a company, organization, or family member(s) will believe these individuals or groups owe them something, regardless of the facts. In this way they justify their dishonest or violent behavior. Therefore, they can justify killing a girlfriend, spouse, children, other relatives, or co-workers when they believe they have been wronged. This may have been the motivation for Thomas Hamilton, who murdered 16 school children in Dunblane, Scotland, in 1996. He was a dishonest man who engaged in questionable practices with boys in his boys' clubs as well as numerous misrepresentations of himself and his organizations. I discussed this case at length in *Blind-Sided*, noting that he was not allowed to participate in an organization because of these practices and later blamed it for what he perceived to be its subversion of his business ventures. In the end, he justified killing school children, the very people he said he loved and wanted to help, because they represented the organization that had "wronged" him. He hurt the organization through these school children.

Over these past many years I have consulted with businesses both large and small. Among them are Delta Airlines, U.S. Airways, the Tennessee Safety and Health Council, Mannington Carpets, Westinghouse Corporation, and Johns Manville, maker of a variety of building materials. I have also worked with law enforcement agencies around the world, both formally and informally, assisting them in establishing criteria for hiring and firing in order to increase the security of their respective sites and personnel. In these many interactions, I have observed numerous situations where businesses have made it easy for perpetrators to commit their crimes. They have minimal security or no security at all. For example, I was once at a business that had a guard stationed at the entrance to the factory delivery area. However, visitors to the main offices did not have to pass by the guard's post. I traveled to and from the main parking area in front of the business several times. The area was in clear view of the guard's post, but I noticed that the guard never once looked up from whatever he was doing in the guard station. Therefore, even though a security guard was posted at the site, a perpetrator could easily have driven right up to the front door of the business, unloaded weapons, and walked in without being seen. I suggested to the business that they require their guard at least to look up and notice who was coming into the business. If a perpetrator exited a vehicle with a rifle or other obvious weapon, the guard would at least have a few seconds to call for help and to notify the occupants of the office building.

This business was run by very well intentioned managers and, all things considered, was one of the better businesses with whom I have consulted. Not all businesses are quite so well intentioned, however, and even though I would never blame anyone or any group for the behavior of an individual, it is clear to me that a business can create circumstances that make events either more or less likely. For example, as a parent, I know that I cannot fully control my children. They are free-thinking individuals and have the ability to choose their behaviors. However, if I often threaten to punish them, but never follow through when they disobey me, I make it more likely that they will disobey me. My behavior has not determined their behavior, but it has made some of their behaviors more probable.

Businesses do the same thing. A nurturing, caring business where employees are treated fairly and respectfully generates an atmosphere of return respect. Especially when employees believe that they have some control over their lives and that their opinions matter, they are much more likely to pursue their grievances through established, appropriate channels than they are to destroy company property or to shoot supervisors and co-workers. The reverse is also true. A company that treats its employees disrespectfully, gives them little or no say over their situations, and has no clear or functional procedures for expressing grievances will more likely be the target of vandalism or murder.

Some years ago I was asked to present a workshop on workplace violence at a business. The business had thousands of employees around the world, and I was asked to visit one of their plants where they were about to lay off 3,000 employees. The business worked with chemicals and had a number of Ph.D.-level chemists and managers in its employ. While I was there, I noticed a clear discrepancy in how upper-level management and middle managers were treated. The middle managers, professional people with Ph.D.'s in chemistry and nuclear science, were permanently housed in mobile trailers. Their permanent bathroom facilities were port-a-potties outside their trailers. These professional men and women had to go outside to use the bathroom. That wouldn't have been so bad in and of itself, but the executive office building was drastically different. Security to get into the building rivaled airport security. The offices were not extravagant, but they were very nice and consistent with what one would find in businesses of comparable size around the country. The discrepancy between these two levels was so stark that it was clear to me that executive management was unconcerned about middle management. If both upper and middle management were cutting corners and their facilities were not so disparate, the middle managers would not have resented their facilities as much. The message the executives sent to their employees was, "We have money for our comfort, but not for yours."

Yet that was just the beginning of the problems at this plant. I presented my workshop to about 50 men and women. The workshop was open to all managers, both executive and middle-level. Just as I finished my workshop, two upper-level managers came into the room. They proceeded to do a number of things that I had just spent two hours telling the other managers not to do because they were disrespectful to employees and fostered resentment. These two managers, using all the terms and phrases that one might learn in a workshop on how to make employees think you care about them, proceeded to explain that during the workshop, they had been searching the employee cubicles for Occupational Safety and Health Association (OSHA) violations. They explained that they just "cared about the safety of the employee" and that they were "all on the same team."

Needless to say, the members in the room were livid. Tempers flared, and the expressions on the faces of these two managers told me that they truly did not understand why everyone was so angry. These employees knew a layoff was eminent, which is why I had been called to do the workshop, but the company would not confirm that a layoff was pending. The company provided minimal facilities for these men and women to do their job. One man even had to repair the glass in his office window himself because the company was unresponsive to his work order requests. Yet these two managers used words that made it appear that they really cared about the employees. Perhaps these two did care at some level, but actions speak louder than words. This was all compounded with the fact that these managers should have been in my workshop, but chose to use the workshop time to covertly invade the workspace of their employees. I have never seen a workplace so perfectly primed for disaster. This worksite could easily have been the source of many *Dilbert* cartoons. As a side note, indicative of the way this company operated, it reneged on its contract with me and still has never fully compensated me for my two-day trip to the site.

The purpose of this discussion is not to belittle this company, but rather to demonstrate how a company can disrespect employees and foster an environment of frustration and hostility. Highly functioning employees will find a way to cope with circumstances even as bad as the ones I have just described. They will not shoot supervisors or blow up buildings because they have numerous coping strategies and problem-solving skills at their disposal. More likely they will find employment in a less hostile environment. On the other hand, socially inept employees with few coping strategies and problem-solving skills are less likely to leave on their own. They pose the highest risk because their lack of coping strategies and problem-solving skills leaves them frustrated, yet with no outlet for their frustration. The more helpless this type of employee feels, the more likely he or she will act out aggressively.

Unlike the company I have just described, many companies are well organized and good places to work, but they still find themselves the victims of workplace violence. There is no guarantee that a nurturing work environment will prevent a workplace shooting. In fact, in two of the workplace homicide cases I have studied, the kindness of a supervisor eventually led to his death. In one case a very kind supervisor allowed a dysfunctional employee to remain on the payroll, and in another case, a gracious boss allowed a former employee to return to the workplace after being fired. The only motivation in both of these cases was to be kind and helpful to the employee, but that kind behavior eventually led to the death of the supervisor when the employee shot and killed them. In the first of these two cases, an employer who was less concerned about the feelings of the employee would have dismissed the man sooner, and in the second case, a less thoughtful supervisor would have refused to interact with him after he had been dismissed. Despite these exceptions, a nurturing environment makes workplace homicide less likely.

JIAN CHEN

Businesses are at risk from disgruntled employees when the environment is abusive and when the employee has weak coping skills. The life of an employee who has few coping skills, weak social skills, and a weak support system may revolve almost completely around his job. He has few friends, no hobbies, and minimal goals for the future. When the employee is fired or when he believes he has been unfairly treated, he perceives that the last remaining vestige of his life is over. He has nothing left to lose and blames his boss, co-workers, or employer.

The risks that businesses face from disgruntled employees also apply to colleges and universities. College students invest many dollars, a great deal of time, and a lot of energy preparing for their careers. College is very expensive, it is stressful, and it is time-consuming. Students are almost totally controlled by the whims of what may be eccentric or sometimes downright cruel professors. If they are unhappy with a professor, they have little recourse other than moving to another college or university, but changing colleges could result in lost curricular hours, time, and money. The stakes get higher as students pursue advanced degrees. Most graduate programs, for example, have comprehensive examinations that a student must successfully pass at the end of his or her program. In Ph.D. programs, these exams last for days. When I took my comprehensive exams for my doctorate, in response to my exam questions I wrote almost 100 pages over three days, eight hours each day. Several weeks later, I was required to sit for my oral exams, during which my professors could ask me anything related to my six years of course work as a doctoral student or anything else they chose. Students in most Ph.D. programs are given two chances to pass their written and oral exams. If the student does not pass, he or she is out of the program. If that happenes, the student has lost several years of study and basically risks having to change careers. Just as in the workplace, students who are stable and have effective coping and problem-solving skills find ways to deal with the stress of graduate school and the eccentricities of their professors.

Students who function less effectively are at higher risk for acute mental disorders, stress-related health problems, and general dissatisfaction. In such circumstances, the stress of exams, pleasing faculty, and so forth can be equal to or greater than the challenges employees face in the workplace. Failing a class or program in college is very similar to being fired from a job. As a college professor and a supervisor of graduate students doing their clinical internships, I know that a poor grade on a paper, exam, or course could cost a student a job, a raise, or a scholarship. Even worse, it could cost the student his or her career. This is what happened to Jian Chen.

Chen was a medical resident at the University of Washington. He was in his second year of what often is a four- or five-year program. Chen had spent his first year of residency at the University of Mississippi, but transferred to the University of Washington when the opportunity arose. Chen's professor, mentor, and supervisor was a world-class physician named Rodger Haggitt. Haggitt was known around the world for his expertise in gastrointestinal pathology. Those who knew him extolled his exceptional skills as a physician, and one colleague claimed that he had "won every award there is to win in pathology and academics."[1]

Chen's duty at the University of Washington did not go as smoothly as he had hoped. His command of the English language was very poor, and many residents and students had difficulty communicating with him. But when the university offered him free English tutoring services, he refused the offer. Some who knew him said that Chen believed he was fluent in English when, in fact, his English skills were poor.[2] He reportedly did not take direction well, and after less than one year in the program he was informed that his contract would not be renewed for the following academic year. He was encouraged to pursue other placement for the remainder of his residency. The hospital staff tried to assist him in pursing placement and offered counseling, but Chen did not take any initiative to follow up on their efforts.

Losing his position in the hospital could have potentially harmed his career, and the university did not want Chen's trouble at their hospital to follow him to other residency programs. They carefully worded his dismissal to ensure Chen's possibilities of being hired by another university to complete his residency requirements. Chen, however, took no consolation from their efforts. Asian cultures tend to be lineal, and the activities of children reflect on their parents. He experienced depression and perhaps feared shaming his family at home because of his failure at the University of Washington.

There is some indication that some of the other residents were even afraid of Chen. They knew that he was aware that his contract was not being renewed for the coming academic year. He was difficult to communicate with and had refused counseling services to help him deal with stress. A fellow resident told reporters that Chen and Haggitt had engaged in arguments several times. "We all heard about the yelling conferences they had with each other about not being able to find another program," said one resident.[3] Even though Chen may have wanted to enter another program, he took no initiative to get into one.[4] Either he believed that Dr. Haggitt, because of his reputation, would get him into another residency without any effort on Chen's part, or he had already resigned himself to the fact that he would take his own life. Then, in May 2000, colleagues discovered that Chen was planning to buy a gun. When the university police confronted him, Chen told them that America was a dangerous place and he wanted the gun for self-protection.

Chen purchased a .357-caliber Glock pistol on June 6. After a mandatory six-day waiting period, he picked up the weapon from the gun shop on June 12. A little more than two weeks later, he used the weapon to take his own life and that of his teacher.

On June 28, Chen had scheduled an afternoon appointment with Dr. Haggitt. After Chen entered Haggitt's office he locked the door behind him. According to some reports, shouting was heard behind the closed door, but the most reliable information was that there were no shouts until after the first shot around 3:45 P.M. At that time, a witness heard Haggitt yell, "Oh my God." Then several other shots followed. After the third or fourth shot, someone in an adjacent office called security. It was nearly 25 minutes before the police entered Haggitt's office, at which time they found both men dead. The .357 Glock was on the floor near their bodies. Haggitt had been shot four times in the body and Chen had one gunshot wound to the head.

I am not sure that initially Chen intended to kill Haggitt. Chen respected him and perceived him as a mentor. A suicide note he left in his apartment indicated that he had planned to take his own life, but allow Haggitt to live. However, something apparently changed his mind after he entered Haggitt's office and locked the door. Some have speculated that Haggitt was shot as he tried to prevent Chen from killing himself, but the number of gunshot wounds to Haggitt's body implies that the shooting was at least in part deliberate. Perhaps Haggitt did try to stop Chen from killing himself and was injured in the process, and when Chen realized that Haggitt had been shot, he decided to finish the job and then took his own life. We will never know.

Shootings like this one have happened at colleges and universities around the country over the past several years. As in the workplace, the stakes are high in academia.

KENNETH MILLER

In Lincoln Park, Michigan, a resident of a retirement high-rise complex had been accused of harassing other residents and making crude comments. The board that oversaw disagreements between residents scheduled a hearing in April 2000 with the two complainants and the accused, a 56-year-old man named Kenneth Miller. Miller risked being evicted from the 14-story complex. After the meeting got under way, Miller became enraged at the accusations made against him and stormed out of the room after only a few minutes.

The deputy director of the facility, Phyllis McLeon, said that during the meeting Miller was making threats and that he would "take care of" this situation.[5] About ten minutes after Miller stormed out of the meeting, a maintenance man called over a two-way radio to say that Miller was coming back with a weapon. Miller allegedly shot and killed one of the women who had brought the accusations against him, but he also allegedly killed a woman who did not even live in the facility. Marilyn Higgins was delivering donated food to the residents and was shot and killed in a doorway. Unfortunately for her and her family, she was in the wrong place at the wrong time. At some point during his shooting spree, Miller allegedly put a gun to the head of another resident and said, "I will show you what this does," but for some reason he chose to let the woman go unharmed.[6]

After the shooting, Miller fled to the top floor and hid in an apartment. Police found him quickly and negotiated with him for over two hours. Miller had taken some painkillers and fell asleep while he was talking on the phone to a negotiator. SWAT members broke into the apartment where he was hiding and found Miller asleep. He was arrested.

Miller reportedly had no history of violence, but there was a history of mental illness. He stated on his housing application that he "suffered from schizophrenia and was on antidepressant medication."[7] Depression and schizophrenia alter a person's ability to think rationally and could have contributed to his extreme response to the accusations against him, especially if he believed he was about to be evicted from his home. To a rational mind, the shooting seemed senseless. McLeon said that the shooting took place all because of a dirty joke.[8] But just like a person losing a job or being dismissed from an academic degree program, Miller may have believed that his life was over. For a person who has minimal coping skills, compounded by mental illness and the threat of eviction, this was much more than an argument over a dirty joke.

ALAN EUGENE MILLER

In August 1999 in a town near Birmingham, Alabama, Alan Eugene Miller's mother kissed him goodbye as he left for work with his usual 7-UP and sausage biscuits. Around 7 A.M., the 350-pound man shot two of his co-workers and then drove a few miles away to a business where he was once employed and shot a third man.

Neighbors said Miller was a nice guy, and relatives said he never bothered anyone. Yet that day Miller, a truck driver for Ferguson Enterprises, went to work armed with a pistol. There, he shot two of his co-workers. One of his victims at Ferguson Enterprises was 32-year-old Lee Holdbrooks. Miller shot him three times in the face and chest, and one of the gunshot wounds was at nearly point-blank range. Holdbrooks dragged himself along a hallway after being shot, but eventually died. Miller's second victim at Ferguson was 28-year-old Scott Yancy. Yancy was the dispatcher and Holdbrooks was a fellow driver. Apparently, Miller believed that Yancy and Holdbrooks were conspiring against him by Yancy giving Holdbrooks better routes.[9]

After shooting Yancy and Holdbrooks, Miller drove a few miles away to his former employer, Post Airgas, a company that sells various forms of gas, some used in the welding trade. Miller had worked at Post Airgas until 1999, when he was laid off because of downsizing at the business. At Post Airgas, Miller confronted a former co-worker, 39-year-old Terry Jarvis. Miller was heard to say, "I'm tired of hearing rumors about me."[10] It was never clear what rumors he was referring to, but after confronting Jarvis, Miller shot him several times.

Police received their first 911 call just after 7 A.M. Then, just minutes later, they received calls from Post Airgas. The description of the shooter was the same in both cases, and they very quickly identified Miller as a suspect. Police spotted his vehicle on Interstate 65. After being pursued for several miles, Miller was arrested.

Workplace shooters almost always determine a target ahead of time when they decide to commit violence. Sometimes the target is the company itself. When this is the case, the shooter will destroy both people and property. They will kill anyone they see. This was the case when Mark Barton conducted his rampage in Atlanta in 1999. Barton shot employees, computers, and walls. Some of his victims were known to him and some were not. His target was anything that represented his workplace. Other shooters select specific targets within the workplace. When this happens, they will walk calmly past one employee only to shoot another. Miller was this type of killer. In each of the two locations where he shot co-workers, another worker came into the room as the shooting was going on. In both cases, Miller allowed them to leave. Miller allegedly even told one of the men where he could seek safety.[11]

Miller was charged with murder. His attorney claimed that he was "at best, very slow, and should be in a mental health facility instead of Alabama's electric chair."[12] A jury disagreed, however, and deliberated only 20 minutes before convicting him of capital murder. They recommended the death penalty.

BRYAN UYESUGI

Hawaii is one of the safest places in the United States to live in terms of homicide rates. In 1998 there were only 24 homicides. Some cities in the United States have that many homicides in a week. In less than five minutes on November 2, 1999, 40-year-old Bryan Uyesugi was responsible for single-handedly killing one-third of Hawaii's 1998 homicide victims, making it the worst mass shooting in Hawaii's history.

Uyesugi worked for Xerox Corporation for 15 years. He traveled to various businesses that owned Xerox equipment and repaired copiers, fax machines, scanners, and other equipment. During his 15-year history with Xerox he had few documented problems. He was arrested for drunken driving in 1985, but only once were problems at work significant enough to warrant company intervention. In 1993, while on a service call, he became angry, threatened a co-worker, and kicked an elevator door, damaging it. Xerox required him to participate in anger management counseling, and that year he was diagnosed with a delusional disorder.[13] He completed the two-week anger management course as required, and after mental health professionals determined that Uyesugi was not a threat to co-workers, he was allowed to return to work. In the six years between 1993 and 1999, there were no reported problems with his behavior.

The company had scheduled a meeting at its warehouse in Honolulu to discuss workloads. According to company officials, Uyesugi was not going to be fired or even disciplined, but one reason for the meeting was to address the fact that Uyesugi was not "working as hard as his colleagues."[14] A company spokesman said that he "didn't know of any problems with Uyesugi's work."[15] Ordinarily there would only have been a handful of employees in the warehouse, but because of the scheduled meeting, more people were there than normal. Mental health experts who testified at his trial said that Uyesugi's delusions caused him to believe that his co-workers and supervisors were conspiring against him.[16] He sought revenge on November 2, 1999.

The day before, he bought extra ammunition and an extra clip for his 9mm Glock.[17] According to testimony at his trial, Uyesugi carefully selected his targets, all members of his technical team. On the morning of November 2, a witness said that just after 8 A.M. he heard gunshots and saw a fellow employee slump at his desk. The witness then saw a second employee scrambling to escape the area when he, too, was shot. Just before he fled the scene, the witness said he saw Uyesugi in the room where the shots had originated. After shooting these two men, Uyesugi then went to a conference room and shot five members of his technical working group. He then fired at a seventh person in a stairwell, but missed that victim. Uyesugi then fled the scene in a company van. For almost two hours, police searched for the shooter. At 9:45 A.M. they received a call from a female who had been jogging near a nature center. The woman had seen the van nearby in a neighborhood. Police immediately responded to the scene, where they found Uyesugi still sitting in the vehicle. They negotiated with him for five hours, even bringing his brother into the negotiations. In the meantime, police prepared to evacuate two groups of grade school students who were on a field trip to the nature center. Several homes were also evacuated, but some residents of the neighborhood sat in chairs on their front lawns and watched the negotiations. Seven hours after the shootings began, Uyesugi exited the van with his hands in the air and was arrested.

After his arrest, police found 25 more guns at Uyesugi's home. At the scene seven men were killed. Uyesugi fired 28 times and struck victims 25 of those times.[18]

People who knew him described Uyesugi as mild-mannered. He was a bachelor who lived with his brother and widowed father. His grief-stricken father, angered by reporters' questions, told them after Uyesugi's arrest, "I'm going to bring him another gun so he can shoot himself."[19]

Uyesugi was charged with only one count of first-degree murder because that charge covers a mass murder. He was also charged with seven counts of second-degree murder as well as attempted murder. His trial lasted only ten days, during which time his lawyer attempted to convince the jury that Uyesugi was innocent by reason of insanity. Mental health experts testified that Uyesugi suffered from schizophrenia and a delusional disorder that caused him to "believe that he was being persecuted by others."[20] He had long been troubled by mental dysfunction. Information during the trial revealed that a Buddhist minister had once conducted an exorcism to rid Uyesugi of the "black shadow that haunted" him, and psychiatrist Park Deitz, a world-famous violence expert, testified that Uyesugi had "no concept of the terrible thing he had done."[21] The prosecutor agreed that Uyesugi suffered from mental illness, but claimed that Uyesugi knew right from wrong, the legal definition of sanity.

The prosecution's psychologist testified that Uyesugi made "scathing re marks about the seven dead men" when he was asked what he would say to the victims if he could.[22] This is indicative of someone who is either cruel or does not understand what he has done. A lawyer for his defense said that Uyesugi did not fully understand his actions, therefore making it difficult for him to express remorse.[23] At the conclusion of the trial, however, the jury did not accept the insanity defense. After deliberating an hour and 20 minutes they convicted Uyesugi of murder and sentenced him to life without parole. Hawaii has no death penalty.

The day before the jury handed down its verdict, Uyesugi's father issued a public statement apologizing to the victims and their families. "Please accept my deepest apologies for this tragedy. I know that no words can bring back your loved ones. Please accept my prayers for the anger, grief and sorrow this has caused you and your families. I am sorry."[24]

A year after the shootings, Xerox was cited by the Hawaii Occupational Safety and Health Administration (OSHA) for failing to have "an effective workplace-violence program" and for failing to "properly train managers to recognize and reduce potential hazards."[25] The company was not fined and adamantly disagreed with the OSHA findings.

Mental illness often plays a role in murder. In the case of Bryan Uyesugi, there is little doubt that his delusions caused him to perceive that his co-workers were conspiring against him. This, of course, does not justify his use of violence to resolve his problems. It does not appear that Xerox Corporation was unkind in its dealings with Uyesugi and even though OSHA found that the company had failed to train managers to reduce potential hazards, Xerox at least made a reasonable effort to ensure that Uyesugi was not a threat to his co-workers. The company allowed him to return to work after the 1993 incident only after being assured by mental health workers that Uyesugi was not a threat. I believe that all businesses should have a violence response plan, especially when an employee has made threats. If Xerox failed its employees, it was in this respect. Our biggest enemy is not the potential shooter, but failing to believe that it could happen to us.

KEVIN WILLIAM CRUZ

When I lecture law enforcement personnel on workplace violence, it is satisfying to tell them that these perpetrators almost always are easy to catch. They may take their own lives at the scene, force police to shoot them (called "suicide by cop"), or simply lay their weapons down and wait to be taken into custody. Occasionally, they flee from the scene, as in the case of Bryan Uyesugi, but it is only a matter of time before the police catch up with them. Rarely do these perpetrators try to conceal their identities. An exception to that rule was 30-year-old Kevin William Cruz, who was accused of killing two men and wounding two others in a shooting at a shipyard in Seattle, Washington.

At 10:32 A.M. on November 3, 1999, one day after Bryan Uyesugi shot his colleagues in Hawaii, a gunman walked calmly into an office at the Northlake Shipyard, opened fire with a handgun, and then walked out. He was wearing sunglasses, a black baseball cap, a dark coat, and camouflage clothing. To some witnesses, he appeared to be wearing a mask. Police searched the area for the gunman for days, even searching house to house, but they were unable to locate the suspect, who had fled the scene on foot. It quickly became apparent to investigators that the attack was not random, and they sought a connection between the unidentified gunman and the boatyard. Police detained a suspect briefly in the evening on the day of the shooting, but the man was eventually released when police realized he was not connected with the case. Within a few days of the investigation, it became evident to investigators that the attack was "sparked by a grudge."[26]

Several weeks later, a bicyclist found a backpack near the shipyard that contained a holstered 9mm handgun, ammunition, and several items of clothing that matched the description of the clothing worn by the assailant. Ballistics tests identified the gun as the one used in the attack at the shipyard. Two days later, investigators arrested and questioned Cruz, who initially admitted that the backpack was his.[27] Cruz, however, later denied that the backpack belonged to him and also said he knew nothing about its contents.

In May 2001 prosecutors announced that DNA evidence from skin cells found on the holster directly linked Cruz to the shooting, and police also claimed that Cruz was a suspect in a burglary during which the weapon had been stolen prior to the shooting at the shipyard.[28] Prosecutors claimed that Cruz was angry over an investigation of a disability claim by his employer. Allegedly, Cruz had made a disability claim and collected money for the injury, but he was videotaped performing activities that proved he had faked his injuries.[29] Cruz was fired over the incident.

One of the two men killed was a marine engineer, and the other was the general manager of the yard and the owner's nephew. The unique thing about this attack is that Cruz allegedly not only attempted to wear a disguise, but in the months between the time he was fired and the day of the shooting, he let his hair grow long and grew facial hair in order to disguise himself.[30] It worked, too, because none of his co-workers recognized him the day of the shooting. Following the attack, he shaved and cut his hair. Of the homicides I have studied that have taken place in the workplace, this is the only one I have seen where a suspect has gone to such lengths to conceal his identity.

Cruz denied any involvement in the crime and pleaded innocent to charges of aggravated first-degree murder. The judge refused a request by Cruz's attorney to lower the $4 million bail because of his "record of assault, domestic violence, and escape."[31] He was convicted in February 2002 and could receive the death penalty when sentenced.

FRED WILLIAMS

A six-year veteran of the Memphis Fire Department, Fred Williams was also a newlywed. He and his wife Stacey had been married on Valentine's Day. The couple had a young daughter, and Stacey had a son from a previous marriage. As they sought a place of their own, they all moved in with Stacey's mother, Gwen Jones. After just one week in that home, Williams took Stacey's life, the lives of two fellow firefighters, and the life of a police officer.

In early March 2000, Williams had returned to work from an extended disability leave from the fire department, but he had the day off on March 8. Stacey Williams, a postal worker, came home from work at 12:30. As she entered the house, Williams met her in the kitchen and shot her to death with a shotgun. Williams then started a fire in the home, perhaps to conceal the murder. Neighbors saw smoke coming from the home and contacted Williams, but he told them that everything was OK.

Gwen Jones arrived home just minutes after Williams had killed her daughter and started the fire. She pulled into her driveway not knowing that her house was on fire and her daughter was dead in the kitchen. Before she could exit her vehicle, Williams emerged from the garage and fired the 12–gauge shotgun in the air.[32] He motioned at Jones to leave, which she did. She then drove a short distance away and called 911. When she drove back toward her house, she heard gunshots and saw emergency vehicles.

A female pedestrian had seen Williams waving the shotgun around and firing it in the air, and police were called. A sheriff's deputy responded to the scene. As he approached, the pedestrian tried to warn him that Williams had a gun. But before the officer could prepare himself, Williams began firing at him in his vehicle. The deputy was struck four times, at least once in the head, and was killed. His patrol car crashed through a fence on the property and came to a stop. The pedestrian was wounded in the face and ran across the street to a residence seeking cover and help. The woman inside the home, however, refused to open the door. She could see that Williams was still outside with the gun and she feared for her life. In fact, her house was hit five times by gunshots.

The fire department had been called and was responding to what they thought was a routine fire. They were unaware that the deputy had been killed. As the firemen prepared to attack the fire, one climbed down from the truck. Williams came outside with a pump-action shotgun and was screaming, "Get away! Get away!" He shot the fireman in the head, killing him. A second fireman was shot in the head and was killed as he sat in his truck. Williams threatened the other firefighters as they attempted to help their fallen colleagues. Within minutes more law enforcement officers arrived and tried to talk Williams into surrendering his weapon. When he refused, officers engaged him in gunfire. Williams was shot four times and was critically injured.

The motive for these killings remains unclear, but Williams had a history of emotional difficulties that were clear to many who knew him. He had been arrested once after a "domestic disturbance" the previous year and was about to appear in court on that charge.[33] After this assault on Stacey, Williams' fiancée at the time, Williams told Gwen Jones that he had been diagnosed with bipolar disorder.[34] According to a friend, Williams had attempted suicide in November by eating rat poison.[35] In the months prior to the incident, Williams' godfather said he had not been himself and had "lost his mind."[36] Mental illness may have precipitated this attack and played an important role in Williams' behavior. Williams was charged with four counts of first-degree murder, one count of attempted murder, and one count of aggravated arson. His trial is pending as of this writing.

CONCLUDING REMARKS

Many psychological principles allow the perpetrators to justify committing the crimes I have described above. Chapter 10 addresses hate crimes and terrorism. Even though the cases I have addressed in this chapter are not hate crimes, the principles are much the same.

It is easy to be frightened by the outrageous behavior of the criminals discussed in this chapter, and we might readily call into question our own security. I remember as a child reading about the Tate-LaBianca murders. When Charles Manson and his followers were arrested for this crime, I feared for my own safety even though I lived more than 2,000 miles away. I was only a boy at that time, but the generalization of fear I experienced is common even among adults. The realistic truth is that you are about as likely to be struck by lightning as you are to be the victim of a mass murder. Yet we shouldn't allow this statistic to cause us to believe it could not happen to us. Reasonable awareness and attention to warning signs can be the decisive factor as to whether your name appears on the list of victims or the list of survivors should you ever be confronted with a mass murderer.

NOTES

1. "Signposts pointed to possible bloodshed at U of WA; colleagues afraid of doctor," *In the Line of Duty, www.lineofduty.com/blotter/july00/jul-1-7/7100–9.htm*, July 2000.

2. "Signposts pinted to possible bloodshed at U of WA; colleagues afraid of doctor," *In the Line of Duty, www.lineofduty.com/blotter/july00/jul-1-7/7100 9.htm*, July 2000.

3. Robert L. Jamieson, Jr., and Ruth Schubert, "Two die in UW medical school shooting," *Northwest, www.seattlep-i.nwsource.com/local/pathweb.shtml*, June 29, 2000.

4. Robert L. Jamieson, Jr., and Ruth Schubert, "Two die in UW medical school shooting." *Northwest, www.seattle-i.nwsource.com/local/pathweb.shtml*, June 29, 2000.

5. "Arrest made after Detroit-area shooting leaves two dead," *CNN Online, www.cnn.com/2000/US/04/18/detroit.shooting.04*, April 18, 2000.

6. "Gunman in Michigan senior complex kills two in rampage," *CNN Online, www.cnn.com/2000/US/04/19/detroit.shooting.ap/index.html*, April 19, 2000.

7. "Gunman in Michigan senior complex kills two in rampage," *CNN Online, www.cnn.com/2000/US/04/19/detroit.shooting.ap/index.html*, April 19, 2000.

8. "Arrest made after Detroit-area shooting leaves two dead," *CNN Online, www.cnn.com/2000/US/04/18/detroit.shooting.04*, April 18, 2000.

9. "Report: Anger over truck routes may have triggered shooting," *CNN Online, www.cnn.com/US/9908/08/AM-AlabamaShooting.ap/index.html*, August 8, 1999.

10. Marlon Manuel, "Prosecutor says killer spared two," *Atlanta Journal/Constitution*, August 7, 1999, p. A3.

11. Marlon Manuel, "Prosecutor says killer spared two," *Atlanta Journal/Constitution*, August 7, 1999, p. A3.

12. "Death penalty sought in Alabama shootings," *Atlanta Journal/Constitution*, August 15, 1999, p. A9.

13. Ken Kobayashi, "Jury rejects insanity defense in murders of seven co-workers," *Honolulu Advertiser*, June 14, 2000, p. A1.

14. "Prosecutor: Accused Xerox gunman about to be reprimanded in meeting," *CNN Online*, www.cnn.com/US/9911/09/xerox.shootings.ap/index.html, November 9, 1999.

15. "Honolulu shooting suspect to be arraigned today," *CNN Online*, www.cnn.com/US/9911/03/honolulu.shootings.02/index.html, November 3, 1999.

16. Ken Kobayashi, "Jury rejects insanity defense in murders of seven co-workers," *Honolulu Advertiser*, June 14, 2000, p. A8.

17. Sally Apgar, "Xerox jurors reluctant to discuss case," *Honolulu Advertiser*, June 4, 2000, p. A7.

18. Ken Kobayashi, "Jury rejects insanity defense in murders of seven co-workers," *Honolulu Advertiser*, June 14, 2000, p. A8.

19. "Honolulu shooting suspect to be arraigned today," *CNN Online*, www.cnn.com/US/9911/03/honolulu.shootings.02/index.html, November 3, 1999.

20. "Xerox repairman found guilty of Honolulu workplace killings," *CNN Online*, www.cnn.com/2000/US/06/13/bc.xeroxshooting.ap/index.html, June 13, 2000.

21. "A look at history of massacre," *Honolulu Advertiser*, June 14, 2000, p. A8.

22. Ken Kobayashi, "Jury rejects insanity defense in murders of seven co-workers," *Honolulu Advertiser*, June 14, 2000, p. A8.

23. Ken Kobayashi, "Jury rejects insanity defense in murders of seven co-workers," *Honolulu Advertiser*, June 14, 2000, p. A8.

24. Sally Apgar, "No words can explain deeds of son, brother," *Honolulu Advertiser*, June 14, 2000, p. A1.

25. "Xerox Hawaii cited unsafe in connection with mass shooting," *CNN Online*, www.cnn.com/2000/LAW/11/07/xeroxshootings.crim.ap/index.html, November 7, 2000.

26. "Investigators say shipyard shooting was result of grudge against victim," *Corpus Christi Caller Times*, www.caller.com/1999/november/06/today/national/613.html, November 6, 1999.

27. "$4 million bail set for shooting suspect," *thesunlink*, www.thesunlink.com/news/2000/january/0106a5b.html, January 6, 2000.

28. Ian Ith, "DNA link in shipyard slaying being checked," *Seattle Times, archives.seattletimes.nwsource.com/cgi-bin/texis/web/vortex/display?slug=shipyard 16m&date=20010516&query=kevin+cruz*, May 17, 2001.

29. "Fired worker held in shipyard shooting," *APBNEWS.COM*, www.apbnews.com/newscenter/breakingnews/2000/01/05/shipyard0105_01.html, January 5, 2000.

30. "Fired worker held in shipyard shooting," *APBNEWS.COM*, www.apbnews.com/newscenter/breakingnews/2000/01/05/shipyard0105–01.html, January 5, 2000.

31. "$4 million bail set for shooting suspect," *thesunlink*, www.thesunlink.com/news/2000/january/0106a5b.html, January 6, 2000.

32. David Waters, "The night before, 'They both were so happy,'" *Commercial Appeal, www.gomemphis.com/newca/special/shoot/12stacnu.htm*, May 17, 2001.

33. Teresa M. Walker, "Colleague's rampage leaves city's firefighters stunned," *Atlanta Journal/Constitution*, March 3, 2000, p. A3.

34. David Waters, "The night before, 'They both were so happy,' " *Commercial Appeal, www.gomemphis.com/newca/special/shoot/12stacnu.htm*, May 17, 2001.

35. "Police try to determine sequence, motive of gunman's rampage," *khou.com, www.khou.com/news/stories/1559.html*, May 17, 2001.

36. Tom Sharp, "Firefighter had been on extended leave," *Atlanta Journal/Constitution*, March 10, 2000, p. A10.

CHAPTER **8**

IMPULSIVE MURDER: AIR RAGE, ROAD RAGE, SPORTS RAGE

For a long time it had seemed to me that life was about to begin–real life. But there was always some obstacle in the way, something to be gotten through first, some unfinished business, time still to be served, or a debt to be paid. Then life would begin. At last it dawned on me that these obstacles were my life.

—Alfred D. Souza

Many types of murder might be appropriately classified as "impulsive," but I would argue that the term certainly applies to road rage and air rage. Road rage and air rage appear to be anomalies in our violent world. Most of us give little thought to aggression committed by people who are engaged in criminal activities or people with violent histories. However, the seemingly impulsive act of road rage or air rage captures our attention because these perpetrators are our neighbors, co-workers, and friends. They look like us, have jobs like us, and live lives like ours. They are not part of some distant world of thugs and criminality. Their lives overlap ours, making us wonder if we, too, are capable of committing such behaviors.

As my first book clearly demonstrated, this is an unrealistic fear. Violence is not a disease. It is not something you catch from someone else, like a virus. More likely, it is something that one plants, nurtures, and cultivates. Air rage and road rage are the harvests of fields that have been sown with the seeds of selfishness, hedonism, and thoughtlessness. It is as improbable for a person to wake up one morning and commit murder out of the blue as it is for a farmer to wake up one morning and reap a harvest without planting, fertilizing, and tending the crop.

How many times have you heard someone describe an acquaintance by saying, "He is such a nice guy, but when he gets behind the wheel, he changes into someone completely different?" This is a myth and has no basis in fact. People who commit road rage and air rage are not magically transformed into irrational or rude people in the blink of an eye. They do not enter the cabin of an aircraft, the driver's seat of an automobile, or the bleachers of an athletic arena as one person and then suddenly metamorphose into another creature. People who commit these acts are demonstrating their deeper character. Most mature adults, if they choose, have the ability to hide who they are deep down inside. Their true character is displayed in times of testing—when they are stressed, tired, or threatened. Yet one's true character is regularly displayed through little things. A person who would shoot at another driver, try to break into the cockpit of an aircraft, or punch a little league umpire is a person who will park his car wherever he chooses, regardless of whom he inconveniences. He will do what he wants, follow rules when he chooses or when it is convenient, and deny or rationalize his failure to follow rules when it is convenient. He may seem an unlikely candidate to commit crimes of road rage or air rage because he is not routinely forced to show his true character to those who do not know him well. People like this have no qualms about telling "white" lies. They smoke in no smoking areas and will not correct a cashier who makes an error when giving change if the error is in their favor. They will pursue their own personal goals, both professional and recreational, at the expense of their spouses and children. In short, they are self-seeking at their core.

We use rationalization and denial to help us cope with life. For instance, people will argue with me about how "nice" someone was before they committed a murder. When I probe a little bit into their experience with the perpetrator, I either find that they did not know the murderer very well or that they had ignored or rationalized symptoms of aggression, normalizing otherwise abnormal behaviors.

This doesn't mean, of course, that such people cannot be kind at times or that they are incapable of changing, maturing, or empathizing. Quite the contrary. The most mystifying thing of all is that these people may be able to shift between their empathetic selves and their hedonistic selves quite quickly. Yet their hedonistic selves will always take control when they are threatened, stressed, or tired. Many times, these people are passive-aggressive. They are afraid or incapable of showing their real emotions, especially anger. Therefore, they find other ways to release their frustration on others. In the safety of an automobile, they can display their real emotions without having to confront another person face-to-face.

Many people have little gratitude for what they have. The individualistic culture I addressed in Chapter 2 is clearly at work. For example, with air rage, instead of being grateful that we arrive at our destination alive, we are angry that we are 30 minutes late. Instead of being grateful that a flight shortened a trip that would have taken six hours longer if we had driven or taken a bus, we begrudge the loss of 30 minutes. Our individualistic approach to life then makes us believe that the airline owes us something for "our trouble." By the same token, instead of being grateful for the privilege of driving, we perceive it to be a right. When we realize how much more difficult our lives would be without our cars, we begin to appreciate them and possibly be more tolerant of the few delays we actually have. In the following pages, note the role that individualism, lack of gratitude, denial, rationalization, hedonism and coping skills play in each of the case studies.

AIR RAGE

At any gathering of airline security personnel, stories of outrageous passenger behavior flow freely. Passengers have defecated on service carts, spat on flight attendants, wrestled for the controls of the aircraft after breaking into the cockpit, tried to open exterior doors while the plane was in flight, and thrown hot coffee on flight attendants and other passengers. They have threatened to kill other passengers and crew, punched and urinated on other occupants of the cabin, and thrown books and magazines. Some have tried to break the window glass with their heads. Once, in 1999, a passenger even stabbed to death the pilot of an Asian aircraft as it left Tokyo. These are only a few of the unbelievable behaviors that airline crews experience. Much of what we call "air rage" is a federal offense. It is defined as "threats, assaults and interference with flight crews in the performance of their duties while on the airplane."[1]

In the late 1990s, the corporate security director for one of the companies I have served as a consultant asked me to investigate the phenomenon of air rage. Initially, I did not think that studying air rage would be any different from studying other types of violence, but I was wrong. My first thought was that alcohol would be a present in most cases, but even though alcohol is a factor in about one-third of the documented cases of air rage, in two-thirds of the cases no alcohol was involved at all. My second thought was that most passengers who exhibited air rage would have a clear history of aggressive behavior. Yet again, this was not always the case. I was left shrugging my shoulders at conferences when airline security personnel asked me what I thought caused air rage. Here are a few examples of air rage.

- While Continental Airlines Flight 120 was on its way from Anchorage, Alaska, to Seattle, Washington, a 38-year-old woman threw a beer can at a flight attendant and bit a crew member on the arm, forcing the captain to return the plane to Anchorage. There, the woman was charged with interfering with the flight crew and assault. The incident allegedly began after she had an argument with her boyfriend. The flight attendant asked her to calm down. At that point, she threw the beer can, showering beer over the crew and passengers, including a three-month-old baby. As the crew tried to restrain her, she bit a crew member. Passengers kept her restrained until the plane landed in Anchorage.[2]

- In July 1998, a 38-year-old female passenger on a Spirit Airline flight from Ft. Lauderdale to Atlantic City was said to have exhibited "unsettling" behavior even before takeoff.[3] She was complaining about an odor in the rear of the plane, and sprayed perfume in the area. She cursed at a flight attendant who asked her only to spray the lavatory area. She later kicked the seat of a 14-year-old passenger in front of her and threatened to sue him as well as kill him because he reclined his seat. The woman was convicted of assault and was sentenced to three months of house arrest and five years of probation, and fined over $16,500.[4]

- In Newark, New Jersey, an angry traveler body-slammed a Continental gate manager into the floor, breaking his neck.[5] The passenger was arrested and tried for aggravated assault, but was acquitted.

- An American Airlines flight from Dallas to London made an unscheduled landing in Boston, where a 33-year-old male passenger was arrested. During the flight the man was drinking and shouting vulgarities. He allegedly poked a flight attendant and refused to calm down, even after the co-pilot had a discussion with him.[6]

- A 19-year-old male on a short flight from Las Vegas to Salt Lake City died after being restrained by passengers. Originally, it was thought that he died of a heart attack.[7] The man tried to break into the cockpit and hit other passengers when they tried to subdue him. When the plane landed, he was taken into custody, where he died. Marijuana was found in his system. The attorney for the man's family said passengers kicked and strangled him.[8] No charges were filed against the passengers involved.

- A 39-year-old man broke into the cockpit of an Alaska Airlines flight in 2000 and lunged for the controls of the aircraft. He reportedly began "babbling incoherently, stripping off his clothes, and wandering from seat-to-seat."[9] The man was arrested, but received a pretrial diversion because experts testified that his outburst was the result of an extremely rare reaction to encephalitis. The pilots momentarily lost control of the aircraft, but passengers restrained the man.[10]

- On an America West flight from Ft. Lauderdale to Las Vegas, a 32-year-old male threw a cup of ice and a beer can at a flight attendant, forcing the pilot to divert the plane to Albuquerque, New Mexico, where the man was arrested. Fifteen other passengers were also removed from the plane for name-calling and out-of-control behaviors.[11]

- The pilot of a Delta flight from Atlanta to England chose to return the plane to Bangor, Maine, when a 42-year-old male groped a flight attendant and threw food. The British man was convicted of assault, but failed to return to the United States to serve his six-month sentence.[12]

Per passenger, incidents of air rage are relatively rare. Of an estimated 600 million passengers a year, well below 1 percent (4,000 to 5,000) engage in air rage.[13] Still, 4,000 to 5,000 incidents a year is significant, and that number is on the rise. According to the International Transport Workers' Federation, "air rage incidents have increased from 1,131 in 1994 to 5,416" in 1997.[14] Research by the Federal Aviation Administration (FAA) has yielded similar results.

Complete and accurate information on air rage episodes is very hard to come by for several reasons. First of all, airlines do not want the potential bad publicity of these episodes. Since there is no required reporting of air rage incidents, an airline risks being the only one to report such events; hence making it look less competent. Not only does it present the potential impression that the flight crews cannot handle the passengers, but diverted flights mean potential delays. If an episode of air rage endangers the lives of passengers, such as occurred on the Alaska Airlines flight mentioned above, customers may be reluctant to fly with that airline. Jurisdiction also complicates air rage events. When the plane is in the air on international flights, the laws governing the behavior of the persons on board are those of the country where the airline is based. If a behavior is illegal in the home country, but not illegal in the country where the plane lands, the authorities may be helpless to file charges. In some international episodes, the behavior may be illegal, but authorities in the foreign country may be unwilling to arrest or prosecute.

A number of causes of air rage have been proposed. As is always true when analyzing any form of behavior, no single cause accounts for all incidents of air rage. Rather, a multifaceted approach is necessary to account for most incidents. These causes can be grouped into physical factors, airline industry problems, and personal factors.

Even though alcohol is not an issue in many cases, it is perhaps the biggest single physical factor. In one study by Swissair in 1999, one-third of all aggressive incidents on its planes could be attributed to alcohol.[15] A study of disruptive passenger behavior conducted by the Federal Aviation Administration found similar results, claiming that alcohol was a factor in one-third of all serious incidents it examined.[16] We know that alcohol lowers inhibitions and makes aggression more likely. One does not have to be legally intoxicated to have lowered inhibitions. Even one drink can have that effect, especially if the individual has an empty stomach and is already prone to aggressive behavior.

Smokers have a physical disadvantage. Smoking is an addictive habit, and withholding the drug (nicotine) creates nervousness, irritability, and anxious behavior. Even on a short flight, they may be required to refrain from smoking for several hours. For example, the flight may only be 45 minutes long, but passengers are prohibited from smoking from the time they enter the gate area until they deplane and leave the gate area at their destination. Delays on the tarmac, runway, or landing, can extend one's sabbatical from smoking to several hours. The 1999 Swissair study mentioned above noted that nearly one-third of aggressive behaviors on Swissair flights could be attributed to smoking-related issues.[17]

A final physical cause has to do with the conditions in the cabin of the aircraft. One expert in the field suggests that dehydration, air pressure, altitude, and air quality contribute to air rage. Michael Emmerman, an expert in the field of SCUBA, has applied his knowledge of the physiological effects of diving to air travel. He has noted that the quality of the air in the cabin is poor and has a lower oxygen saturation than on the ground. These issues, combined with dehydration caused by air pressure and poor air circulation routinely experienced by passengers during a long flight, contribute to impaired thinking, hence increasing the possibility of air rage. He suggests that passengers avoid alcohol, caffeine, and sugared drinks, eat light meals, and drink plenty of water while flying.[18] He also advocates that airlines improve the quality of the cabin air they provide. In short, altitude affects the body by reducing the efficiency at which the lungs can exchange gases, most notably, oxygen and nitrogen.[19] Plus, most airlines circulate between 40 and 60 percent fresh air, leaving the remaining cabin air reprocessed, circulating pollutants and 'pre-breathed' air.[20] In other words, much of what we are breathing in an airline cabin is air that has already been exhaled by other passengers. Increasing fresh air could reduce these negative effects.

The airline industry contributes to occurrences of air rage as well. The industry has changed a great deal in recent years, especially since deregulation. Prior to that time, fares were higher, but airlines provided more services. One former airline pilot said that at one time passengers were "treated like royalty."[21] For example, to minimize discomfort from changing barometric pressure during descent, this pilot said that they never exceeded 300 feet a minute descending.[22]

After deregulation, airfares were subject to more competition across carriers. Airlines reduced services and cut personnel to make lower fares possible. The flying public was willing to fly with fewer perks for the convenience of flying more cheaply. One former pilot stated that "traveling by jet these days is rarely, if ever, the hedonistic comfort-fest airlines pretend it is in their commercials."[23] In fact, most people who fly frequently do not enjoy the experience. It is a necessary activity that most travelers find stressful. We endure long lines to check bags, to board and exit the aircraft, and then to retrieve our luggage.

Airlines overbook flights, playing the odds at having a full aircraft. Crowded planes mean cramped conditions. Not only does overbooking make for a crowded flight, but it may lead to passengers having to give up their seats. More than once my own departure has been delayed because the airline overbooked the flight and all booked passengers checked in. The plane could not leave until several passengers volunteered to give up their seats and wait for later flights. Even though airlines routinely offer perks to inconvenienced passengers, overbooking often causes delayed departures.

Except in business class, airplanes are very cramped even if the plane is not full. Even with the seat fully reclined (only 18 degrees on most planes) there is just over two feet of room between seats. Passenger aggression sometimes stems from arguments over who owns the space between the seats. A passenger will try to recline his seat, only to be kicked by the passenger in the seat behind. Both passengers believe that their freedom/space is being invaded by the other. Lack of control over your own space creates helplessness and resentment. Some experts in the field have suggested that seats be locked into position permanently to avoid this issue altogether.[24]

All of these issues are compounded with unexpected and unavoidable occurrences such as mechanical problems and foul weather conditions that lead to delays or cancellations. In short, passengers have high expectations, but perceive the service to be poor. But it would be completely irresponsible to blame air rage on the airlines. The issues addressed above set the stage for violence by passengers, but do not cause it. It is analogous to a person leaving an open purse on the front seat of an unlocked vehicle in a supermarket parking lot. A thief could easily open the door and steal the purse without attracting any attention. The person does not cause the thief to steal, but she sets the stage for the activity.

Yet even though there are physical contributions to air rage, and even though the airlines can make things worse, the most important factors are personal ones. A combination of high expectations for service and low cost has put the airline industry in a bind. People expect to pay little, while enjoying the same amenities they have had in the past. When they perceive service to be of low quality, regardless of what they paid for their ticket, they feel justified being angry. Sometimes expectations are high, but reasonable. When expectations move beyond the reasonable, the industry is forced to say no to requests. For example, if a flight is cancelled or exceptionally late, airlines may provide vouchers for free travel, food, and hotel rooms. Yet some passengers expect such expensive perks even for routine and unavoidable inconveniences such as a flight that is a few minutes late due to heavy air traffic or foul weather. They may ask for cab fare, hotel expenses, reimbursement for their time, "punitive damages" such as those awarded in a tort case in court, and other unreasonable forms of compensation.

Personal stress contributes to air rage. Ever-looming concerns over delayed departures, cancelled flights, and lost luggage add to our stress. When flights are delayed departing or arriving, we may receive bad information, or worse, no information, from the airline, leaving us feeling completely helpless.

Fearing that the airline will lose their luggage, more and more passengers are carrying their bags with them. Thus, the limited space in the overhead compartments is at a premium. Even though airlines regulate the size of bags that can be carried on, argumentative passengers sometimes manage to circumvent their rules, creating more crowding, delaying departure, and infuriating other passengers who were required to check their oversized bags. On a full flight, the overhead compartments may fill, forcing passengers who had planned to carry on their luggage to check their bags as they board the aircraft, further increasing their frustration and anger with the airline.

Our lives are so busy and tightly scheduled that we do not allow time for unforeseen interruptions. It would be unrealistic to expect every flight to leave and arrive the exact minute that it was scheduled. Some problems can be avoided, but inevitably there will be delays that can not be helped. Some passengers react to these interruptions as if they think the airline has deliberately delayed the flight to personally inconvenience them.

People choose their behaviors from a pool of options. Poor coping skills lead to poor choices. Options available to the cabin crew for dealing with unruly passengers are limited. As one airline professional said, "At 30,000 feet you can't call the police. You're at the mercy of those around to help. When a situation occurs or escalates on a plane you can't walk away or tell the person to go somewhere to cool off."[25]

Unruly passengers believe that because they have paid for a ticket, the airline staff must tolerate their childish actions. On the aircraft a passenger's personal space is invaded by sights, sounds and odors that are unpleasant. Because they have purchased a ticket, they expect airline personnel to satisfy them, even if such an expectation is unreasonable or impossible.

Airlines have made little headway in dealing with passenger violence, but they are trying. Japan Airlines has instated a policy that allows cabin crews to tie up unruly passengers, Air Canada withdraws mileage points from violent passengers, and British Airways crews are allowed to issue "warning cards" to passengers, notifying them of potential fines or arrest.[26] Several airlines have plastic flexible cuffs available to restrain aggressive passengers. Perhaps most extreme of all, Swissair has equipped its planes with plastic handcuffs and allows its flight attendants to "slap passengers who sexually harass them" and to "retaliate against other unruly passengers by tying them up in their seats."[27]

The government has intervened and raised the fines for air rage from $1,000 to $25,000.[28] Disruptive passengers who are responsible for flights being diverted so that they can be deplaned may also be held liable for the cost of that diversion. The cost of diverting a flight to deplane an unruly passenger could exceed $10,000.[29]

In summary, to change the rising trend in incidents of air rage, the industry must address several issues. First, they need to accommodate their passengers' desire to drink alcohol, but with reasonable limits. I personally would advocate the prohibition of alcohol altogether in both the aircraft and the terminal, thus removing the issue from the formula. Encouraging passengers to drink noncaffeinated beverages, especially water, and providing a higher concentration of fresh oxygen could also help reduce tensions in the aircraft. Airlines need to give gate agents the authority to deny a passenger the right to board an aircraft at all if the passenger's behavior in the terminal area provides clear signs of aggression or intoxication. The airlines already have a great deal of authority over the passengers, so this would have to be carefully supervised to avoid abuse by airlines or their employees.

Limiting carry-on baggage more than airlines already do could help in several ways. It would speed the process of boarding and deplaning and reduce crowding in the cabin. Limiting carry-on luggage could also reduce dissatisfaction and disagreements over what little luggage space exists.

To stay fiscally solvent, the industry must consider profits, but airlines should also consider how hedging their bets by overbooking is damaging their reputations and contributing to air rage. Better planning could avoid some delays, and a more customer friendly approach by the industry would be helpful.

Finally, individuals have to recognize their own expectations, denials, rationalizations, and coping strategies. The airline can do little to change the aggressive passenger. Ideally, the aggressive passenger will address the issue before ever boarding an aircraft, but that requires self-awareness and motivation to change. This may be the most outrageous suggestion of all.

ROAD RAGE

It is fascinating how some people seem to change when they slip behind the wheel of a car. People who are ordinarily mild-mannered and quiet may become aggressive when they drive. There is something about the isolation and power of the automobile that can bring out the worst in our behavior.

I once took a defensive driving course as required by my employer. Over the several days of the course, the instructor showed us that among many ways to prevent accidents was simply to get out of the way of an aggressive driver. At the time I remember thinking how odd his instructions sounded. In almost all other areas of life, what he said made sense, but when it came to driving, I realized that defensive strategies are not the norm.

We do things in a car we would never do in any other environment. Imagine maneuvering a shopping cart through the grocery store the same way you drive your car. You would never run through the supermarket pushing your cart as fast as possible just because you were in a hurry. If someone was moving too slowly down the aisle, you would not get right up on their heels with your cart and intimidate them into either speeding up or getting out of your way. If there was a long line waiting for the cashier, you would not bypass the line of customers, pretending not to see the others waiting and then signal to be let in at the front. We wouldn't think of cussing at another shopper or gesturing obscenely if we did not like the way someone else was maneuvering his or her cart. Yet for some reason these behaviors seem reasonable on the streets and freeways around our country.

One of my FBI friends told me a story that brings this point home. Bill (not his real name) was on his way home in his unmarked bureau car. He had just returned from a tactical exercise and had his pistol holstered and his MP-5 machine-gun on the seat beside him. While he was driving down a two-lane rural road, another driver passed him. The other driver, a man in his forties, drove a few miles down the road and then stopped his truck sideways in front of Bill's vehicle, blocking the road. The driver exited his vehicle and was heading toward my friend's car. At that point, Bill flipped on his grill lights and hit the siren. He opened the door, identified himself as a federal agent, and drew his weapon, ordering the man to stop. The driver nearly fainted.

In the minutes that followed, Bill determined that the man was angry because he did not like the way Bill looked at him when he passed him. His plan was to "kick his ass" and teach Bill a lesson. Instead, he spent some very tense minutes with a federal agent and later with state police. Before Bill radioed state police, the man said, "Can't we just forget this whole thing?" This driver had not even begun to see the significance of what he had just done.

Bill explained to the man that he had his machine-gun on the seat beside him. What would have happened, he asked the man, if instead of being a law enforcement officer, he had been a criminal? The driver would have ended up dead in a ditch along that deserted stretch of highway, all because he did not like the way someone looked at him.

When I lived in Tennessee, an angry driver actually bumped my motorcycle with his car as we drove along a winding highway. Fortunately, I did not lose control of my motorcycle. He was apparently angry because I was not driving fast enough even though it was night and I was exceeding the speed limit already. A few years later, an angry interstate driver bumped the rear of my car when my family and I were driving in a rain storm. Again, I was apparently not driving fast enough even though visibility was nearly zero. By far my most frightening personal experience, however, was one occasion when a man, clearly in his fifties or sixties, waved a gun at me on the exit ramp from a limited access highway. To this day I still do not know what I did to enrage him. Many times I've seen angry drivers nearly losing control of their vehicles in an attempt to demonstrate their rage at others with whom they are sharing the road.

The National Highway Traffic Safety Administration (NHTSA) defines aggressive driving as "an assault with a motor vehicle or other dangerous weapon by the operator or passenger(s) of another motor vehicle or an assault precipitated by an accident that occurred on a roadway."[30] Between 1990 and 1997, incidents of aggressive driving rose by 51 percent, and the U.S. Department of Transportation has estimated that nearly two-thirds of all driving fatalities can be attributed to aggressive driving.[31] Aggressive drivers are old and young, male and female, and of various races. The significance of the problem is demonstrated by a poll done in Washington, D.C., which showed that residents perceived aggressive drivers to be a larger threat than drunk drivers.[32] Here are some documented cases of aggressive driving.

- In Eagan, Minnesota, a physician punched a 69-year-old woman on an on-ramp to an interstate when she cut him off. The woman stopped when the angry doctor stopped his vehicle because she said she thought she may have hit his sports car. He cursed at the woman and then slapped her before getting back in his vehicle and speeding off. He was later charged with assault.

- In December 1999 in Manassas, Virginia, a 17-year-old girl was convicted of second-degree murder after an altercation with another driver. The teenaged girl was parked in the street, blocking passage of other vehicles. When the driver approached, she honked, and then the victim, a passenger, yelled something out of the car window as they passed. The teenager then sped past them and blocked their way a second time. The victim stepped from the vehicle, reportedly to protect the other passengers, which included three children, ages two, four, and ten, as well as young teenagers. The angry teenager then bashed the woman's head into the sidewalk and kicked her. A second teenager also kicked the woman in the head as she lay injured on the sidewalk, suffering brain trauma. The woman died two days later. The second teen was convicted of manslaughter in connection with the altercation.[33]

- In Chestertown, Maryland, a 73-year-old woman was shot to death by an unknown perpetrator as she returned home from Christmas shopping in 1999. The perpetrator followed the victim, her 67-year-old cousin, and a third occupant for nearly 30 minutes, honking the horn, tailgating, and flashing headlights.[34] The perpetrator then pulled alongside the victim's car and fired two or three shots into the vehicle. It is unknown what prompted the driver's rage.

- In Los Angeles, California, in April 2000, a vehicle pulled alongside a Mustang driven by a 19-year-old woman. In the car were a seven-year-old boy and a two-year-old girl. The driver of the Mustang cut off another vehicle before the suspect's vehicle pulled up beside her and shots were fired into the Mustang. The two-year-old was shot in the foot.[35]

- In Philadelphia, Pennsylvania, in November 2000, a teenager was killed over a traffic altercation. The episode began after a fender-bender when the perpetrator pulled out of a parking space. Words were exchanged between the 25-year-old perpetrator and the 18-year-old victim. The perpetrator left his vehicle, came up to the victim's vehicle, and demanded that he get out. The victim had seen him withdraw something from his vehicle and feared for his life. When he tried to shut the car door to drive away, the perpetrator shot him once in the chest. The victim, still alive, tried to drive away with his girlfriend and one-year-old in the car, but he crashed into a parked car a few blocks away, where he died. The perpetrator was arrested later outside his home and charged with murder.[36]

- In 1994, 56-year-old Donald Graham became angry when he saw another driver flash his lights at another vehicle, so he decided to follow the car. Eventually, both men pulled over and the 42-year-old man in the other car, an EMT, walked over to Graham's car. As he approached, Graham shot him with a cross-bow. Graham was convicted of first-degree murder and sentenced to life without parole.

- In Chicago in 1999, a driver became enraged with a man on a bicycle. The cyclist punched the driver's vehicle when he was cut off. The driver let the cyclist in front, rammed him with his vehicle, knocking him off his bike, ran over him, and fled the scene. The driver later turned himself in to police.[37]

- In Birmingham, Alabama, in November 1999, a 40-year-old woman on her way home from work tailgated another woman for several miles. The victim eventually stopped on an exit ramp and walked back toward the perpetrator's vehicle. As she approached, the 40-year-old woman shot the victim in the face and killed her. The woman was later convicted of manslaughter and sentenced to 13 years in prison.[38]

- A 38-year-old man was found lying against the median wall of an Atlanta area interstate, dead of a gunshot wound to the chest. A witness said the victim was driving an SUV in the high occupancy vehicle (HOV) lane when he slammed on his brakes, causing another motorist in a Pontiac to also brake suddenly. The victim left his vehicle and ran back toward the Pontiac. Nothing else was witnessed, but someone in the Pontiac apparently shot the man either out of rage or out of fear.[39]

- In San Jose, California, Sara McBurnett accidentally bumped another driver's vehicle in stop-and-go, bumper-to-bumper traffic on a rainy night in April 2000 when the driver cut her off and she was unable to stop. The driver approached McBurnett's vehicle and she rolled her window down to apologize. The driver, however, was in no mood for apologies. He spouted profanities at McBurnett and then reached into her vehicle through the open window and grabbed her 10-year-old dog, a bichon frise, by the collar and the neck. He threw the tiny dog into traffic and, while a horrified McBurnett watched, the dog was struck and killed by another vehicle. The man then drove away. More than $120,000 was raised as a reward to find the suspect.[40]

An anonymous tip led to the arrest and indictment of a 27-year-old man from San Jose.

- In April 2000, an 18–wheeler driven by Jeremy Grimes attempted to merge into the same lane with a red Ford on an interstate near Atlanta, Georgia. The driver of the other vehicle let Grimes into the lane, but later pulled alongside his truck and fired into it. Grimes' two-year-old son was in the sleeper of the 18–wheeler having a pillow fight with a cousin. The toddler was struck in the shoulder and cheek. The boy barely survived after many weeks in the hospital, at one point being given only a 50/50 chance of survival. The driver of the red Ford was never caught.[41]

I propose two major groups of causes for aggressive behavior behind the wheel—psychological, or internal causes, and environmental, or external causes. Psychologically, automobiles give us a sense of power and anonymity. One writer notes that people who ordinarily feel powerless and frustrated can change all that when they get into a 3,000-pound vehicle.[42] This sense of invincibility is fueled by the power of the vehicle as well as by the autonomy that a vehicle provides. Especially in large vehicles, it is easy to perceive oneself as invincible. Vehicles allow us the freedom to go where we want, when we want, and for how long we want. We mistakenly expect that our progress should never be interrupted. When other drivers get in our way, we take it personally, supposing they are deliberately impeding our progress, in essence attempting to steal our freedom. Leon James and Diane Nahl, experts on aggressive driving, note that our freedom is contradicted by natural impediments of driving. "On one hand, we can get into cars and drive where we please, the very symbol of freedom and independence. But on the other hand, we encounter restrictions and constrictions like regulations, congestion, and the unexpected actions of other motorists that prevent us from driving as we wish."[43]

Aggressive drivers imbue other drivers with motives. They suppose that a slow driver is deliberately doing something aggressive to them personally. A driver who absentmindedly pulls out in front of an aggressive driver may be perceived to have done it deliberately. The reader may find it interesting that some of these victims were elderly. One reason the elderly may be victims of road rage is that they tend to drive slower, thus frustrating aggressive drivers who are in a hurry. Because aggressive drivers falsely construe the motives of other drivers, they may incorrectly assume that these older drivers are deliberately trying to slow them down.

Different cultures have different expectations on the road. While in Mexico recently, I noticed that traffic signs were largely ignored. Lane markings, speed limits, stop signs, one-way streets, and so forth were routinely ignored. The cultural expectation there appeared to be that the largest vehicle made the rules. When one has become accustomed to driving in one culture (e.g., Mexico) and then transitions to the United States, problems are bound to occur.

For example, if a Hispanic driver pulls out in front of an American driver, it may be that the Hispanic driver has been acculturated to "make a space" whenever possible. Yet the American driver may misinterpret the other driver's behavior as rude or confrontational. Likewise, drivers who are both part of the same culture could misinterpret the other's behavior. For example, one male client of mine was attacked by another driver. As my client was driving down the road, attempting to pass the driver in front of him, he flashed his lights to let the other driver know that he was about to pass. The other driver, however, misinterpreted my client's behavior as a confrontation and forced him off the road.

Perhaps one of the biggest problems with aggressive drivers is that they do not see themselves as aggressive. In one NHTSA study, only 15 percent of aggressive drivers believed that aggressive driving contributed to accidents, while 53 percent of nonaggressive drivers believed that aggressive driving contributed to accidents.[44] Since aggressive drivers do not think they are the problem, they will be unlikely to take responsibility for changing their behavior.

The availability of weapons in our culture does not help the problem. Someone who is angry, who feels justified in that anger, and who feels the need for retribution is a very dangerous person. Firearms are impersonal weapons that allow us to distance ourselves from the results. The self-justified driver doesn't necessarily see himself shooting at another person. More likely he sees himself shooting at another vehicle, making it easier to pull the trigger.

Other drivers on the road are faceless, nameless, and sometimes invisible. A driver sees another vehicle rather than another person. It is much easier for a person to vent rage, especially in the case of passive-aggressive individuals, on an inanimate object than on a living creature. A person who would never kick the dog or strike a spouse might readily throw a golf club or break a dish. It is easy to make the mistake of seeing another vehicle as "driverless"—that is, forgetting that a human being is in the driver's seat. Even when an aggressive driver knows that, there is a "deep psychological urge to release aggression against an anonymous other," notes Richardo Martinez of NHTSA.[45] One psychologist tells the story of two drivers who were prepared to fight one another until they pulled off of the road and realized they were neighbors.[46] When the other driver is humanized, aggression is less likely.

We take our driving seriously and most of us think we are good drivers— that we drive the "right way." For example, a driver who tends to speed away from a stop light will get frustrated if she is behind a driver at a stop light who tends to accelerate slowly. If an aggressive driver allows for the possibility that other ways of driving are acceptable, the likelihood of aggression is reduced.

Younger drivers may incite anger in aggressive drivers because they are less experienced, may drive too fast, and may not pay attention. Their inexperience leads them to tailgate and fail to follow other road courtesies such as dimming one's high beams. Likewise, because they are less skilled behind the wheel, they don't plan for traffic hazards and may end up cutting off other drivers in an attempt to avoid obstacles that a better driver would have planned for earlier. Even very experienced drivers are a greater hazard on the road when they are doing several things at once—multitasking—such as tuning the radio or talking on a cell phone. Younger drivers are even riskier on the road when they have passengers or when they try to multitask while driving. Their immaturity may also lead them to lose their tempers. Numerous studies have shown that younger, less experienced drivers commit more driving errors and are involved in more fatal crashes than any other age group.[47] It is also interesting to note that in one study, while younger drivers, ages 16–20, perceived behaviors like running a red light and speeding as dangerous, they perceived these behaviors as less dangerous than did older drivers.[48]

Environmental and behavioral factors also contribute to road rage. Multitasking while driving not only makes us more dangerous, but it is indicative of the hurried lifestyles that contribute to rude driving and aggressive driving—multitasking includes dashboard dining, talking on cell phones, mobile computing, reading, and adjusting the radio or CD player.

The roads on which we drive are becoming more and more crowded. Between 1987 and 1997, "the number of miles of roads has increased just 1 percent while the miles driven have shot up by 35 percent."[49] Also, the Federal Highway Administration (FHA) has noted that as more people move out of major metropolitan areas into the suburbs, congestion increases. The roads in these communities were not designed to handle the volume of traffic that they now have to accommodate.[50]

Defensive Driving

Research indicates that aggressive drivers are more likely to drink and drive, speed, and drive unbelted. Their concern for other motorists is low and they do not consider the consequences of their actions. They run stop signs, disobey red lights, speed, tailgate, weave in and out of traffic, pass on the right, make unsafe lane changes, flash their lights, blow their horns, or make hand and facial gestures.[51] We, however, do not have to drive without defenses.

Some incidents of road rage take victim drivers completely by surprise. They have no idea what they have done to anger another driver until they see the enraged person in their mirror or next to them. Often, however, the situation is avoidable, and I could list countless documented cases of such events. One-third of all driving injuries can be attributed to aggressive driving.[52] Aggressive drivers feel the need to "police" the road, slowing down other drivers by blocking their progress. If an aggressive diver antagonizes another aggressive driver, the episode may escalate. An altercation in Atlanta in July 2000 was just such an event, ending with no injuries and one man arrested. On a crowded Atlanta area interstate, a 31-year-old man was stuck in a traffic jam due to a fatal car accident ahead of him. He admittedly attempted to block the emergency lane with his vehicle, thus preventing other drivers from using it to bypass traffic. Another driver who was attempting to skirt the traffic jam was forced back into the interstate lanes. He then pulled up along the left side of the 31-year-old's vehicle and said, "Now what? You scared, right?" When the driver said no, the man then aimed a pistol at him. The driver, however, continued to taunt the man saying, "You shoot me, you still going to be stuck in traffic. So where you going to go then?" The offender was arrested several miles away after the man reported the incident to a nearby state patrolman.[53]

This driver made several mistakes. First of all, it was not his responsibility to keep other drivers from breaking the law. It is frustrating to follow the rules, waiting your turn, all the while seeing others "cheating," but if you want to stay alive, mind your own business. Second, he antagonized a driver who had already demonstrated his temper, even after the man had brandished a weapon. Verbally taunting the man was analogous to lighting the fuse of a stick of dynamite. Many of us lose our tempers, but once the weapon was displayed, this driver still did not have the good sense to keep his mouth shut. Fortunately for him, the story had a positive ending.

Drivers can take a number of steps to reduce anxiety, stress, and anger while driving. First of all, give yourself plenty of time for your trip. Second, relax in your vehicle. Adjust the temperature, radio, and other comfort settings to your preferences before you leave your house. Listen to soothing music or an entertaining program. Third, keep your eyes open for signs of aggressive drivers. Frequent lane changes, tailgating, speeding, flashing lights, and so forth indicate the potential aggressive driver. Get out of the way of an aggressive driver when you can. Keep in mind that your goal is to get where you are going, not to instruct or correct the behavior of other drivers.

Drivers create stress for themselves by failing to allow enough time for their travel, setting unrealistic expectations for the trip, and by refusing to adjust their time schedules to accommodate impediments to their travel. When you find that you are stressed, breathe deeply and slowly. When another driver makes you angry, think before you react. Finally, examine your own behavior for the possibility that you are an aggressive driver. If you are, admit it and get help.

Community Prevention

The NHTSA held a symposium on aggressive driving in early 1999 and considered possible steps for addressing the problem. Participants concluded that three issues needed be addressed: education, enforcement, and judicial response to aggressive driving. Under enforcement, they suggested that communities could take advantage of applied technology, such as Red Light Running (RLR) cameras, unmanned radar, use of nontraditional law enforcement vehicles, and establishing tip lines where other drivers could report road rage they have witnessed. These participants also suggested that the judicial system take a more serious approach to dealing with aggressive driving. They noted that the automobile is a deadly weapon and suggested that drivers who are reckless with a vehicle be sentenced according to the "risk taken and the lives endangered and destroyed thereby."[54]

Gresham, Oregon, was the first place to enact a law specifically against road rage, making the offense of road rage punishable by a fine of up to $2,500 or six months in jail.[55] According to their law, passed in February 1999, a person commits the act of aggressive driving if he or she "intentionally harasses, annoys, or alarms" another driver by changing speeds, changing lanes, following too closely, impeding the other driver, or endangering other drivers in some manner.[56] In less than two months, the first charge was filed against a driver who was tailgating another driver and moving "as if he were going to ram" the other car.[57] The aggressive driver was arrested and eventually convicted. He was sentenced to 18 months bench probation, required to receive anger counseling, and fined $200.

Leon James has noted that some communities have begun a CARR program (Children Against Road Rage) that works something like Mothers Against Drunk Driving (MADD). "Its purpose is to form local organizations of children, supervised by adults, in which they learn to develop emotionally intelligent road behaviors as pedestrians, cyclists, vehicle passengers, and later, as student drivers."[58]

The NHTSA Web site provides a self-test for aggressive driving, allowing the reader to test his or her level of aggressiveness.[59] The items range from "mentally condemning other drivers" to "killing someone." Interested individuals can access the Web site and check their own attitudes about aggressive driving, allowing them to determine if they need to seek help for aggressive driving. Such an instrument should be a part of driver education and certainly a part of defensive driving courses.

In conclusion, the driver would be wise to monitor himself. In the words of Leon James, "One sure sign of a high road rage tendency is the strong desire to let the other person know how you feel."[60]

SPORTS RAGE

A few years ago I had a conversation with a man whose sons participated in T-ball, a pre-baseball sport for very young children. The man was describing how he and other coaches "scouted" for the T-ball "draft" and how he hoped that his sons would make the advanced team. I told him that I thought T-ball, a sport for four- and five-year-olds, was supposed to be fun, recreation, and a way to learn the game of baseball, and I questioned the need for a draft. He told me it was a noncompetitive draft. That seemed contradictory to me, so I asked him why they felt the need to "scout" if it was noncompetitive.

"So better kids could play with other kids of their level."

"Why?" I asked. After all, we were talking about kindergarteners.

"So they can be more competitive," he answered.

"But I thought it was noncompetitive," I said.

"It is, but we want the better kids to play with each other and the kids who aren't as good to play with each other."

"Why?" I asked again.

"So they can play on better teams the next year."

"Why?"

"So they can play with better kids."

This conversation went on for several minutes just like this. This well-meaning parent could not see that he was doing the very thing he said he was avoiding. He was driving his children to play on better teams just so they could play on better teams. He argued that they would then be better athletes when they were older, but when I told him that the literature on development did not support his supposition that being drafted in T-ball made his sons more likely to be great high school and college athletes, he discounted it. If he wanted his kids to play competitive ball and they enjoyed it, there is nothing wrong with that, but what became evident in this conversation, and is indicative of many youth sports programs, is that the game was not about the game. It was about prestige, parents' wishes, and things other than fun, sportsmanship, and learning.

It may seem outrageous to you that parents can be so wrapped up in their children's little league games that they commit murder, but it happens. In the early 1990s, John Hills, a father and coach of a little league baseball team, was attacked by an angry parent at a game. The attacker was then joined by several relatives who were also present at the game. They beat Hill with a baseball bat and kicked the man into unconsciousness. It would be nearly ten years before Hill was able to return to his career as a plumber, and even then his injuries still plagued him. The attackers were charged with battery and sentenced to 40 hours of community service. Hill sued the attackers as well as the little league association and was awarded $757,710.[61]

Michael Costin was a 40-year-old single father of four children. When Michael was 15, his father stabbed his brother to death. Costin became an alcoholic, and had a checkered past that included seven stays in prison. By 2000, he had gotten his life together, according to those who knew him, and on July 5 of that year he was directing a youth hockey practice at a rink in a small town a few miles north of Boston. Watching from the stands was Thomas Junta, a

42-year-old truck driver, whose son was involved in the practice. There was a no-contact rule for the practice, and when Junta's son was checked by another skater, he yelled at Costin to do something about it. Costin skated over to the stands and yelled at Junta, saying that contact was part of the game. Angry, Junta ran onto the ice, and the two men argued. After they left the ice, the verbal confrontation continued and developed into a physical fight that was broken up by rink employees who kicked Junta out of the arena.

Sometime later, Junta returned to the rink and confronted Costin near the vending machines. In front of Costin's sons, Junta attacked him, punching and kicking him. The 6'2", 275-pound Junta, who also had an arrest record, pinned the 5'11", 175-pound Costin to the floor. With his knee in Costin's chest, Junta beat him about the face and bashed his head against the floor. A visitor to the arena finally pulled Junta of the unconscious man, while Costin's sons screamed for Junta to stop. Costin slipped into a coma and never regained consciousness. The autopsy revealed that he was brain dead before he ever left the ice rink. Police arrested Junta and charged him with assault, but two days later, Costin died and the charge was changed to manslaughter. Junta claimed he was only defending himself after he had returned to the rink to pick up his children. He pleaded not guilty but was convicted in January 2002 and sentenced to six to ten years in prison.

One newspaper columnist wrote that this case is quite typical of those who do not understand the language of violent behavior. After noting that Junta's wife was a swimming coach and that both of their children were actively involved in sports programs, the columnist opined that, "when Junta wasn't acting like a monster, he was probably a nice guy."[62] Unfortunately, the very same thing was true of Ted Bundy. Junta did not become a murderer the moment he attacked Costin—he had been preparing, although not consciously, for that moment for much of his life. Junta had been arrested and charged with destruction of property (he was found not guilty) and arrested for assaulting a police officer (no finding has been made in this case). I am not suggesting that Junta walked around looking for someone to harm. Rather, I believe that aggression was a part of his life skills that culminated with the death of Michael Costin.

A relative said that Junta was "a big gentle giant" who "walks away from fights."[63] This relative said that Costin had "seriously provoked [Junta], giving him a hard time."[64] While this is a possibility, provocation does not condone beating a man to death, and this is a perfect example of the kind of rationalization addressed at the beginning of the chapter.

In sports leagues around the country, stories abound of individuals who have screamed profanities at each other as well as officials, fired weapons at participants, parents, and officials, and engaged in a host of other unbelievable misbehaviors. Victims have received broken bones, lacerations, and black eyes, and in some cases have been permanently injured or, like Costin, lost their lives. In defense, officials can now buy assault insurance. The problem has grown to the point that the National Association of Sports Officials offers assault insurance to its members for injuries "suffered when an official is the victim of an assault and/or battery by a spectator, fan or participant."[65] The people losing control of their behavior at these events are parents, coaches, and managers, not the children in the game, as one might expect.

Some of these aggressive individuals get so wrapped up in the game that they forget it is a game. They do not want their children to be hurt, either emotionally or physically, and they feel the need to defend them. Sports psychologist Frank Smoll notes that parents experience a "reverse dependency trap." In normal circumstances, children look to their parents for self-esteem.[66] But in reverse dependency, parents are embarrassed if their children sit on the bench. They live out their own unresolved past through their children, and anything that might interrupt the future greatness of their children is perceived as a personal attack on the parent.

Most violent fans, coaches, and parents, however, are undoubtedly aggressive people in other areas of their lives. They may yell at their neighbors and co-workers, drive aggressively, and most likely verbally assault the officials and coaches in their own adult athletic events. Their child's athletic event provides only one of many forums for their aggression to be displayed.

One study has shown that almost three-quarters of the 20 million children who play youth league sports will quit by age 13 because of the atrocious behavior of parents, many of them their own parents.[67] Youth sports leagues around the country have tried to combat the problem of poor parent conduct by requiring ethics education before children can play, requiring sportsmanship training programs, adopting a code of conduct, and employing other systemic methods in an attempt to change the culture. These programs address the inability to cope with one's frustrations effectively as the root of this problem.

CONCLUDING REMARKS

It should be evident that the aggression displayed in the aircraft cabin, on the highway, and on the athletic field has many causes. But whether we are talking about a passenger who assaults a flight attendant, a driver who rams another vehicle with his own, or a parent who assaults an umpire at a little league baseball game, these people have one thing in common. They have within their behavioral repertoire the language of aggression. The day they assault the flight attendant, bump the other vehicle with their own, or punch the umpire is not the first time they have committed an aggressive act. Whether they restricted their aggression to words, punching furniture, throwing golf clubs, or hitting other people, they know the language of aggression. Even though they may function normally under many or even most conditions, the language of violence is present. Their aggression has its root in character, coping skills, hedonism, individualism, social context, and personal decisions to act the way they do.

NOTES

1. "Air rage: Rare but rising," *CNN Online, www.cnn.com/1999/TRAVEL/NEWS/12/21/air.rage./index.html*, December 21, 1999.

2. "Unruly passenger forces flight to return to Anchorage," *CNN Online, www.cnn.com/2000/US/07/05/unruly.passenger.ap/index.html*, July 5, 2000.

3. Bruce Frankel, Alex Tresniowski, Karen Grigsby Bates, Matt Birkbeck, Susan Gray, Margery Sellinger, and Ellen Tumposky, "Stormy skies,"*People* (Internet edition), July 31, 2000.

4. "Air rage," *Reader's Digest*, March 2000, p. 115.

5. Michael Meyer, "Flying wildly out of control," *Newsweek* (Internet edition), November 29, 1999.

6. "Passenger aboard American Airlines flight arrested for unruly conduct," *CNN Online, www.cnn.com/US/9911/25/plane.emergency.01/index.html*, July 7, 2000.

7. "Passenger, 19, dies after charging cockpit," *Atlanta Journal/Constitution*, August 13, 2000, p. A5.

8. "Teen killed by airplane passengers who restrained him," *CNN Online, www.cnn.com/2000/US/09/16/passenger.dead.ap/index.html*, September 16, 2000.

9. "Psychiatric tests ordered in jetliner cockpit attack," *SF Gate, www.sfgate.com/cgi-bin/article.cgi?file=/chronicle/archive/2000/10 . . . /5SR5BA7. DT*, October 27, 2000.

10. "Lawyers reach settlement in Alaska Airlines cockpit attack," *CNN Online, www.cnn.com/2000/LAW/12/19/cockpitattack.civ.ap/index.html*, December 19, 2000.

11. "Pilot makes unscheduled landing after ruckus on airliner," *CNN Online, www.cnn.com/2000/US/11/30/ruckus.aboard.02/index.html*, November 30, 2000.

12. "Briton convicted in 'air rage' assault skips punishment," *CNN Online, www.cnn.com/2000/LAW/09/08/airrage.ap/index.html*, September 8, 2000.

13. "Air rage: Rare but rising," *CNN Online, www.cnn.com/1999/TRAVEL/NEWS/12/21/air.rage./index.html*, December 21, 1999.

14. "Flight attendants worldwide rally against 'air rage,' " *CNN Online, www.cnn.com/2000/TRAVEL/NEWS/07/06/air.rage.03.ap/index.html*, July 6, 2000.

15. "Swissair attendants can slap sexual harassers," *CNN Online, www.cnn.com/2000/TRAVEL/NEWS/12/21/swiss.attendants.reut/index.html*, December 21, 2000.

16. "Seeing red over air rage," *Consumer Reports Travel Letter* (Internet edition), February 1999.

17. "Swissair attendants can slap sexual harassers," *CNN Online, www.cnn.com/2000/TRAVEL/NEWS/12/21/swiss.attendants.reut/index.html*, December 21, 2000.

18. Michael Emmerman, "Air travel," *Esquire*, September 1989, p. 142.

19. Michael Emmerman, "Air travel," *Esquire*, September 1989, p. 142.

20. Michael Emmerman, "Air travel," *Esquire*, September 1989, p. 142.

21. Len Morgan, "Deplorable air rage," *Flying* (Internet edition), September 1998.

22. Len Morgan, "Deplorable air rage," *Flying* (Internet edition), September 1998.

23. Joe Chidley, "Uncivil aviation," *Canadian Business* (Internet edition), February 21, 2000.

24. Christopher Elliott, "Ticked at seat kickers?," *CNN Online, www.cnn.com/ 2000/TRAVEL/VIEWS/elliott/07/26/index.html*, July 26, 2000.

25. Carla Smithson, "When passengers explode," *Report/Newsmagazine (Alberta Edition)* (Internet edition), February 7, 2000.

26. "Kitsch Report," *Time, www.time.com/time/asia/asia/travel_watch/ 980907/kitsch_report.html*, September 7, 1998.

27. "Swissair attendants can slap sexual harassers," *CNN Online, www.cnn.com/ 2000/TRAVEL/NEWS/12/21/swiss.attendants.reut/index.html*, December 21, 2000.

28. Bruce Frankel, Alex Tresniowski, Karen Grigsby Bates, Matt Birkbeck, Susan Gray, Margery Sellinger, and Ellen Tumposky, "Stormy skies," *People* (Internet edition), July 31, 2000.

29. Carla Smithson, "When passengers explode," *Report/Newsmagazine (Alberta Edition)* (Internet edition), February 7, 2000.

30. "Aggressive driving fact-tip sheet with talking points," National Highway Traffic Safety Administration, *www.nhtsa.dot.gov/search97/cgi/ s97_cgi.exe*.

31. Jason Vest, Warren Cohen, and Mike Tharp, "Road rage," *U.S. News & World Report* (Internet edition), June 2, 1997.

32. Leon James, "Aggressive driving and road rage: Dealing with emotionally impaired drivers," *www.aloha.net/~dyc/testimony.html*, 2001.

33. "Virginia teen denies she intended to kill during fight over traffic dispute," *CNN Online, www.cnn.com/1999/US/12/21/traffic.beating.ap/index.html*, December 21, 1999.

34. "FBI investigates fatal shooting of woman on rural Maryland road," *CNN Online, www.cnn.com/1999/US/12/07/road.shooting.ap/index.html*, December 7, 1999.

35. "Two-year-old shot in California 'road rage' incident," *CNN Online, www. cnn.com/2000/US/04/05/crime.roadrage.reut/index.html*, April 5, 2000.

36. Thomas J. Gibbons, Jr., "Phila. teen is shot dead in traffic dispute," *www.web. philly.com/content/inquirer/2000/11/15/pa_west/proad15.htm*, November 15, 2000.

37. "Driver charged with running over cyclist he cut off in traffic," *CNN Online, www.cnn.com/US/9904/28/AM-BRF—RoadRage.ap/index.html*, April 28, 1999.

38. Jay Reeves, "Woman convicted in 'road rage' slaying," *Atlanta Journal/Constitution*, October 4, 2000, p. A8.

39. Bill Montgomery, "Cops: Slaying linked to traffic altercation," *Atlanta Journal/Constitution*, January 29, 2000, p. F3.

40. "Road-rage dog killer eludes California police," *CNN Online, www.cnn.com/ 2000/US/04/25/life.dog.reut/index.html*, April 25, 2000.

41. David Pendered and Gita M. Smith, "Toddler shot in driver's fit of road rage on I-20," *Atlanta Journal/Constitution*, April 22, 2000, p. C1.

42. Cathy Free, "Make their day," *People Weekly* (Internet edition), September 1, 1997.

43. Leon James and Diane Nahl, "Road rage and aggressive driving," *www.aloha. net/~dyc/booktoc.html*, 2001.

44. "Put the brakes on aggressive driving," National Highway Traffic Safety Administration, *www.nhtsa.dot.gov/search97/cgi/s97_cgi.exe*.

45. Jerry Adler and Theodore Gideonse, " 'Road rage': We're driven to destruction," *Newsweek* (Internet edition), June 2, 1997.

46. Jerry Adler and Theodore Gideonse, " 'Road rage': We're driven to destruction," *Newsweek* (Internet edition), June 2, 1997.

47. "Traffic safety facts," (Washington, DC: U.S. Department of Transportation/National Highway Traffic Safety Administration, 1994).

48. Leon James, "Facts and statistics by Dr. Driving," *www.aloha.net/~dyc/ facts.html*, 2001.

49. Jason Vest, Warren Cohen, and Mike Tharp, "Road rage," *U.S. News & World Report* (Internet edition), June 2, 1997.

50. Jason Vest, Warren Cohen, and Mike Tharp, "Road rage," *U.S. News & World Report* (Internet edition), June 2, 1997.

51. "Aggressive Driving and the Law: A Symposium," National Highway Traffic Safety Administration, *www.nhtsa.dot.gov/search97cgi/s97_cgi.exe*, January 22–23, 1999.

52. Kevin Anderson, "Getting a handle on road rage," *Black Enterprise* (Internet edition), January 1999.

53. Brad Schrade, "Two drivers wanted same lane on I-20—and one had a gun," *Atlanta Journal/Constitution*, July 28, 2000, p. D1.

54. "Aggressive Driving and the Law: A Symposium," National Highway Traffic Safety Administration, *www.nhtsa.dot.gov/search97cgi/s97_cgi.exe*, January 22–23, 1999.

55. " 'Aggressive driving' law is nation's first," *American City & Country* (Internet edition), April 1999.

56. "Ordinance No. 1469," *Gresham News* (City of Gresham Online), *www.ci. gresham.or.us/news/ordinance1469.htm*, 1999.

57. "First aggressive driving arrest results in guilty plea," *Gresham News* (City of Gresham Online), *www.ci.gresham.or.us/news/062399a.htm*, June 23, 1999.

58. Leon James, "Aggressive driving and road rage: Dealing with emotionally impaired drivers," *www.aloha.net/~dyc/testimony.html*, 2001.

59. "Aggressive driver self-test," National Highway Traffic Safety Administration, *www.nhtsa.dot.gov/people/outreach/employer/nets98/pdf_2/Agdriv.pdf*, 1998.

60. Leon James and Diane Nahl, "Road rage and aggressive driving," *www.aloha. net/~dyc/booktoc.html*, 2001.

61. William Nack and Lester Munson, "Out of control," *Sports Illustrated* (Internet edition), July 24, 2000.

62. Froma Harrop, "Abusive parents ruining children's sports," *Providence Journal* (Internet edition), *www.thehollandsentinel.net/stories/071800/opi_ruining.html*, July 18, 2000.

63. Jessica Heslam, "Hockey dad freed on $5G bail, victim's kin outraged," *CNN Online*, *www.cnn.com/2000/LOCAL/northeast/07/11/boh.hockey.death/index.html*, July 11, 2000.

64. Jessica Heslam, "Hockey dad freed on $5G bail, victim's kin outraged," *CNN Online*, *www.cnn.com/2000/LOCAL/northeast/07/11/boh.hockey.death/index.html*, July 11, 2000.

65. National Association of Sports Officials Web site, *www.naso.org/benefits/--sos.htm#AssaultProtectionProgram*,. 2001.

66. William Nack and Lester Munson, "Out of control," *Sports Illustrated* (Internet edition), July 24, 2000.

67. William Nack and Lester Munson, "Out of control," *Sports Illustrated* (Internet edition), July 24, 2000.

CHAPTER **9**

MURDER FOR HIRE: HIRED ASSASSINS, ORGANIZED CRIME

Don't think there are no crocodiles because the water is calm.
—Malayan proverb

Hiring a hit man is often the core of movies and novels. However, most of these fictitious stories exaggerate the real nature of murder-for-hire. Rarely are hired gunmen the suave, globe-hopping, sophisticated characters with endless resources and unlimited access to technology found in movies like *The Jackal*. Similarly, most of them do not commit their crimes for exorbitant amounts of money like the assassin in Ian Fleming's James Bond film *The Man with the Golden Gun*, who earned $1 million for each job. Instead, most people hired to commit murder are punks, thieves, and derelicts who are willing to do the dirty work of dishonest cowards for as little as a few hundred dollars.

Individuals who hire hit men wish to pursue their own goals at someone else's expense, yet they are too afraid to commit the crime themselves. They wish to avoid getting their hands dirty, while at the same time distancing themselves from the crime. Often, those who seek the services of a hit man are not professional criminals. They reach into the marginal corners of their lives for potential accomplices—chat rooms, prisons, bars, or even Internet sites. In the Coen brothers' black comedy *Fargo*, an embezzling car dealer hires two men to kidnap his wife. His initial contact in his attempt to find someone to carry out the plot is a man who worked as a mechanic in his automobile dealership.

Even though this movie is fiction, this part of the story is not far from how such contacts are made. Someone knows someone who knows someone, and so forth. What these cowards fail to recognize is that it is their very attempt to distance themselves from the crime often leads to their own arrest and conviction when the hit men they hire go to police and divulge the plot. The risk that someone will disclose the plan to authorities or the victim increases with every person who knows of the plot. Once the plot is uncovered and authorities are involved, undercover agents are utilized to establish a prosecutable case. Many times, a person who believes he or she is talking to a hit man hired through a third party is actually talking to an undercover police officer or federal agent.

There is no distinct profile of those who hire people to kill others. They are professional and lay people, male and female, and of varied ages. Perpetrators are not limited to any socioeconomic class. Doctors, lawyers, drug dealers, homemakers, actors, mobsters, clergy, and college professors have all been found guilty of plotting the demise of another human being.

Contracts in murder-for-hire plots range from the promise of a few hundred dollars to thousands of dollars. Deals are made in restaurant parking lots, alleyways, and over the telephone. People who are willing to commit murder for money are dishonest; hence, they cannot be trusted to keep a secret. If it is in their best interest to keep the secret they will, but as soon as it becomes evident that they have something to gain by talking about the plot, they will. For example, one man was hired by a woman to kill her ex-husband. She met the potential killer in an Internet chat room and promised him $4,000 for the job. The woman provided the hit man with a layout of her husband's home and a picture of him. She also gave the hit man a down payment, which he used to pay off some credit card debt. When the potential hit man's wife saw the credit card statement reflecting the payment, she questioned him about the money, eventually accusing him of having an affair. In order to save his own marriage, he revealed the murder plot to his wife and eventually went to police. The woman who tried to hire him was convicted and sentenced to ten years in prison for conspiracy to commit murder. The intended victim was not injured in the plot. I find it interesting that this potential hit man thought it would be better to admit he had been hired to kill someone than to say he had an affair. I wonder how long that marriage lasted after this revelation.

Just as those who hire hit men can't trust those they hire, hired guns cannot necessarily trust the people who hire them. Murderers have been promised money in the hundreds of thousands of dollars from life insurance settlements, only to find out that no such potential ever existed. Others have been promised thousands of dollars, yet when the job was done, they were paid only a few hundred dollars. You can't call the Better Business Bureau or go to small claims court when someone fails to honor a contract of this nature.

Most murder-for-hire plots are motivated by one of six reasons: revenge; financial gain; illness or mental instability; relationship complications; self-protection or avoidance of prosecution for a crime; and organized crime.

REVENGE

One may seek revenge because of bad business deals, betrayed relationships, or what one perceives to be a miscarriage of justice. In 1999 an agent with the Drug Enforcement Administration (DEA) hired a hit man to kill the person he thought was responsible for the death of his cousin in a carjacking. A 17-year-old male was eventually charged with the carjacking and murder. The teen was convicted of the crime, but the conviction was thrown out, and after two mistrials the prosecutor decided not to pursue the case. Subsequently, the agent offered $10,000 to one of his drug informants to kill the teen. The plot was discovered and the agent was arrested. He pleaded guilty, was convicted for planning the murder, and was sentenced to seven years in prison. As a DEA agent, the man had plenty of shady contacts as he sought someone to kill on his behalf. Lawyers, policemen, and others who routinely work with criminals may not find it difficult to find someone willing to kill for money.

Ordinary citizens, however, find ways to hire hit men as well. A mother was convicted of hiring two Mexican hit men to kill her daughter's boyfriend because she was upset by the breakup of the relationship between her daughter and the victim. She was convicted of the crime and sentenced to 20 years in prison, but after 2 years in jail her sentence was overturned. Later, however, she was recharged with the crime.

FINANCIAL GAIN

This is perhaps the most common reason someone hires a hit man. In this category, the perpetrator stands to receive some fiscal benefit at the death of the victim, often related to life insurance or inheritance. For example, in 1992 a Texas woman hired a man to kill her father and stepmother because she did not get along with them and she believed that she would inherit $12 million upon their deaths. She offered a hit man $1 million to commit the crime. The man beat the stepmother to death and intended to do the same to the woman's father. Even though he was severely beaten, the father survived. The assassin was tried and convicted for the crime, and in 2000 he was executed. The woman who plotted the scheme, along with her boyfriend, was sentenced to life in prison.

People have plotted murders for much less than the $12 million in the previous case. In 1999 a 16-year-old discussed hiring a man to kill his father because he wanted his father's gun collection. The son changed his mind and tried to back out of the plot, but the man hired for the murder went ahead with it anyway. He shot the teen's father in the face, killing him. After killing the father, the hit man and his accomplices turned on the son and cut his throat. The teen survived and the hit man was arrested, convicted, and given a life sentence. The son was convicted of solicitation for capital murder and was given a two-year sentence in juvenile prison.

In another case where the motive for the murder-for-hire scheme was money, a couple hired an ex-convict to kill a woman for her insurance money. The man stabbed the victim 12 times and cut her throat, killing her. The man was told he would be paid $12,000, but was paid only $400. He was convicted and sentenced to death. The couple who hired him are still awaiting trial. Sadly for the victim, she had once before been the target of an aggressor. More than 20 years earlier, her husband shot her in the back, and she was permanently paralyzed from that injury.

In 1998 a millionaire tried to hire someone to kill his former business partner, giving a former employee $75,000 to hire a hit man. Instead of hiring a hit man, the employee told the intended victim of the plot, and the plotter was arrested and eventually found guilty of criminal solicitation.

In 2000 a 39-year-old Kentucky woman unknowingly hired an undercover officer to kill her 80-year-old husband. She had been married for only four months and the alleged motive was the man's money. In negotiations with an undercover agent that she thought was a hit man, she offered him $4,500 to kill her husband and to make it look like an accident. The case has not yet been fully adjudicated, but the prosecution believes that the woman, pregnant with the man's child, feared her husband would cut her out of his will. Her attorney has said that her name was not on any life insurance policy or will. The case is still in court.

As one final example of financial gain as a motive in murder-for-hire plots, actress and former model April Goodman was sentenced to 30 years and fined $25,000 for trying to hire a hit man to kill her ex-husband. Her ex-husband, who was not injured, claimed that Goodman was unhappy with money from her divorce settlement. The FBI became aware of Goodman's plans, but what makes this case unique is that the FBI warned her they knew of her plans. Even so, she waited a year and tried again to hire a hit man to kill her ex-husband. Goodman planned to remarry her millionaire ex-husband and then have him murdered on their honeymoon so that she would inherit his fortune. She was tape-recorded talking to an undercover detective whom she thought she was hiring to commit the murder for $6,000. Her boyfriend tipped police that Goodman was planning the job. She was convicted of solicitation for murder and sentenced to 30 years in prison. She apparently had considered killing her first husband, who was so afraid for his life that he wore a bulletproof vest.

Goodman carried a $50,000 life insurance policy on her first husband even after they were divorced.

ILLNESS OR MENTAL INSTABILITY

Courtney Duval Jacob had been married to Bobby Kimbrough only three months when she hired an undercover Georgia Bureau of Investigation agent to kill him. She gave the undercover agent $500 and promised $20,000 more, telling him he could make the murder look like an accident. She suggested he either push her husband in front of a tractor or strike him with a crowbar and then arrange the scene to make it look like a vehicle had fallen on him. Sitting in a vehicle at a McDonald's restaurant with the undercover agent, she gave him $500, a box with a gun, and photos of her husband and his vehicle. She was arrested after this videotaped conversation with the undercover agent. Prosecutors claimed she did it for insurance money, but her attorney claimed she was mentally ill, due in part to a head injury. All of the mental health experts involved in the case, including psychologists for the prosecution, agreed Duval suffered from personality disorder. Mental health experts said that her mental illness caused her to believe that her husband was trying to kill her and to falsely believe that he was abusing his children from a previous marriage.

The prosecution's claim that she planned the scheme for money seemed to fall apart when it was revealed that her children were the sole beneficiaries of her husband's estate. Since her arrest, her mental illness has been treated and her condition has improved. In court, she watched the videotape of her conversation with the undercover agent and said that "it was like watching a movie of someone else."[1] She confessed to the plot in court and her husband testified on her behalf, saying he wanted to save their marriage. Jacob was sentenced to three years in county prison and seven years on probation, and was fined $3,000. Her husband remains devoted to her and anxiously awaits her release.

RELATIONSHIP PROBLEMS

One might argue that almost all murders stem from relationship problems in one way or another, but the murder-for-hire plots discussed in this section were committed specifically to end or to conceal relationships. In these cases, financial gain or revenge was either absent or of secondary importance to the perpetrators. An anesthesiologist plotted the murder of his wife of 14 years so that he could pursue a relationship with his lover of 9 years. Unfortunately for the doctor, he himself was killed during the attack on his wife. Having arranged the time and location of the murder, the hit man fired several times into the couple's vehicle, killing not only the doctor's wife, but killing him as well. The physician reportedly had asked several people to commit the murder.

Eventually, he hired the boyfriend of his own lover to do the job. Apparently, the physician's mistress and her boyfriend concocted the plan to make money on the murder, getting the doctor out of the picture at the same time.

Other plots have gone awry as well. In 1998 a hired gunman inadvertently shot and killed the wrong man. He had been hired by a man who was angry because of a love triangle involving the intended victim. The accidental victim resembled the intended victim and worked in the same business. The gunman was sentenced to 10 years in prison, but the man who hired him was sentenced to a minimum of 47 years in prison.

In Michigan in 1999, a 46-year-old woman offered two men $15,000 to kill the wife of her former lover. The victim was shot to death in a parking lot. The woman had had an affair with the victim's husband, but he eventually ended the extramarital relationship and reconciled with his wife. The woman had tried other means to get the man to come back to her, once claiming that she was pregnant and another time claiming that she was mentally ill. As of this writing, the trial has not yet concluded, but all perpetrators face life in prison if convicted.

In December 2000, a 17-year-old high school student allegedly hired a friend to kill his mother for $250, reportedly because he and his mother were having relationship problems. In fact, his mother had told a relative that she feared her son might harm her and that he would be the likely culprit if anything ever happened to her.[2] The woman was shot to death, and both the shooter and the woman's son were arrested. Their trial is pending.

Gina Lynn Spann is currently serving a life sentence with no chance for parole for arranging the murder of her husband Kevin, who was a staff sergeant in the army. When she was 31 years old, she began a relationship with a teenaged boy who had moved in with them. As the teen and Gina played video games together, she talked to the 18-year-old boyfriend about her thoughts of killing her husband and then committing suicide. She was frustrated in her marriage and talked of ways to end it. Her boyfriend told her that he knew two friends who would kill Spann's husband, but she did not think he was serious.[3] On Mother's Day weekend of 1997, Spann, her boyfriend, and Spann's 12-year-old son from a previous marriage came home to find Kevin Spann shot to death in front of their home. The boys who actually committed the murder were convicted and sentenced to prison. Spann still insists that she did not intend for her boyfriend to commit the murders and that she was only thinking out loud when she made comments about killing her husband.

A 54-year-old rabbi in New Jersey allegedly plotted to kill his wife so that he could pursue a relationship with another woman with whom he had engaged in a two-year affair. His 54-year-old wife was bludgeoned to death in her home in November 1994. Six years later, two men pleaded guilty to the murder. One of them, a member of the rabbi's synagogue, said that the rabbi had offered him $30,000 to kill his wife, whom he described as "an enemy of Israel."[4] The rabbi allegedly feared that a divorce would harm his position in his synagogue. The rabbi was charged with murder and conspiracy. The trial began in September 2001.

One final example of murder-for-hire was the case of 30-year-old Eric Bullock. He hired two men, paying them $400, to beat his pregnant girlfriend. Bullock's intention was that the hit men kill the fetus because, according to prosecutors, he feared the pregnancy would interrupt his relationship with another woman. The mother survived the beating, but the baby was born dead. Bullock was convicted of capital murder and sentenced to life in prison.

SELF-PROTECTION

As in movies and suspense novels, there are cases where criminals attempt to have prosecutors, witnesses, and judges assassinated to increase the likelihood that they will not be found guilty during their trials. In one such case, an ex-broker, jailed on a $100 million fraud case, hired a fellow jail inmate to kill the judge who was supposed to hear his case. The judge had a strict reputation, and the ex-broker feared he would lose his case and receive a harsh sentence. The man offered a fellow inmate $50,000 for the hit, provided the man with information about security near the judge's courtroom, gave the man a phone number where he could get paid, and devised a code for the timing of the hit. The plot was uncovered and the judge was not injured. The broker was found guilty of second-degree conspiracy.

ORGANIZED CRIME

An amazing story of political corruption and one man's attempt to clean up a community unfolded in Youngstown, Ohio, in 1996. In a case that rivals the plot of *Serpico*, newly elected District Attorney Paul Gains vowed to both clean up both the mob-infested community and weed out corruption from the political scene. The case is very complicated and involves corruption ranging from the sheriff's office to the federal government. The mafia allegedly controlled a "chief of police, the outgoing prosecutor, the sheriff, the county engineer, members of the local police force, a city law director, several defense attorneys, politicians, judges, and a former assistant U.S. attorney."[5] Also involved in this case was a diligent FBI agent who had spent much of his career battling organized crime. This story provides a telling example of how real life and the movies are not all that far apart.

The Youngstown area was riddled with mob contacts throughout the community. It has been reported that "as late as 1997, in the small city of Campbell, [the mob] controlled at least 90 percent of the appointments to the police department."[6] When their attempts to get Gains to accept a place on their payroll failed, the mob intended to have Gains murdered and then replace him with a DA who would be sympathetic to their interests. Not only was Gains a threat to their organization, but he had planned to hire as his chief investigator FBI Special Agent Robert Kroner. Kroner had spent most of his FBI career attempting to shut down the Youngstown mob, but had little success.

The mob don ordered a lieutenant to take care of the murder of Paul Gains. This lieutenant then hired Jeffrey Riddle to do the job. Riddle hired two cronies, Mark Batcho and another man. The three of them were the ones who actually carried out the attempt on Gains' life on Christmas Eve in 1996. That evening, while the other two waited outside, Batcho entered Gains' home through his open garage door. Gains' was in his kitchen talking on the telephone when Batcho walked in and shot him twice, once in the forearm and once in the side. He attempted to shoot him again, but the gun jammed and Batcho fled. When Batcho told his accomplices that he was unsure if Gains was dead or not, the men planned to return and finish the job, but they heard on a scanner that police were on their way to Gains' residence. Gains survived, but the case went unsolved for several months until a former girlfriend of a mobster called Gains and told him she knew who had conducted the hit. That phone call broke the case, and most of the men involved in the attempt, including the mob boss, are now in prison.

Even though this story sounds like something you might see in a movie, the similarities end with the plan. The actual murder attempt was a debacle from the beginning. The men planned to keep in touch with each other by walkie-talkie during the hit, but the walkie-talkies wouldn't work. The first time they went to Gains' home he wasn't there, so they left and came back later in the evening. Batcho shot Gains twice with a .38-caliber pistol. When he tried to shoot him a third time, he aimed at his heart and pulled the trigger, but the gun jammed. Frustrated and not knowing what else to do, Batcho ran out of the house. His accomplices asked if Gains was dead, but it wasn't until they were driving away that they realized that he wasn't. By that time it was too late to return to the scene because they heard the police call on their scanner. As if that weren't enough, Batcho left a speed loader for his gun at the crime scene as well as a footprint. The only way they could have made the case against them much easier would have been to leave their wallets at the scene.

As the above cases have demonstrated, men and women as well as adults and children have plotted murders. The public is especially stunned when the perpetrator is rich, well known, or powerful. Such was the case in 1999 when rising football star Rae Carruth was arrested and charged with plotting the murder of his girlfriend.

RAE CARRUTH

The world of professional sports is a complicated one of which most people see only a segment. From our living rooms and stadiums around the country we watch our favorite athletes and follow the progress of their careers as they sign professional contracts. Few people know about the many challenges that face these men and women as they begin their careers. Athletes are recruited while in high school by colleges and universities. From these beginnings they are courted, wined and dined, and provided with special privileges by recruiters who hope to secure the athlete's commitment to play for their university. Recruiters have often ignored rules that prohibit perks for prospective players, giving the recruits the impression that they are above the rules. Once these athletes are in college and have taken their places on the court or playing field, the perks continue. Even without illegal contributions or provisions from coaches, the university, athletic boosters, or alumni, athletes are given special privileges. They are often housed in facilities separate from other students, they have tutors provided by the university exclusively for them, and they are often treated as if they were untouchable by students and faculty alike.

Once the lucky few have risen to the top of the national rankings in their sports, recruiters and coaches from professional teams court them with lucrative signing bonuses and contracts. Yet that is only the beginning of their financial boon. Companies seek endorsements from well-known athletes, enabling some of them to make as much money from advertising off the court as they do on the court. Granted, few can draw the kind of paycheck a veteran like Michael Jordan can, but these young men begin earning millions of dollars very early in life.

In their home towns and around the country, everyone knows them, and the red carpet is rolled out in department stores, restaurants, and shopping malls. Even people in their entourage derive a level of fame by mere association. Drugs, women, and parties can be found any minute of any day.

Their age, lack of wisdom, and inexperience are their enemies. Imagine being 21 years of age and having an unlimited expense account. These men are often immature and unskilled in money management. They are thrust into a cutthroat world where gold-diggers and con men are not hard to find. Women regularly throw themselves at these athletes, some merely hoping to sleep with them. Others have darker motives. It is well known among professional athletes that women seek sexual relationships with them, hoping to be impregnated, thus either forcing the athlete into a permanent relationship or, more likely, suing for child support running into millions of dollars.

One should note, of course, that not all professional athletes live lives like this, but it should be no surprise that many of these young men are quickly drawn into bad business deals, drugs, and unhealthy partnerships with women. How can we expect them to know, at such a young age, how to deal with the fame and fortune that has befallen them? Their money, power, and popularity convince them that they are invincible. Perhaps some of these variables led to the downfall of one of football's superstars in the late 1990s, Carolina Panther Rae Carruth.

On the evening of November 16, 1999, Rae Carruth and his pregnant 24-year-old girlfriend, Cherica Adams, went to a movie. After the movie, they returned to Carruth's home to get his vehicle. Apparently, they had planned for Carruth to spend the night at Adams' home. As they drove along a dark and winding stretch of highway, Carruth in his Ford Expedition in front of Adams in her black BMW, Carruth suddenly slowed to a stop, blocking the highway. A third vehicle pulled up alongside Adams' car. In the vehicle were three men: Van Brett Watkins, 44, Michael Kennedy, 24, and Stanley Drew Abraham, 19. As the car containing the three men came alongside Adams' vehicle, five shots rang out. When the shooting ended, Adams was fatally wounded, shot four times in the neck and chest. Carruth watched from his vehicle as the shooting took place and then fled, as did the vehicle containing the three men.

Adams rolled her car off the highway into the yard of a home belonging to a man named Farrell Blalock. In pain and bleeding, she dialed 911 on her cellular phone.

"He was in the car in front of me, and he slowed down, and somebody pulled up beside me and did this," she told the 911 operator. When asked who "he" was, Adams told the operator, "Rae Carruth. He plays for the Panthers."[7] This began a chain of events that would lead to the death of Cherica Adams and days of conflicting of testimony that eventually resulted in the conviction of all four men.

Rae Carruth grew up in Sacramento, California. He played high school football and eventually went on to become a first-round NFL draft pick in 1997, where was picked up by the Carolina Panthers as a wide receiver. During the 1990s, Carruth had relationships with several women. In 1994 he lost a paternity suit brought by a Sacramento woman named Michelle Williams. Carruth paid $3,500 each month to care for their son, Rae Carruth Wright.[8] Other than making his paternity payments, Carruth had little interaction with Williams or their son. Later, Carruth allegedly impregnated a second woman named Amber Turner. At his insistence, she had an abortion.[9] After this relationship, he dated yet another woman, Candace Smith, who would become an important part of the prosecution's case against him in the Adams murder trial.

Carruth suffered a broken foot during the opening game of the season in 1998. That year he missed all but two games. Carruth had a reputation as an introvert and, referring to missing so many games, said of himself, "I can honestly say I wasn't part of the team."[10]

Carruth began dating Cherica Adams, a 24-year-old exotic dancer, and she became pregnant early in 1999. Carruth allegedly urged her, as he did with Amber Turner, to have an abortion, thus freeing himself from further paternity payments. Adams, however, refused to have an abortion. According to court testimony, it was around that time that Carruth began to plan her murder. He first discussed his plan to have Adams killed with Van Brett Watkins. Watkins was admittedly a violent man who reportedly stabbed his own brother and pistol-whipped another man.[11]

Watkins said Carruth forced him to participate in the scheme. "I was very afraid of Rae Carruth," he said.[12] Watkins said Carruth offered him $5,000 to assault Adams and hurt her baby and that the planning began six months before the shooting. "This wasn't a one-day affair," Watkins said during the trial. "It was six months. He dragged me into something I didn't want to be involved in."[13]

Carruth then recruited Michael Kennedy, but when Kennedy hesitated, Kennedy said that Carruth threatened his life.[14] Kennedy also said that Carruth asked him where he could buy a gun and gave him $100 to acquire it. Carruth told Kennedy that he needed the gun because he had gotten a woman pregnant and that "she was trying to juice him for the money."[15] Kennedy was later recruited to drive the rented vehicle from which Watkins would fire upon Adams.

On the evening of November 16, Watkins, Kennedy, and Abraham waited for Carruth and Adams to leave the movie theater and to get Carruth's vehicle. When Carruth left his house, he contacted Watkins and the other two men by cell phone, informing them that he and Adams were in separate vehicles. Abraham was unaware of the scheme until late in the evening. The threesome had stopped at a convenience store and Watkins had gone inside, leaving Abraham and Kennedy alone. It was then that Kennedy told Abraham of the plan. Abraham allegedly wanted no part of it, but when Watkins returned to the vehicle, Kennedy was afraid that there wasn't time to make any changes, and the three left together to follow Carruth and Adams. Just after midnight, Carruth blocked Adams' way with his vehicle and Watkins fired five rounds into her vehicle, striking her four times. Adams, eight months pregnant at the time, began screaming. Watkins reported that he "could hear a gurgling sound" as she struggled to breathe and began drowning in her own blood.[16] After the shooting, Watkins claimed that Carruth called him to tell him he was OK and not to tell the police anything.[17]

Adams drove her car off the road and called 911, and responding emergency personnel found the bleeding woman still conscious. Several witnesses heard her identify Carruth as the person responsible for the shooting. A 12-

minute tape of Adams' call to 911 recorded her statement to the operator that Carruth had stopped his Ford Expedition in front of her car when "somebody pulled up beside me and did this . . . I think he did it. I don't know what to think."[18] Farrell Blalock, on whose front lawn Adams' car stopped, said that he overheard her identify her "boyfriend" to police as her attacker."[19] In court, Blalock testified that Adams, when asked who shot her, said, "My husband, I mean my boyfriend."[20] Nicole Michaels, a paramedic who was the first to reach Adams, testified in court that a police officer asked the victim if she knew who shot her, and Adams answered, "Rae, my baby's daddy."[21]

The dying pregnant woman was rushed to the hospital, where surgeons delivered her baby, Chancellor Lee Adams, by Caesarian section. While she lay in the hospital, a breathing tube in her mouth, she motioned to a nurse for a pen and paper. The nurse, Tracy Willard, said that Adams wrote on a piece of paper that Carruth "was driving in front of me and stopped in the road and a car pulled up beside me and he blocked the front and never came back."[22] When Willard asked Adams who "he" was, Adams wrote "Rae."[23]

At the hospital, Carruth, who had arrived along with several friends, reportedly never asked about the condition of his girlfriend or child.[24] Carruth was arrested, as were his co-defendants. The judge set bail at $3 million, which Carruth posted, after which he was released. The other three defendants were released on $1.5 million bail. Nearly a month after the shooting, on December 14, Cherica Adams died from complications of the gunshot wounds. Carruth had been free on bond just under a week and a half when Adams died. The day after her death, Carruth skipped bail and for 24 hours remained a fugitive. Acting on a tip from his mother, FBI agents located Carruth at a motel in Wildersville, Tennessee, a town about 100 miles north of Memphis. In the company of a female friend of Carruth's, agents were told that he was hiding in a vehicle. "When she [Carruth's female friend] started to open the trunk, she told us he was in there, for his safety," said FBI agent Mark Post. "He just had his hands up in the air."[25] Authorities arrested Carruth at 5:45 P.M. on December 15, 1999, hiding inside the trunk of the car along with $3,900 in cash. He reportedly had spent 21 hours hiding in the trunk.

The Trial

On November 14, 2000, two days short of the one-year anniversary of the shooting, opening arguments were presented in 26-year-old Rae Carruth's trial. The prosecutor's case included motive, history of aggression and threatening behavior by Carruth, confessions by the triggerman and another accomplice, the dying woman's 911 call during which she identified Carruth as being responsible, as well as repeated statements by the victim that Carruth was involved, and testimony that Carruth confessed to a former girlfriend to plotting the murder. According to the prosecutor, the motive for the assassination was that since Adams would not have an abortion, Carruth wanted to avoid paternity payments to her and his son. He was already paying $3,500 a month to Michelle Williams in California, and a second suit would have further eroded his financial situation. "He wanted her to have an abortion, but she was adamant in her refusal. She wanted to have that baby," said prosecutor Gentry Caudill.[26]

Officer Peter Grant testified in court regarding Adams' statement. Could she have been confused or perhaps been misunderstood? This was unlikely, according to Grant, who said, "I asked her [Adams] point blank if her boyfriend was the one who shot her and she said yes, he was."[27] Also testifying in court was Farrell Blalock, who heard Adams identify Carruth as her attacker to police; Nicole Michaels, the paramedic who also heard that conversation; and Tracy Willard, the nurse who provided the pen and paper for Adams, who wrote a statement implicating Carruth. Perhaps most damaging was the 12-minute 911 recording where Adams identified Carruth as responsible for the shooting.

Candace Smith, Carruth's former girlfriend said that Carruth confessed to her about his involvement in the shooting, giving an account of the episode that agreed with Watkins' testimony.[28] Smith confirmed the prosecutor's hypothesized motive, saying Carruth told her he was upset at Adams' decision not to have an abortion.[29] Smith also testified that Carruth "paid the guys some money over a period of time. . . . He saw the guys pull up and shoot into her car," and that Carruth told her he doubted the baby was his.[30]

The defense questioned why Smith waited several months to come forward with her story of the confession. Candace Smith said she wasn't angry or jealous of Adams. She said she was afraid, but former NBA player Charles Shackleford confirmed in court that Candace Smith told him about Carruth's confession back in November 1999.[31] "He basically confessed to her at the hospital about what happened," Shackleford said.[32]

During his testimony, triggerman Van Brett Watkins said, "He hired me as a hit man. He hired me to kill Cherica Adams and the baby. . . . I couldn't bring myself to kill the baby. I shot at the top [of the car], not through the door."[33] Watkins said Carruth instructed him to take Adams' belongings after she was shot to make the attack look like a robbery. "If he would kill his own girl and their baby, what would he do to me?" Watkins told the court.[34]

Damaging to Carruth's reputation during the trial was the testimony of his former girlfriend, Amber Turner, who became pregnant while dating Carruth. According to Turner, Carruth threatened her and demanded that she have an abortion. She also said that Carruth "joked about killing his oldest son and the child's mother" and expressed concern to her about child support for the child Cherica Adams was carrying, saying, "I ain't going to have no more kids with someone I ain't going to be with. . . . Don't make me send somebody out there to kill you. You know I'll do it."[35] In reference to having someone kill his eldest son, Turner said, "I heard him on the phone talking to people, saying he had people out in California who would do it for him."[36] Also damaging to his reputation was the testimony of Michelle Williams, the mother of his first child, who said Carruth once told her, "Don't be surprised if you get into a car accident," referring to her discussion of a visit to his Carolina home with their son.[37]

The Defense

The heart of the defense's argument was to challenge the prosecution's supposition about the motive for the murder. While in jail, Watkins allegedly told a Mecklenburg County sheriff's deputy that he killed Adams because she made a gesture at him. According to the defense, Kennedy had arranged to borrow $5,000 from Carruth to buy marijuana.[38] When Carruth backed out of the deal at the last minute, Watkins became furious. Driving behind Carruth that night in 1999, Watkins allegedly told the deputy that he drove up beside Adams' car to find out where Carruth was going. He motioned at her and she slowed her vehicle. According to the sergeant's testimony, Watkins said Adams made an obscene gesture at him that enraged him and he shot her to death. Watkins said that the shooting was Carruth's fault, saying, "If he had just given us the money none of this would have happened."[39] In court and under oath, Watkins denied that he ever made this confession. The defense argued that Watkins, the primary witness against Carruth, was a drug dealer with a history of mental illness.[40] Carruth's attorney had a difficult job trying to convince jurors that Watkins was a liar, but at the same time convincing them that they should believe his alleged confession to the sergeant.

The defense said that on the night of the shooting, Carruth had intended to spend the night with Adams, but on their way from his home, she pulled alongside his car and said she did not want him to spend the night with her. Carruth then went to the home of Panthers teammate Hannibal Navies. From there, he was paged to come to the hospital.[41] According to a defense witness, Carruth arrived at Hannibal Navies' house, played video games, and joked around. Tanya Ferguson, Navies' girlfriend, said "no" when asked by the defense if Carruth seemed upset as if he had come from a murder scene.[42]

Renowned forensic scientist Henry Lee provided evidence that called into question the possibility that Watkins fired at a stationary vehicle, as it would have been if Carruth blocked the road. But he also added that if the vehicle was moving, how could Carruth's vehicle have avoided damage?[43] The defense also claimed that Carruth had no financial motive to kill Adams. They called to the stand a trainer for the Panthers who said Carruth's injury did not threaten his pro career. Therefore, it was likely that paternity payments for a second child would have had little impact on his financial status.

Character witnesses argued that Carruth "loved children," coached T-ball, and had "a good heart."[44] A fellow Carolina Panther, Muhsin Muhammad, testified that Carruth wanted to bond with his son, especially since he had missed that opportunity with his first child.[45] Finally, a psychologist testified that police and family members asked Cherica Adams leading questions and distorted her memory of what happened the day she was shot.[46]

A Complicated Decision for the Jury

The Carruth case presented an interesting dilemma for jurors. Many witnesses for the prosecution had reason to lie, and much of the prosecution's case was built on circumstantial evidence. Had it not been for the 911 call from Cherica Adams and her statements to various individuals implicating Carruth, he almost certainly would not have been convicted. Yet even these statements could have been interpreted in other ways.

I am reluctant to include case studies like this one in my books if I am not convinced that the person accused was, indeed, guilty of the crime. As I evaluated the evidence in this case, I decided that the most credible position is that Carruth did, in fact, orchestrate this murder. Most convincing is the web of people who would have had to coordinate their stories in order to create a coherent deception. Watkins and Kennedy could easily have concocted the story that led to Carruth's conviction and both of them certainly had reason to deceive—trying to save their lives. Yet also included in any plot to frame Carruth would have been Stanley Abraham, Candace Smith, Amber Turner, and Charles Shackleford. There would be no clear motive for any of these four to lie. Likewise, Adams' comments to the 911 operator could have been the words of a delusional woman who was in shock, pain, and struggling for her life. Yet she made almost identical comments on at least two other occasions. She too, in a sense, would have had to be in on the plot to frame Carruth—a highly unlikely scenario.

Watkins was potentially not a credible witness. He was an admitted liar. Even though he had been diagnosed with a mental disorder, he said he faked the condition so he could serve time in a mental hospital instead of prison.[47] The prosecution claimed that he told a jail guard that he killed Adams because she made a gesture at him, but Watkins denied that this confession ever took place. Watkins lost his temper on the witness stand once or twice, and perhaps most significant regarding his credibility was the fact that he was a state's witness. He saved his own life by implicating Carruth. Watkins, familiar with the prison system, would have known that he could make a deal with prosecutors if he could give them something they wanted. Hence, making up the story of

Carruth's involvement would have been to his advantage. Kennedy potentially had the same motive to lie. Likewise, the prosecution's account of Watkins' motive is plausible, but as the prosecutor pointed out, it is very unlikely that a woman by herself would have stopped on a dark, winding road when strange men in another car motioned for her to do so.

Watkins testified that Carruth had planned to have Adams killed on another occasion outside a restaurant. "He said he would run off and act like he was trying to get help inside the restaurant and leave her there for dead."[48] This plan failed, but lends potential credibility to Watkins' story that the plan to kill Adams took several months.

It is possible that Candace Smith was jealous of Carruth's association with Adams and used the woman's death as a way to exact revenge on Carruth. It is also possible that Amber Turner's statements about Carruth's threatening behaviors and words were the work of either an overactive imagination or a jilted lover trying to get revenge. But it is unlikely that these women lied. Their stories were similar, and they either conspired together against Carruth (unlikely, because if they were jealous, why would they work together?) or they were telling the truth.

Assuming they were telling the truth, why would someone joke about arranging the killing of one's former girlfriend and child? Why would Carruth joke about a former girlfriend "getting into an accident," and why would he say "you know I'll do it" in reference to threats to have someone killed? These statements are not funny and are representative of one who has the potential to do exactly what he "joked" about.

Part of the prosecution's case involved the fact that Carruth never asked about the condition of Adams or their child while he was at the hospital. However, one could argue that if he had asked about them, then prosecutors could have said that he was "too concerned," as if he was afraid they would live. This may have been one of those situations where he would lose no matter what he said or did not say.

If he was innocent, why would Carruth have left a message on Tanya Ferguson's voice mail not to cooperate?[49] His high school football coach said, "Rae is not stupid. How could a person throw all that away?"[50] Yet one could suppose that if he felt invincible, he did not believe he was throwing it away. Many men and women in history have traded their places of prestige for a jail cell, or even death, because they believed they could not be touched. Napoleon was beaten at Waterloo in part because he believed that he was invincible. Richard Nixon foolishly and unknowingly contributed to his own downfall, arranging and then lying about the Watergate break-in. Again, he believed he was in total control and unable to be touched.

Finally, it is possible that Adams did not mean for her statements to implicate Carruth. Perhaps she only meant that he was her baby's father. In fact, what she said during her 911 call is open to question: "I think he did it. I don't know what to think."[51] It is also possible that her impression at the moment the shooting occurred—that Carruth was involved, even though he was not—was embedded in her mind, accounting for the fact that she implicated him more than once. The 911 call prompts other questions as well. For example, she stated that Carruth shot her when it was never even suggested by the prosecution that Carruth handled the gun in any way.

Regardless of the conflicting information, it seems evident that the most logical conclusion in this case is the one that the jury reached. Carruth hired these men to kill Cherica Adams because he wanted to avoid the complications of having fathered a child. Unfortunately for him, not only did his plan fail, but his life was forever changed by his poor decision making.

Summary and Sentencing

The jury was composed of seven white men, three black women, and two white women. Jurors initially were divided on all four charges against Carruth—first-degree murder, conspiracy to commit murder, shooting into an occupied vehicle, and using an instrument to destroy an unborn child. After three days of deliberation, deadlocked jurors explained the impasse to the judge. "We voted on all four charges, and we are split on all four charges," said a note from the jurors.[52] The judge ordered them to keep trying to reach a verdict. The next day, after 20 hours of deliberation over four days, the jury reached a verdict, acquitting Carruth of first-degree murder, but convicting on the other three charges. He was sentenced to 18 years and 11 months in jail with no possibility for parole.

In exchange for his testimony against Carruth, Van Brett Watkins was spared the death penalty. Watkins pleaded guilty to second-degree murder, conspiracy to commit first-degree murder, attempting to kill an unborn child, and shooting into an occupied vehicle and was sentenced to minimum of 40 years and 5 months and a maximum of 50 years and 8 months in prison. Michael Kennedy also pleaded guilty to second-degree murder, conspiracy to commit murder, shooting into an occupied vehicle, and attempting to kill an unborn child, and was sentenced to a minimum of over 11 years in prison. Stanley Abraham pleaded guilty to accessory charges and was given the lightest sentence of all, 90 days in jail and 5 years probation.

The claims lawyers make during murder trials never cease to amaze me. Kennedy testified that Carruth was present during the entire attack and that Kennedy was the one who acquired the gun, picked up Watkins and Abraham, and drove the vehicle. He also was the one who received the call from Carruth saying he was leaving his home with Adams behind him. In other words, he acknowledged his part in this scheme, yet his attorney had the audacity to suggest that this criminal was "heroic" because he stepped forward to testify, ensuring that the "Adams family would know what happened."[53] I see nothing heroic in gunning down a pregnant woman and then testifying to protect yourself.

Carruth was in the third year of a four-year, $3.7 million contract, more money than most people will make in a lifetime. Yet he traded a life of affluence, prestige, and stardom for a prison cell. Even if he had won his case, the charges destroyed his financial life. He was declared indigent by the court because he had spent much of his money posting his bond. His assets were briefly frozen because of a custody suit over his younger son.[54] He lost his house to foreclosure.[55] The state eventually paid more than $120,000 for his lawyers and legal services.[56]

Rae Carruth maintains his innocence, and prosecutor Gentry Caudill noted that "Carruth has shown 'not one ounce of remorse' for Adams' death."[57] Since the shooting, Saundra Adams, Cherica's mother, said she has wondered whether Carruth's seeming interest in the baby "may have been just all part of the plan."[58] Carruth's son survived the shooting, but he suffers from developmental problems and cerebral palsy. He is living with Saundra Adams, who sued Carruth for custody and child support.[59] Unfortunately, what began as a promising professional career in athletics—a career that young men dream about—ended with a dead woman, a baby with physical limitations, and an athlete in jail. Of course, the most significant loss was the loss of life. Adams' parents said that Cherica had been selling real estate and was doing well. The Adamses lost a daughter and Chancellor lost a mother.

CONCLUDING REMARKS

The list of cases involving people who have hired assassins is a very long one. Those cases discussed in this chapter illustrate the various motives for murder-for-hire, and more could be included if space allowed. These perpetrators often show no remorse, but rather contempt for both their victims and the court. Some have made outrageous requests of the court. For example, an attorney who was convicted of arranging a murder-for-hire plot against two of his former clients unbelievably asked the government to return the money that he paid undercover agents for the assassination. He had paid undercover agents $11,000 for the plot, but after being convicted and sentenced to eight years in prison, he asked for the money back. This is demonstrative of the egocentric worldview of those who hire assassins.

Although many people have hired assassins and some have undoubtedly succeeded in their plans, murder-for-hire is relatively rare. Some of the six motives for murder-for-hire that I have addressed are common problems, but healthy, well-functioning people find productive means to deal with their relationships and difficulties. As is always true, the more productive one's coping strategies, the less likely one will pursue an extreme behavior like murder-for-hire.

NOTES

1. John Munford, "Woman who hired assassin gets three years in jail, probation," *The Citizen*, January 31, 2001, p. 1A.

2. "Michigan teen charged with plotting mother's shooting," *CNN Online*, *www.cnn.com/2000/LAW/12/20/mother.slain.ap/index.htm*, December 20, 2000.

3. "The murderer," *Atlanta Journal/Constitution*, March 12, 2000, p. C6.

4. Marilyn Silverstein, "Pair of alleged 'hit men' confess to slaying rabbi's wife," *Jewish Bulletin News* (Online edition), *www.jewishsf.com/bk000505/ushitmen.shtml*, May 5, 2000.

5. David Grann, "Crimetown USA," *New Republic*, July 10, 2000, p. 23.

6. David Grann, "Crimetown USA," *New Republic*, July 10, 2000, p. 23.

7. Lester Munson, "Thrown for a loss," *CNNSI.com, www.sportsillustrated.cnn.com/football/nfl/news/2000/11/28/sc1204/*, November 28, 2000.

8. Scott Michaux, "No killer's profile for Carruth," *Atlanta Journal/Constitution*, December 19, 1999, p. E3.

9. "Carruth trial: Day 25," *CNNSI.com, www.sportsillustrated.cnn.com/football/nfl/news/2000/01/05/carruth_trial_ap/*, January 5, 2001.

10. Scott Michaux, "No killer's profile for Carruth," *Atlanta Journal/Constitution*, December 19, 1999, p. E3.

11. "Carruth trial: Day 19," *CNNSI.com, www.sportsillustrated.cnn.com/football/nfl/news/2000/12/20/carruth_trial_ap/*, December 20, 2000.

12. "Carruth trial: Day 19," *CNNSI.com, www.sportsillustrated.cnn.com/football/nfl/news/2000/12/20/carruth_trial_ap/*, December 20, 2000.

13. "Carruth trial: Day 19," *CNNSI.com, www.sportsillustrated.cnn.com/football/nfl/news/2000/12/20/carruth_trial_ap/*, December 20, 2000.

14. "Day 2," *CNNSI.com, www.sportsillustrated.cnn.com/football/nfl/news/2000/11/21/carruth_tuesday_ap/*, November 21, 2000.

15. "Day 2," *CNNSI.com, www.sportsillustrated.cnn.com/football/nfl/news/2000/11/21/carruth_tuesday_ap/*, November 21, 2000.

16. "Carruth trial: Day 21," *CNNSI.com, www.sportsillustrated.cnn.com/football/nfl/news/2000/12/22/carruth_trial_ap/*, December 22, 2000.

17. "Key witness," *CNNSI.com, www.sportsillustrated.cnn.com/football/nfl/news/2001/11/28/charles_carruth/*, November 28, 2000.

18. "Guilty on three of four," *CNNSI.com, www.sportsillustrated.cnn.com/football/nfl/news/2001/01/19/carruth_trial_ap/*, January 19, 2001.

19. Scott Michaux, "No killer's profile for Carruth," *Atlanta Journal/Constitution*, December 19, 1999, p. E3.

20. "Day 2," *CNNSI.com, www.sportsillustrated.cnn.com/football/nfl/news/2000/11/21/carruth_tuesday_ap/*, November 21, 2000.

21. "Searching for the truth," *CNNSI.com*, *www.sportsillustrated.cnn.com/football/nfl/news/2000/11/20/carruth_trial_ap/*, November 20, 2000.

22. "Searching for the truth," *CNNSI.com*, *www.sportsillustrated.cnn.com/football/nfl/news/2000/11/20/carruth_trial_ap/*, November 20, 2000.

23. "Searching for the truth," *CNNSI.com*, *www.sportsillustrated.cnn.com/football/nfl/news/2000/11/20/carruth_trial_ap/*, November 20, 2000.

24. "Day 2," *CNNSI.com*, *www.sportsillustrated.cnn.com/football/nfl/news/2000/11/21/carruth_tuesday_ap/*, November 21, 2000.

25. "Police catch up to Panthers' Carruth at Tennessee motel," *Atlanta Journal/Constitution*, December 16, 1999, p. A1.

26. "Searching for the truth," *CNNSI.com*, *www.sportsillustrated.cnn.com/football/nfl/news/2000/11/20/carruth_trial_ap/*, November 20, 2000.

27. "Carruth trial: Day 6," *CNNSI.com*, *www.sportsillustrated.cnn.com/football/nfl/news/2000/11/29/carruth_trial_day6/*, November 29, 2000.

28. "Prosecution set to wrap up murder case against former NFL player," *CNN online*, *www.cnn.com/2000/LAW/12/11/carruth.trial.ap/index.html*, December 11, 2000.

29. Leslie Boghosian, "Incriminating testimony?," *CNNSI.com*, *www.sportsillustrated.cnn.com/football/nfl/news/2000/10/28/carruth_testimony/*, October 28, 2000.

30. "Carruth trial: Day 6," *CNNSI.com*, *www.sportsillustrated.cnn.com/football/nfl/news/2000/11/29/carruth_trial_day6/*, November 29, 2000.

31. "Prosecution set to wrap up murder case against former NFL player," *CNN Online*, *www.cnn.com/2000/LAW/12/11/carruth.trial.ap/index.html*, December 11, 2000.

32. "Carruth trial: Day 8," *CNNSI.com*, *www.sportsillustrated.cnn.com/football/nfl/news/2000/12/04/carruthtrial_day8_ap/*, December 4, 2000.

33. "Carruth trial: Day 20," *CNNSI.com*, *www.sportsillustrated.cnn.com/football/nfl/news/2000/12/21/carruth_trial_ap/*, December 21, 2000.

34. "Carruth trial: Day 20," *CNNSI.com*, *www.sportsillustrated.cnn.com/football/nfl/news/2000/12/21/carruth_trial_ap/*, December 21, 2000.

35. "Carruth trial: Day 25," *CNNSI.com*, *www.sportsillustrated.cnn.com/football/nfl/news/2001/01/05/carruth_trial_ap/*, January 5, 2001.

36. "Carruth trial: Day 25," *CNNSI.com*, *www.sportsillustrated.cnn.com/football/nfl/news/2001/01/05/carruth_trial_ap/*, January 5, 2001.

37. "Carruth trial: Day 25," *CNNSI.com*, *www.sportsillustrated.cnn.com/football/nfl/news/2001/01/05/carruth_trial_ap/*, January 5, 2001.

38. Lester Munson, "Thrown for a loss," *CNNSI.com*, *www.sportsillustrated.cnn.com/football/nfl/news/2000/11/28/sc1204/*, November 28, 2000.

39. Leslie Boghosian, "Defense strategy," *CNNSI*.com, www.sportsillustrated.cnn.com/football/nfl/news/2001/01/18/munson_carruth/, January 18, 2001.

40. Nick Charles, "Process begins," *CNNSI.com*, *www.sportsillustrated.cnn.com/football/nfl/news/2001/01/23/profile_carruth_jury/*, January 24, 2001.

41. Leslie Boghosian, "Defense strategy," *CNNSI.com*, *www.sportsillustrated.cnn.com/football/nfl/news/2001/01/18/munson_carruth/*, January 18, 2001.

42. "Carruth trial: Day 10," *CNNSI.com, www.sportsillustrated.cnn.com/ football/nfl/news/2000/12/06/carruth_trial_ap/*, December 6, 2000.

43. "Carruth trial: Day 14," *CNNSI.com, www.sportsillustrated.cnn.com/ football/nfl/news/2000/12/13/carruth_trial_ap/*, December 13, 2000.

44. Scott Michaux, "No killer's profile for Carruth," *Atlanta Journal/Constitution*, December 19, 1999, p. E3.

45. "Carruth trial: Day 14," *CNNSI.com, www.sportsillustrated.cnn.com/ football/nfl/news/2000/12/13/carruth_trial_ap/*, December 13, 2000.

46. "Carruth trial: Day 18," *CNNSI.com, www.sportsillustrated.cnn.com/ football/nfl/news/2000/12/19/carruth_trial_ap/*, December 19, 2000.

47. "Carruth trial: Day 19," *CNNSI.com, www.sportsillustrated.cnn.com/ football/nfl/news/2000/12/20/carruth_trial_ap/*, December 20, 2000.

48. "Carruth trial: Day 20," *CNNSI.com, www.sportsillustrated.cnn.com/ football/nfl/news/2000/12/21/carruth_trial_ap/*, December 21, 2000.

49. "Carruth trial: Day 10," *CNNSI.com, www.sportsillustrated.cnn.com/ football/nfl/news/2000/12/06/carruth_trial_ap/*, December 6, 2000.

50. Scott Michaux, "No killer's profile for Carruth," *Atlanta Journal/Constitution*, December 19, 1999, p. E3.

51. Roger Cossack, "Case against Rae Carruth appears to be springing leaks," *CNN Online, www.cnn.com/2000/LAW/10/columns/cossack.carruth.10.23/*, October 23, 2000.

52. "Deadlock," *CNNSI.com, www.sportsillustrated.cnn.com/football/nfl/ news/2001/01/18/carruth_deadlock_ap/*, January 18, 2001.

53. "Day 3," *CNNSI.com, www.sportsillustrated.cnn.com/football/nfl/news/ 2000/11/22/carruth_trial_ap/*, November 22, 2001.

54. "Picking up the check," *CNNSI.com, www.sportsillustrated.cnn.com/ football/nfl/news/2001/01/07/carruth_taxpayers_ap/*, January 7, 2001.

55. "Picking up the check," *CNNSI.com, www.sportsillustrated.cnn.com/ football/nfl/news/2001/01/07/carruth_taxpayers_ap/*, January 7, 2001.

56. "Carruth trial: Day 26," *CNNSI.com, www.sportsillustrated.cnn.com/ football/nfl/news/2001/01/08/carruth_trial_ap/*, January 8, 2001.

57. "Carruth sentenced," *CNNSI.com, www.sportsillustrated.cnn.com/ football/nfl/news/2001/01/22/carruth_trial_ap/index.html*, January 22, 2001.

58. "Police catch up to Panthers' Carruth at Tennessee motel," *Atlanta Journal/Constitution*, December 16, 1999, p. A1.

59. "Defendant in shooting of Rae Carruth's girlfriend pleads guilty," *CNN Online, www.cnn.com/2000/US/08/01/carruth.shooting.ap/index.html*, August 1, 2000.

CHAPTER 10

INSTRUCTIONS FROM GOD: HATE CRIMES

Be careful who you choose for an enemy for that is who you become most like.

Nietzsche

The most dangerous person in the world is the one who believes he has been called by god to maim, destroy, or kill. If the person believes that a higher power has called him or her to action, no one can persuade him or her otherwise. For example, terrorists who bomb shopping centers or city buses do not perceive their behavior as murder. They believe that they are acting on behalf of god and, therefore, their behavior is righteous. In fact, in some religions, the suicide terrorist earns an automatic ticket to heaven for his or her "holy" behavior. Likewise, doctors who perform abortions have been shot and killed by religious men who believed they were engaged in a holy war to protect the fetus. While I share the desire to protect unborn children, I do not condone the slaughter of any man, woman, or child. Many factors converge that allow a person or group to perceive killing people as a righteous act. I will address each of the following issues in this chapter: self-justification theory, psychological defenses, mental illness, and righteous aggression. Following this discussion, I will provide several cases that illustrate the use of these mechanisms.

SELF-JUSTIFICATION THEORY

People have the need to view themselves and their actions as right and blameless. This is called self-justification. Once we have normalized our thoughts and behaviors, whatever they may be, we can then engage in those thoughts and behaviors without guilt, anxiety, or remorse. Self-justification is a part of our everyday lives, and it is nearly inescapable. Most of the behaviors and thoughts that we rationalize are trivial and have little effect on other people. For example, a man may justify spending some of his working hours playing on the Internet even though he is supposed to be working. He thinks to himself that his search will "only take a few minutes" and that his company won't really be hurt by his momentary disengagement from his assigned duties. No one may ever know what has happened and, for the most part, no one is injured. Other times, our self-justified behaviors may affect others, but those effects are nothing more than irritations. For example, a person may believe that she should correct the grammar of her co-workers, both in meetings and in casual conversation. Her co-workers resent her intrusion, but she sees this behavior as part of her "calling" in life because she believes that she has a better than average understanding of English grammar. In this case, even though it irritates her co-workers, they can cope with it and no one's existence is threatened. In its extreme form, however, self-justification of violent behavior is a serious threat to life and limb. A terrorist who believes god has ordained him to kill is an extremely dangerous person.

Most of us engage in behaviors that we would not accept from others, but justify for ourselves. For example, we may break traffic laws by speeding, rolling through stop signs, or passing in no-passing zones. Or we have affairs, steal, lie, or cheat on our income taxes. Those who engage in such behavior might readily accept that it would be wrong for someone else, but they perceive their specific case as unique. Self-justification makes it possible for the tax cheat or the adulterer to cope with what would otherwise be oppressive guilt. For example, you might hear someone say, "I know that I shouldn't claim this as a deduction on my taxes, but the government has enough of my money already." With this statement, the person acknowledges that he is being dishonest, but justifies the behavior.

PSYCHOLOGICAL DEFENSES

We employ a variety of defense mechanisms that allow us to justify our behavior. Four of these mechanisms are prominent in those who engage in hate crimes: rationalization, depersonalization, desensitization, and the need to affiliate.

Rationalization

Rationalization is the process of making something seem acceptable when it is not. Similar to self-justification, rationalization allows us to justify our behaviors using false logic. When one is rationalizing, one's argument sounds reasonable, but upon close inspection, flaws in one's logic become clear. I once caught two students cheating on a test. One student was allowing the other to copy from his test paper. He rationalized that he really wasn't cheating because he was "minding his own business" even though he knew the other student was looking at his paper. The student tried to argue that he could not control other students and keep them from looking at his test paper. Yet his flawed logic became clear when he conceded that he had agreed ahead of time to position his paper so the other student could see it.

A young Protestant woman came to see me some years ago. Her presenting problem was that she had difficult relationships with men. When we looked closely at her relationships, she confided that she slept with all of her dates. In her conservative faith this was considered sinful, and her promiscuous behavior also could have resulted in her suspension from the college she attended. She rationalized her behavior, however, by pretending she really wasn't doing anything wrong. She said to me that her sexual liaisons didn't really "count" as fornication because she believed that when her faith addressed fornication, it only meant adultery by married persons. Since she wasn't married, she reasoned, the rule did not apply to her. This argument would not have held water for very long with any religious scholar in her faith.

During the Holocaust in World War II, guards and commandants of the death camps exhibited self-justification in order to cope with their assigned tasks. They justified their torturous, inhumane, and murderous treatment of the Jews by any of the following statements: "They would have killed me, too, if I didn't obey," or "They were only Jews," or "I was just doing what I was told," or "I didn't know any better." Each of these statements made their unthinkable behavior thinkable. Not only did those directly involved in the extermination of the Jews exhibit this self-justification behavior, but the citizens who witnessed portions of these atrocities did so as well. In the villages surrounding Auschwitz and Dachau, two of the most notorious extermination camps, the ashes of human remains rained down on the gardens, automobiles, and rooftops of the residents. Yet after the liberation of the camps, the residents claimed that they knew nothing of the activities within the walls of the camp. Further investigation made it evident that many of the residents of these towns knew what was going on, but they chose to pretend it was not their concern. The following statement is often attributed to Martin Niemoller, a German preacher and victim of a Nazi concentration camp:

In Germany, they first came for the Communists, and I didn't speak up because I wasn't a Communist. Then they came for the Jews, and I didn't speak up because I wasn't a Jew. Then they came for the Trade Unionists, and I didn't speak up because I wasn't a Trade Unionist. Then they came for the Catholics, and I didn't speak up because I was a Protestant. Then they came for me—and by that time no one was left to speak up.[1]

Niemoller justified ignoring a responsibility to help his fellow man by supposing that as long as the Germans left him alone, he would mind his own business.

Most of us would like to think that we would not be so easily manipulated, but Stanley Milgram's study, discussed in Chapter 1, demonstrates that this is most likely not the case. Subjects in Milgram's study continued "shocking" their victims because someone in authority told them to do so. In other words, they justified their own behavior by displacing their personal ethic and responsibility on another person. These were ordinary people who found themselves doing unthinkable things. In fact, when the subjects in Milgram's study were told of the real nature of the study and realized what they had done, many were so traumatized by the way they had justified their behavior that they had serious psychological responses to the experiment. Out of a desire to prevent such responses in test subjects in the future, it became unethical to do such a study again.

Religious activists who bomb abortion clinics rationalize breaking the law and taking human life by supposing that they are "at war." Therefore, when one is at war, bombing, killing, and injury are unfortunate byproducts, not cruel behavior or deliberate violations of law.

Depersonalization

Terrorists and hate groups depersonalize the victims of their cruelty. They claim that their targets are not individuals, but governments or groups. Depersonalization is also a regular part of basic military training. New recruits are taught to refer to their opposition as "the enemy." Faceless mannequins and dummy bags are used in hand-to-hand combat practice. When the soldier is then forced to shoot at an enemy, he sees something less than human—a stuffed dummy bag. As long as victims are perceived as "the enemy," the soldier doesn't have to think of them as people with faces, names, and families. Timothy McVeigh, for instance, used a military term when talking about killing children in a day care center housed in the Murrah Federal Building that he destroyed. He called the deaths of these children "collateral damage." Using this term removed their faces from his mind and made it easier to justify their deaths.

The Nazis in World War II dehumanized the Jews by creating the perception of them as subhuman; therefore, they could take their lives without guilt. It is evident that the Nazis perceived the Jews as lower than animals because they would have never done to an animal many of the cruel things that they did to the Jews. In the film *Schindler's List*, the commandant of the Krakow labor camp stepped onto his balcony one morning, stretched, lit a cigarette, and picked up his rifle. He then began randomly shooting inmates. It was all very recreational, yet this same character most likely would not have performed the same act on squirrels, dogs, or cats. In *Speaking with the Devil*, Carl Goldberg addresses this process of dehumanization when he quotes a terrorist as saying, "Once you are able to convince yourself that most of the human race are nothing more than insects, then all the crimes you commit against people are tolerable. You're even proud of yourself."[2] Timothy McVeigh nearly cried as he told reporters about killing a gopher, and he also cried when he watched the tragedy at the Branch Davidian compound in Waco, Texas, but he exhibited no remorse at all for killing women and children in Oklahoma City.[3] To him, his victims were less than human.

Desensitization

When I was a child, I did not live on a farm, but I had a few experiences with farm life. I recall my grandfather killing chickens by chopping their heads off with a hatchet. My siblings and I chased the chickens into the woods after they had been beheaded. I look back on that event and wonder how most city children would respond to the slaughter of farm animals. It is a normal part of farm life, but it would undoubtedly be very distressing to them. Hunters, farmers, and so forth, however, would have no qualms about it because they become desensitized to the death of animals. I have often eaten my lunch while examining autopsy or crime scene photographs. I have seen hundreds of dead bodies, and it doesn't bother me in the least. Students who have never been exposed to death, bodies, and blood not only find it impossible to eat, they sometimes lose their lunch. Again, over time I have become desensitized to such things. My wife and I once lived in a house that bordered an interstate highway, a state highway, and a train track. As if that were not enough, less than two miles away was the Atlanta International Airport. Planes, trains, and automobiles roared past our house at all hours of the day and night. The first few days we lived there, the noise was unbearable. However, after a few weeks, we got used to it. My parents came to visit and in the morning they asked us how we put up with all the noise. "What noise?" we said. We didn't even hear it anymore.

When one affiliates with people who rationalize violent behavior, one will grow accustomed to that violence over time. Behavior that at one time would have been unthinkable eventually becomes normal. People who live in a world where injury, brutality, murder, hate, and destruction are everyday events eventually fail to even see them. "What violence?" they might say.

Need to Affiliate

The need to affiliate is not actually a defense, but it is a part of socialization that affects our behavior and can provide rationalization for dysfunctional, illegal, and/or evil behavior. One of our basic needs is the need to affiliate; in other words, we need to be a part of a group. In order to identify with those with whom they wish to affiliate, people will sometimes engage in behaviors that they might otherwise have found repulsive or distasteful. For example, as I noted earlier, one year all the soccer players I was coaching decided to shave their heads. None of them would have shaved his head if it had not been for the solidarity of the group, and none of them believed that he looked better with a shaved head. The need to affiliate was more powerful than concern about their personal appearance.

Loners are individuals who for one reason or another have failed to develop the social skills that would allow them to engage in normal socialization. They often are people who have extreme ideas and, because they do not have a cohesive social structure around them, their extreme ideas remain unchecked. When these people find one another, they can be very dangerous. Skinheads, for instance, are often loners who have found each other. In other words, even though it sounds contradictory, they are a group of loners. These social outcasts and dysfunctional men and women find meaning in their lives by hating others. What they really seek is affiliation, but they find it in the oppressive doctrines of their hate-filled group. Yet because their members are socially and psychologically dysfunctional, these groups often are unstable. In short, their membership is made up of people who don't get along well with other people.

MENTAL ILLNESS

Some people who commit violence believe that god instructed them to do so. They are delusional, actually hearing voices, and their activities are the result of mental illness rather than the defense mechanisms described above. For example, a woman in the midwestern United States brutally killed her children because she suffered from psychosis. In her psychotic state, she believed that evil spirits possessed her children and that the only way she could free their souls was to brutalize their bodies. She heard the voices of the evil spirits just as clearly as you and I hear voices over the telephone. Political leaders and celebrities are sometimes the targets of mentally ill people who believe they have been commissioned by god to destroy their victim. The United States Secret Service sorts through hundreds of potential threats against political leaders and dignitaries each year. Because their lives are public, they are easy targets for the "righteous anger" of mentally disturbed people who are unhappy with the way these leaders conduct the business of the country or their personal lives.

RIGHTEOUS AGGRESSION

Some people believe they are instructed by god to do terrible things to other people, often their own children, but do not suffer from any delusions. Through their study, reading, and interpretation of holy writings, they become convinced that they are called to action. They perceive their behavior as righteous because they are of sound mind and believe that they are being persecuted or martyred if anyone tries to stop them. For example, I have been a faculty member for almost 20 years at a conservative religious college. Many of our graduates pursue various professional ministries as careers. Many of my students over the years have interpreted a few passages from the Bible as justification for hitting children. In several places the book of Proverbs instructs a loving father not to "spare the rod," and it is from this concept that we get the cliché "spare the rod and spoil the child." However, what some of my students fail to understand is that these words are describing discipline, not hitting in and of itself. Some years ago, one of my students adamantly argued with me when I suggested that if a parent can accomplish the same goals without spanking a child, then spanking in that situation may be unnecessary. He used the Proverbs passages as his justification that he not only *would* spank his children when he had them, but that he *must* spank them. I told him that it appeared that he was choosing to read the passage literally, and he affirmed my observation, I then said to him, "So you believe then that if you spank your children they will never die." He said, "Of course not." I observed that the same book of Proverbs says, "If you punish a child with the rod, he will not die."[4] I reminded my student that he said he was reading the scripture literally, so he must also read that passage literally. If, on the other hand, he chose to read it figuratively, then he could also read the passage I quoted figuratively. My student was not convinced and told me that he would "just do what the Bible says." One can see how easy it would be to justify cruel behavior in the name of religion.

This interchange with my student may seem like a trite example, but it has serious ramifications. Ricardo Davila and his wife, Joseta Davila, were arrested for cruelty to children and eventually sentenced to prison for torturing their son. They beat him, crushed his feet with a sledge hammer, left him for a week in a bathroom blindfolded, with a bucket taped to his head, and forced him to eat his own vomit.[5] The couple believed that they were "trying to make a good man to God and to society."[6] In Georgia in April 2001, an entire church came under fire from the department of family and children's services when it became known that they were beating their children. These church members were publicly whipping each other's children in the church, and nearly 50 of the children were eventually removed from their homes by family services. The judge told the parents they could have their children back if they would agree to suspend their public beatings, but the church leaders and parents refused to agree to that request. The children remained in foster care.

Many people do not like to hear that religious people are some of the most biased on the planet. Much of the research on prejudice and religion indicates that discrimination and prejudice increase as people become more religious, and that the more right-wing, authoritarian, dictatorial, dogmatic, and fundamentalist a religion is, the more prejudice is likely. This happens because various religions give their members permission to hate, exclude, and shun (rationalization, self-justification). Gordon Allport once said that religion "makes prejudice and unmakes prejudice. . . . Some people say the only cure for prejudice is more religion; some say the only cure is to abolish religion."[7] White supremacist groups justify their hate with the same religious writings other religions use to emphasize tolerance and brotherly love.

Of course, it should be emphasized, just as Allport suggested, that not all religion promotes prejudice, discrimination, and hate. It simply has that potential because, as I have said, people who believe god justifies their behavior and thoughts will not easily change them.

FEAR AND CHAOS

Terrorists seek to create fear. Their behavior is aimed not against the victim alone, but also against the group of people who are represented by the victim. Therefore, an anti-Semite who murders a rabbi is not just killing the rabbi, but also attempting to communicate hate and fear to the Jewish community. In essence the terrorist is saying, "I can strike anywhere and you might be next." For this reason, victims of terrorism do not have to be members of the military. The western European view of battlefield ethics maintains that civilians should not be direct targets of military operations. In Vietnam, soldiers regularly shot and killed the Viet Cong, but the tragedy at My Lai was an atrocity solely because the victims were civilians. However, depending on the specific goals of the terrorist group, almost anyone can serve as a representative of the fear that the terrorist seeks to instill in the actual target. As former FBI profiler Robert Ressler says, "Terrorism is aimed at the people watching."[8] For this reason, terrorists can blow up school buses, civilian airplanes, and restaurants without compunction. Their larger target is not the people they kill any more than it is the building or vehicle they destroy. Those are secondary to presenting a message that says, "We are here among you. Be afraid."

Westerners have a difficult time understanding how the terrorists of the Middle East could justify killing "innocent" women and children. However, their behavior is not so far removed from our own religious teachings as we might think. Even the Old Testament contains stories where God instructs the Israelites to completely annihilate a group of people. In one case God speaks to the king of Israel and commands him not only to kill his enemy, but to kill men, women, children, infants, ox, sheep, camels, and donkeys.[9] In case God's words may have been misunderstood, His prophet later reminds the Israelite king that God intended for him to "utterly destroy the Amalekites and fight against them until they are exterminated."[10] Such examples are not uncommon in the Christian Bible or in other religious histories. In fact, one could look to the Crusades, the Grand Inquisition, and the Salem witch trials to see how religious people have condoned horrifying behaviors against other human beings. As a current example, even in this new millennium, many religious people are passive-aggressive toward homosexuals who have contracted the AIDS virus, believing that God has sent the virus to punish them for what they consider to be a sinful lifestyle. In other words, they have no empathy for these suffering people because they do not want to interfere with what they see as God's punishment for the victim's behavior.

ROBERT ERIC RUDOLPH

Eric Rudolph has been accused of the bombing in Centennial Olympic Park during the 1996 Olympic Games as well as the bombings of a gay nightclub and two abortion clinics. Rudolph has been described as a loner and a participant in the ideology of the Christian Identity movement, a white supremacist organization. The leader of this group has said, "If you are an enemy of God, I am obliged to kill you."[11] Note the use of the word "obliged." As I have stated before, people like this believe that their perceived spiritual calling justifies overriding any human law or code of conduct. A man like Rudolph, if he is guilty of these crimes, could easily justify wounding or killing visitors to the Olympics, a security guard at an abortion clinic, or patrons of a gay nightclub, believing that these people are less than human and enemies of god. There is a $1 million reward for the capture of Rudolph, and several federal and local agencies have been searching for him unsuccessfully for several years.

TIMOTHY McVEIGH

Timothy McVeigh was convicted in the bombing the Murrah Federal Building in Oklahoma City that killed 168 people in 1995. That year I recall walking into my classroom, where I found my students glued to a television set. Together we watched the smoldering building and rescuers rushing to and fro. Ironically, the class I was teaching was called "Violence in America." The bombing in Oklahoma City was originally thought to be the work of foreign terrorists, but it became evident that it was a domestic terrorist who was responsible for the deadliest terrorist attack in American history up to that time.

195

McVeigh, a former military man and a veteran of Desert Storm, hated the government. He was deeply distressed over the government's behavior at Ruby Ridge and Waco, Texas. He selected the Murrah Federal Building because it housed several government offices and thus for him represented the government. He rationalized his terrorism by believing that he was at war with the U.S. government. McVeigh never showed any remorse for his behavior, and he even refused his father's request that he apologize.[12] McVeigh, 33 years of age, was scheduled to be executed by lethal injection on May 16, 2001. However, just prior to his execution date, it was revealed that the FBI had failed to turn over hundreds of pages of documents to McVeigh's defense attorneys. A stay of execution was granted and the execution date was rescheduled. On June 11, 2001, McVeigh was executed by lethal injection.

RUSSELL HENDERSON AND AARON McKINNEY

Sexual orientation is perceived by some to be a legitimate cause for violence. Some religious leaders, who claim to be messengers of Jesus' grace and love perpetuate this hate. In 1998 a young homosexual man named Matthew Shepard was brutally killed by two thugs. At Shepard's funeral, men and women picketed with signs that read, "No Fags in Heaven" and "No Tears for Queers."[13] The Reverend Fred Phelps of the Westboro Baptist Church in Topeka, Kansas, was behind the picketing, and his organization maintains a Web site whose address is godhatesfags.com. On this Web site, the number of days Shepard has been "in hell" is maintained, and the site says, "All the fag cater-wauling, candlelight vigils, court orders, etc., can't buy Matt one drop of water to cool his tongue."[14] On this same site, in an alleged "memorial" to Shepard, the page shows a picture of Shepard's face with flames beneath it as if he were burning in hell, and an audio segment is available called "Matthew's message from hell."[15] The audio segment consists of several seconds of a man screaming in agony. Actually, this audio segment would be more appropriately titled "The sound that Matthew made when he was being beaten to death by two hate-filled, homophobic men."

People who engage in gay-bashing are exhibiting their homophobia, not their bravery. Gay-bashers are so afraid of homosexuals that they feel the need to go out and find them and beat them up. I suggest that those individuals who feel the need to harm homosexuals are actually trying to destroy their own homosexual thoughts or drives. They experience sexual interest toward members of the same sex at either a conscious or an unconscious level and in order to prove to themselves that they are not homosexual, something that they fear, they seek out homosexuals, lure them into vulnerable positions, and then beat them up or kill them. This may have been part of what led to the brutal death of gay college student Matthew Shepard.

On October 6, 1998, in Laramie, Wyoming, Aaron McKinney and Russell Henderson lured 21-year-old Matthew Shepard, a freshman at the University of Wyoming, from a bar by pretending to be gay. Earlier in the evening in the bathroom, McKinney and Henderson decided they would pretend to be gay in order to rob Shepard.[16] Investigators said that the original plan of the pair was to rob the 5'2", 105-pound Shepard, but when Shepard got into their truck, he made a sexual advance toward McKinney. In a rage, McKinney told Shepard, "We're not gay and you're going to get jacked."[17] He then began beating the young man.

Around midnight, the pair drove Shepard to an isolated spot where they tied him to a fencepost and beat him into unconsciousness with their fists and with a .357-caliber handgun while Shepard begged for his life. They kicked him repeatedly in the groin. Finally, they asked the semiconscious man if he had seen the license plate of their truck. Shepard repeated their tag number. McKinney then beat him again before he and Henderson left him there to die.

After leaving Shepard, they got into a fight with two teenaged males during which time McKinney received a head wound. McKinney allegedly struck one of the two men on the back of the head so hard that he later required surgery. Later, McKinney and Henderson went to the home of McKinney's former girlfriend, Kristen Price. She heard someone outside her window and when she looked, she saw McKinney covered in blood. When she asked him what was wrong, he said, "I think I killed someone."[18] McKinney washed off a wallet and other items in her sink. Later, Price, Henderson, and Henderson's live-in girlfriend, Chasity Pasley, drove to Cheyenne, where they threw the men's bloody clothing in a dumpster.

Eighteen hours after the pair left Shepard tied to the fence in freezing temperatures, a college student riding his mountain bicycle found the man's body. Shepard was taken to a hospital where it was discovered that he had suffered numerous skull fractures. He never regained consciousness and died five days later.

Price and the other three had rehearsed a story to tell police, but Price's conscience eventually drove her to tell police about her ex-boyfriend's involvement in the murder. During a search of McKinney's truck, police found Shepard's credit card, and they later found Shepard's wallet in McKinney's apartment and blood on McKinney's gun, in his truck, and on his jacket.

McKinney claimed that methamphetamine and "gay panic" syndrome led to his actions, but he was an aggressive man who allegedly once offered to have a woman's ex-husband murdered.[19] The gay panic defense suggests that some people are prone to an uncontrollable, violent reaction when propositioned by a homosexual.[20] There is nothing in the mental health literature that I am aware of that supports this claim. Responding to the defense's argument that they should be allowed to use the "gay panic" defense, the judge said, "If I'm a lousy, rotten human being, and I use that as a defense, then the legal system becomes a shambles. Everyone will come in arguing that they aren't guilty of premeditated murder because they are a lousy human being."[21] McKinney's attorney wanted to present to the court that he had "suffered a homosexual advance" as a child, but the judge would not allow that testimony, saying such evidence was not permitted by Wyoming law.[22]

McKinney, age 22, was acquitted of first-degree murder, but was convicted of felony murder, aggravated robbery, and kidnapping. After McKinney was convicted he apologized to the Shepard family, saying, "I really don't know what to say other than that I'm truly sorry to the entire Shepard family. Never will a day go by I won't be ashamed for what I have done."[23] The prosecution had intended to seek the death penalty, but Shepard's mother urged the judge to be lenient in sentencing, sparing his life. He was sentenced to two life terms with no possibility of parole.

Henderson pleaded guilty in April 1999 to murder and kidnapping and was given two life sentences in prison. Chasity Pasley, 21, received an 18-month sentence after pleading guilty to being an accessory after the fact. Kristen Price was the last person to be tried for actions related to the death of Matthew Shepard. Like Chasity Pasley, she was charged with being an accessory after the fact, but she pleaded guilty to a misdemeanor charge of interfering with police. She received 180 days in jail, but was credited with 120 days. The remaining 60 days were suspended.

BUFORD FURROW

An avowed white supremacist, Buford Furrow was 38-years-old in August 1999 when he fired on a Jewish community center in Los Angeles, wounding four children and one adult. He then drove several miles away where he approached a Filipino-born U.S. postal worker. Furrow asked him a question about the mail and then drew a gun and shot him to death. A day later, he turned himself in to authorities in Las Vegas and said that the shootings were a "wake-up call to anti-Semites and hate groups."[24] He told authorities that he shot the postal worker because he was non-Caucasian and was working for the federal government. He said he wanted to "intimidate him and other non-white people from participation in federal employment."[25] Note that Furrow was motivated by a desire to intimidate and to generate fear. Originally, Furrow pleaded not guilty to all charges against him, but later pleaded guilty to murder, civil rights violations, and weapons charges. He was sentenced to 110 years in prison with no possibility of parole and fined over $700,000. Furrow claimed that a history of mental illness was responsible for his behavior, and he expressed deep remorse at his sentencing.

RICHARD BAUMHAMMERS

In a town near Pittsburgh in April 2000, a 34-year-old lawyer and recluse fired upon two synagogues—one housing a day care center—spray painted anti-Semitic graffiti on a synagogue wall, wounded an Indian man by shooting him in the back and neck, paralyzing him, and killed five people. The dead were his Jewish neighbor, an Indian grocer, two Asian men killed at a Chinese restaurant, and a black man killed at a karate school. In just 90 minutes, Baumhammers killed these five people and wounded a sixth before police apprehended him. Authorities were called to the neighbor's apartment because an alarm had indicated a fire, but on the scene they discovered a woman's body. Baumhammers had killed his neighbor and then gone to a grocery store, where he killed an Indian man and injured a second victim. Police realized that the shootings were linked when they got a third call from a Chinese restaurant where Baumhammers opened fire and killed a man. Next, Baumhammers drove to a karate studio and shot a sixth victim, killing him. Witnesses at the karate studio gave police Baumhammers' license plate number and a description of his vehicle. Finally, Baumhammers drove to two synagogues, firing on them and spray painting "Jew" and swastikas on the walls. Witnesses near the synagogues notified police of the incident and gave them the perpetrator's vehicle description and tag number. Soon thereafter, police apprehended Baumhammers. Baumhammers had a history of mental disorder and had been so reclusive that some of his neighbors did not even know he was in town.

Authorities found documents in Baumhammers' apartment that indicated he was attempting to found a "political party opposed to immigration" called the Free Market Party.[26] He allegedly feared that white people would become minorities because of immigration. Authorities found a document in his home computer that read in part, "the descendants of the people who made this nation great are losing a foothold on this nation."[27]

Baumhammers was being treated for paranoid schizophrenia, and he believed that he had been poisoned while he was in Europe. He pleaded innocent to the charges against him. In May 2000 a court found him incompetent to stand trial and ordered a 90-day evaluation. In September, after four months in a psychiatric hospital, he was deemed competent to stand trial. Ironically, Baumhammers was the son of Latvian immigrants, and his law practice specialized in immigration law. His trial began in April 2001. Baumhammers was convicted in May 2001, and the jury recommended the death sentence.

RONALD TAYLOR

Hate crimes are not only committed by white people against minorities. A few weeks before Baumhammers killed his victims, Ronald Taylor, 39, a black man, opened fire at his apartment building and two fast-food restaurants just outside of Pittsburgh, killing three white people and injuring two others. He then held several people hostage at an office building that housed, among other things, a day care center containing 36 children on the third floor. He eventually surrendered and was apprehended, but a lengthy suicide note discovered in his apartment suggested that his intention had been to end his life.

Taylor's shooting spree was triggered when three workers from his apartment building arrived at his apartment to repair a door Taylor had damaged by kicking it in when he had been locked out. Taylor was upset because the door had not been fixed fast enough. He told one of the white workers, "You're all white trash, racist pigs," and then he looked at the other white workers and said, "You're dead."[28] One of the white workers was called to another job, but the other was later shot in the neck and killed. Taylor did not harm the black worker. After Taylor killed the maintenance man, he started a fire in his own apartment. Then he went to a Burger King, where he killed a second person. Then he went across the street to a McDonald's, where he shot a man sitting in his vehicle in the parking lot drinking coffee. He then went inside, shot an employee, and returned to the parking lot, where he shot another person in a vehicle in the drive-thru. He walked further down the street, pausing to reload his .22-caliber revolver, and entered an office building.

On his way to the office building, Taylor encountered a black woman whom he told, "I'm not going to hurt any black people. I'm just out to kill all white people."[29] During his standoff, he put his gun in his mouth several times, but never discharged it. He claimed that "doctors and nurses" were racist, and a suicide note found in his home said, "As long as the system remains racist white and racist Jew, black people will never overcome."[30] Like several other perpetrators discussed in this chapter, Taylor had a history of mental illness, but had no criminal record. However, a white maintenance worker at his apartment complex said about Taylor, "Whenever he saw me, he'd call me a racist pig, or white trash, or he'd make a point of walking past me and brushing up against me. He just didn't like me."[31] Ironically, Taylor's lawyer was white. Taylor was diagnosed with chronic paranoid schizophrenia, and in April 2000 a judge ruled that Taylor was not mentally fit to stand trial. In August, Taylor was deemed competent to stand trial. In November 2001, having been convicted of first-degree murder for these racially motivated killings, he was convicted and sentenced to death by a jury in Pennsylvania. An execution data has not been set.

CONCLUDING REMARKS

This chapter has addressed how self-justification, psychological defenses, mental illness, and righteous aggression contribute to terrorism and hate crimes. Each of the cases discussed here demonstrates one or more of these principles. I have watched hours of overt and covert FBI video footage of gatherings of hate groups. I have heard their vile speeches and watched as they indoctrinated their children with messages of hate and exclusivity. In the movie *Schindler's List*, as the Jews were being herded from their homes to the Krakow ghetto, a young girl of ten or so years of age screams hatefully, "Goodbye, Jews! Goodbye, Jews!" The venom in her words is searing. Where do you suppose she learned to hate so deeply? The answer lies not only in the culture, but in one's home. The place for change is in the home, and no social program or religious organization can be more powerful in curbing hate than the power of a parent's positive words and example. Likewise, no social program or religious organization can be more detrimental than the destructiveness of a parent's hateful example.

NOTES

1. Postcards at the Holocaust Museum in Washington attributed the quote to Niemoller. Also quoted in Michael P. Green, ed., *1500 Illustrations for Biblical Preaching* (Grand Rapids: Baker, 2000), p. 203.

2. Carl Goldberg, *Speaking with the Devil: Exploring Senseless Acts of Evil* (New York: Penguin Books, 1996), p. 223.

3. "Book: McVeigh calls children 'collateral damage,' " *CNN Online*, www.cnn.com/2001/US/03/29/mcveigh.book/index.html, March 28, 2001.

4. Proverbs 23:13.

5. "Parents sentenced to prison in Florida for torturing son," *CNN Online*, www.cnn.com/2001/LAW/01/23/child.tortured.ap/index.html, January 23, 2001.

6. "Parents sentenced to prison in Florida for torturing son," *CNN Online*, www.cnn.com/2001/LAW/01/23/child.tortured.ap/index.html, January 23, 2001.

7. Gordon W. Allport. *The Nature of Prejudice* (Cambridge, MA: Addison-Wesley, 1954, quoted in Ralph Hood, Jr., Bernard Spilka, Bruce Hunsberger, and Richard Gorsuch, *The Psychology of Religion: An empirical approach*, 2nd ed. (New York: Guilford Press, 1996), p. 338.

8. Robert K. Ressler and Tom Shachtman, *I Have Lived in the Monster: Inside the Minds of the World's Most Notorious Serial Killers* (New York: St. Martin's Press, 1997), p. 235.

9. 1 Samuel 15:2–3.

10. 1 Samuel 15:18.

11. John Christensen, "Where's Eric Rudolph?," *CNN Online*, www.cnn.com/2001/US/03/05/wheres.eric/index.html, March 5, 2001.

12. "McVeigh's father says his son won't apologize," *CNN Online*, www.cnn.com/2001/US/04/27/mcveigh.father/index.html, April 27, 2001.

13. "Who killed Matthew Shepard?" *Christianity Today* (Online edition), December 7, 1998.

14. "God Hates Fags," www.godhatesfags.com/main/index.html, May 3, 2001.

15. "God Hates Fags," www.godhatesfags.com/main/index.html, May 3, 2001.

16. "Prosecution rests in Shepard murder trial," *CNN Online*, *www.cnn.com/US/9910/29/gay.attack.02/*, October 29, 1999.

17. Joshua Hammer, "The 'gay-panic' defense," *Newsweek* (Online edition), November 8, 1999.

18. Joshua Hammer, "The 'gay-panic' defense," *Newsweek* (Online edition), November 8, 1999.

19. John Leo, "The top ten victims," *U.S. News & World Report*, January 31, 2000, p. 16.

20. "McKinney gets life in gay student's murder," *CNN Online*, *www.cnn.com/US/9911/04/gay.attack.verdict.03/index.html*, November 4, 1999.

21. "Prosecution rests in Shepard murder trial," *CNN Online*, *www.cnn.com/US/9910/29/gay.attack.02/*, October 29, 1999.

22. Angie Cannon, "In the name of the son," *U.S. News & World Report* (Online edition), November 15, 1999.

23. "McKinney gets life in gay student's murder," *CNN Online*, *www.cnn.com/US/9911/04/gay.attack.verdict.03/index.html*, November 4, 1999.

24. "Furrow pleads guilty to shootings, will avoid death penalty, get life without parole," *CNN Online*, *www.cnn.com/2001/LAW/01/24/furrow.plea.crim/index.html*, January 24, 2001.

25. "Furrow pleads guilty to shootings, will avoid death penalty, get life without parole," *CNN Online*, *www.cnn.com/2001/LAW/01/24/furrow.plea.crim/index.html*, January 24, 2001.

26. "Friend: Pittsburgh shooting suspect made 'outlandish' comments," *CNN Online*, *www.cnn.com/2000/US/05/01/shooting.spree.ap/index.html*, May 1, 2000.

27. "Lawyer: Pittsburgh shooting spree suspect will use insanity defense," *CNN Online*, *www.cnn.com/2000/US/05/02/shooting.spree.ap/index.html*, May 2, 2000.

28. "Third victim of Pittsburgh-area shootings dies; hate crime charged," *CNN Online*, *www.cnn.com/2000/US/03/02/wilkinsburg.shooting.03/index.html*, March 2, 2000.

29. "Third victim of Pittsburgh-area shootings dies; hate crime charged," *CNN Online*, *www.cnn.com/2000/US/03/02/wilkinsburg.shooting.03/index.html*, March 2, 2000.

30. "Paper prints accused killer's note," *Atlanta Journal/Constitution*, March 8, 2000, p. A4.

31. Larry Elder, "When the bad guy is black," *Human Events* (On-line edition), March 31, 2000.

CHAPTER 11

UNWRAPPING THE ENIGMA: HOMICIDE INVESTIGATION

We need education in the obvious more than investigation of the obscure.
—Oliver Wendell Holmes, Jr.

I have demonstrated throughout this book that people communicate information about themselves through their behaviors. The process of interpreting these clues is the same regardless of the context. It doesn't matter if one is a psychologist trying to interpret a client's behavior, a parent trying to figure out whether or not a child is telling the truth, or a homicide detective investigating a crime scene. The process of deduction is much the same. The psychologist reads the behavioral cues clients present. He makes assumptions based on what they wear, how they sit, and the words they choose. The parent reads the behavior of the deceptive child, drawing conclusions based on things such as lack of eye contact, fidgeting, and stammered speech. In fact, these same clues may assist interrogators as they question a suspect. The only difference between what the psychologist or parent does and what the homicide detective does is that the detective cannot always confront the perpetrator in person. Perpetrators of crimes, however, leave information about themselves in their wake nonetheless.

When the investigator has a suspect in front of him, he has the opportunity to listen with both his eyes and his ears, asking himself several questions throughout the process. Does the suspect sound believable? Is the story credible? While almost anything is possible, the question I always ask is, "Is it likely?" The case of Kenny Hardwick provides a perfect example.

One evening in July 1992, as my wife and I watched the local news, there was a story about a man, Kenny Hardwick, who claimed that his seven-month-old daughter, Haley, had been abducted from his truck. He originally claimed that he was assisting some motorists whose vehicle had broken down. He said that he left the child in his truck when he went to see if he could help the motorists, but when he returned the child was gone. The media reported this story as a missing child case, but I told my wife that very evening that the child was dead. I had no involvement in this case, but based only on the television interviews I saw with the father on the evening news I believed Hardwick killed the child. His story and behavior told me all I needed to know as an armchair investigator to make an educated guess about what had happened.

First of all, I found it unbelievable that he would not notice a person approaching his vehicle as he assisted the motorists. Even though it was possible that someone could have walked up to his truck and removed the child without his noticing, it was unlikely. If the abductor had been in a vehicle, the father surely would have noticed another vehicle stopping beside his vehicle.

Second, there was no motive for an abduction. Relatives take most children who are kidnapped. Estranged spouses, lovers, and others battling over custody routinely either violate visitation and are charged with kidnapping, or deliberately abduct their own children in order to have more visitation or to restrict access to the children by their ex-spouses. It is possible that someone seeking to kidnap a child just happened to be in the area, but again, it was unlikely. Even though Hardwick was divorced from his wife, there was no reported indication of custody problems.

Third, his voice was not convincing. He fidgeted as he told the story, and it appeared to me that even he did not believe his own story. Child abductions are unusual in the area where he claimed this occurred, and since neither the circumstances nor the suspect were believable, if I had been investigating that case I would immediately have suspected the father. The man's youthful appearance and manner of dress suggested to me a blue-collar family. Physical abuse, even though it occurs across all sociodemographic groups, is statistically more likely in younger parents and those from blue-collar families. Therefore, I hypothesized that he had hit the child abusively and unintentionally killed her.

For three weeks, the police effectively used the media to keep pressure on Hardwick. They continued to give interviews to the media, talking about how sure they were that they would catch the perpetrator, and they kept the story alive. In doing so, they kept the likelihood of getting caught in the forefront of Hardwick's mind. His story eventually began to unravel. He first confessed to striking the child in the head and said that he had left her in the woods, but he denied that he killed her. He then led investigators to a shallow grave on a riverbank where they discovered her body. The medical examiner determined that the child had received two blows to the head, one to the front and one to the side, either of which could have been fatal.[1] Original accounts suggested that Hardwick buried her alive, but the medical examiner determined she was already dead when she was buried.

Hardwick was charged with felony murder and cruelty to children. In 1994 he pleaded guilty and was sentenced to life in prison, agreeing not to seek parole for 20 years. If I had been investigating this crime, I would have immediately suspected the father, as the police did, and from the beginning I sadly would have had to conclude that the child was probably dead. I can afford to make such guesses in the comfort of my living room, but no investigator could operate on this formula alone. Even when I assist homicide detectives in an ongoing investigation, I remind them that my hypotheses, of course, do not prove who the guilty party is. What I provide for them is information that gives direction to an investigation.

I have three children, each of them about four years apart in age. I can walk into a room and see the results of their behavior and fairly quickly assess who the likely participant(s) were. Most parents can do the same thing. They have seen their children operate and know who is most likely to do what, as well as when, where, and how they are most likely to do it. Investigation or profiling of a suspect is very similar. Even though I don't know the suspect personally, in the way a parent knows his child, I know the *type* of person who would commit a certain act, in a certain place, at a certain time, and in a certain way. In this chapter, I demonstrate how that process works in profiling and investigating a homicide.

HOMICIDE INVESTIGATION: DIFFICULTIES AND POLITICS

I always enjoyed the television series *Columbo*. I was fascinated with the deductive skills of this detective as he methodically tried to make sense out of every clue at the scene of the crime, and I enjoyed watching him gradually corner the murderer in each episode. However, as enjoyable as detective shows can be, investigations of real homicides are much more complicated than what these programs portray. There are many potential complications in the investigation of a homicide. For example, in departments where investigation of homicide is a detective's sole responsibility, he or she will have more than one case on his or her desk at any given time. Even in departments where detectives work in other areas, they are investigating many other cases at the same time they are investigating a homicide. Task forces where detectives work full time on a single case are rare, usually "cold" cases. Investigators usually do not have the luxury that Columbo had of following one suspect around until the case is solved.

Homicides that involve drug deals, armed robberies, and so forth are sometimes difficult to investigate because witnesses refuse to talk. In many cases, both the perpetrator and the victim are criminals. One homicide detective once told me that in cases like these, the difference between perpetrator and homicide victim often boils down to who is the best or quickest shot. This type of homicide may be witnessed by a number of people, yet when the police arrive and start asking for information, mass amnesia seems to settle on the crowd. Because everyone involved may fear police or retribution by one or both sides of the conflict, or because they may have allegiances to the victim, perpetrator, or both, they keep their mouths shut. Even when police know who committed the crime, they have to be able to prove it in a court of law. Knowing who did it and being able to present facts that will convince the district attorney's office, a grand jury, and finally a jury in court are two different things.

Also complicating investigations are competing jurisdictions. In large cities like Atlanta, Los Angeles, or New York, murders happen every week. More often than not, the victims and/or perpetrators are not famous or powerful people. There is little argument across jurisdictions as to who is in charge. In very high profile cases, however, arguments over jurisdiction and jockeying for control are not uncommon. The publicity of a high profile case may cause a smaller department to keep a homicide case where they would ordinarily have referred it to another jurisdiction. Likewise, a high profile case may cause a competing jurisdiction to jockey for control where they ordinarily would prefer to remain uninvolved.

In the JonBenet Ramsey case, for example, the Boulder Police Department was in a quandary. The victim was the daughter of a very wealthy and powerful resident. Most small-town departments do not have a great deal of expertise in homicide investigation simply because there may never have been a homicide committed in their jurisdiction. The December 26 murder was the only homicide committed in Boulder, Colorado, in 1994. Many chiefs of police will hand a case like this over to another agency, such as the county sheriff's department or the state bureau of investigation if the law allows. The police chief in Boulder could have done so, but because of the national publicity the case received, if he handed the case over to another jurisdiction, he risked looking incompetent. If one has aspirations of pursuing public office (sheriff, mayor, governor, etc.), solving a high profile crime like this one, especially when the victim was a cute little girl, could be a powerful catalyst for one's political career. I have no way of knowing if this was one of the police chief's motives or not, but it certainly would not be surprising if he felt pressure to take control of this high profile case.

The victim's father, an influential man locally, had the potential to exert pressure on authorities in this small community. In their attempt to take control and investigate this murder scene, officers made many mistakes. They did not find the girl's body in the house the first time they searched the property. Later that day, when the father found the child's body, he hopelessly contaminated the scene by moving the child to an upstairs room. The detective on the scene at the time should have cleared the house to protect what evidence remained, but she did not, resulting in further contamination of the scene and of the child's body. In fact, she ordered the body covered by a sheet, which could easily have destroyed evidence.[2] Yet another mistake was made when police failed to separate and individually question the Ramseys immediately after the child's body was found.[3] Investigators apparently focused only on the Ramsey family as suspects even when some critical evidence excluded rather than incriminated them. For example, neither the material found under the child's fingernails nor handwriting samples matched the Ramseys'.[4] Blood in the child's underwear allegedly contained DNA samples from two separate unknown individuals, neither of whom was a part of the Ramsey family. Furthermore, DNA from pubic hair found on the blanket in which she was wrapped did not match DNA from any members of the Ramsey family.[5] My opinion, which is shared by others in the field, is that it is unlikely that anyone will ever be successfully prosecuted for this crime except by confession.

Even though Robert Ressler, a renowned expert in homicide investigation, reportedly said that this case should have been "a piece of cake," it may be unfair to point fingers.[6] It would be easy to take these examples out of the context of a complicated homicide investigation and to criticize the investigating officers and agencies. In fact, just as there was evidence to suggest that someone other than the Ramseys committed this crime, there was also evidence that pointed to the Ramseys as the potential perpetrators of the crime. My point is not to belittle those who have struggled earnestly to solve this case, but rather to provide examples of how investigations can be complicated by inexperience and politics.

Law enforcement agencies may refuse to share information even within their own departments. I once was working with one law enforcement agency and I knew they needed the information from a homicide that had occurred in a jurisdiction overseen by the same agency, but in another district. Assuming the information would be sent over, I asked my friend when he would get it. He told me that the agency had refused to surrender a copy of the case. Some detectives are rated based on the cases they personally close. Therefore, sharing information may mean someone else gets the credit for closing the case. If that happens, the detective may be passed over for promotion. As you can see, lack of experience, jealousy, politics, possessiveness, and personalities unfortunately can disrupt the investigative process.

PROFILING A MURDER

I am not a homicide detective, nor was I trained as one. What I do is apply my understanding of human behavior in various settings. That setting may be in therapy, in a business, or in the analysis of a crime scene. In general, I apply many of the same skills I use to interpret the drawings and activities of three- and four-year-old children in my therapy room to the murder scene.

Many homicide cases are easy to solve. Perpetrators leave multiple clues or even turn themselves in and confess, greatly simplifying the investigation. Profilers, whether they are in state bureaus of investigation or with a federal agency, get the most difficult homicide cases. Like them, by the time I am asked to look at a case, the people who investigate homicides for a living have run out of ideas and often have taken the case to profiling units at their state bureaus of investigation or even to the FBI's profiling unit. After all of these people have had a go at solving the case, then I am asked to work on it. When I participate in an investigation, it is not as a homicide investigator per se, but as an investigator of *meanings*. If I can understand what the clues at the scene mean, I can know something about who did it. In the pursuit of meanings, I ask myself why. Why this victim? Why this place? Why this time? Why this weapon? And so forth.

The process of profiling a homicide scene received a lot of attention after the release of the movie *The Silence of the Lambs*. The pioneering work of men like John Douglas, Robert Ressler, and others was brought to the forefront of public attention at that time. This movie portrayed, in general, how the process works, but each profiler operates a little bit differently. John Douglas, for example, has said in his writings that he does not like to have any information on a case before he sees the crime scene photographs. Like Douglas, I do not allow detectives to tell me their theories before I am finished with a case. In fact, I may never know their theories because once I am done with the case there is no need for me to continue asking questions. However, I not only want to see the crime scene photographs, I also want the autopsy reports and photographs, police reports, victim assessment, and witness statements, and I want to visit the scene when that is possible. I once worked a homicide case that was several years old. Unbelievably, the crime scene remained in the exact condition it was in at the time of the crime. I was able to check some of my theories, point out a few clues the investigators had missed, and get a feel for what happened by looking over the location.

I look at every drop of blood, its pattern, and its volume. Many of the things I ask about end up being unimportant, but until I have a complete picture in my mind about what happened, I cannot know what evidence is important and what is not. I want to account for every piece of evidence at a homicide scene. Like a jigsaw or crossword puzzle where all of the pieces not only have to make sense by themselves, but must also interlock with each other, my theories concerning cause, motive, and events, as well as my profile of the perpetrator, all have to wed. I profile the victim as well as the perpetrator. Knowing something about the type of person the victim was may help me in identifying a potential perpetrator.

A crime scene talks to me through all of these pieces of information, whispering clues about who committed the crime. Once in a seminar I was conducting, I described this process and a woman in the back of the lecture hall questioned me, obviously unconvinced that this process worked. The seminar room seated 400 to 500 people, and because she sat toward the back, I could not see her very well. I asked her to play a game with me and allow me to tell her something about herself.

Judging only by her appearance, hairstyle, sweater, and apparent age, I drew some conclusions about her. I told her that she had pierced ears and either wore very small hoops or balls as earrings. I guessed that the face of her watch was a dark color, probably black. I ventured that she drove a small foreign automobile with four doors. I also guessed that she lived with her parents. Everything I said was exactly right except one thing—her earrings were small hoops *with* balls.

She was somewhat shocked that I knew these things about her, but I assured her that I had not done anything mystical. I listened to what her appearance was saying to me. Her conservative hairstyle and very conservative sweater gave me clues to the type of jewelry that she would wear. Because of her black skirt and white sweater, I guessed that the face of her watch would be a conservative color as well. That same information, combined with her young age and the area of the country where the seminar was held, led me to suppose she likely lived at home. Her conservative dress was also a clue as to the type of car she drove. What kind of car does a conservative, responsible young woman drive? A sports car, while certainly possible, would have been less likely than a sedan. Her manner of dress told me that she was sensible, conservative, and cautious. In fact, her choice to sit in the back of the lecture hall itself was a clue that told me she was cautious. While she may have chosen a seat in the back for many reasons, she sat in the middle of the row, not on the end, and I interpreted that to mean she wants to see, but not get too close. I presumed that she was pragmatic and responsible. Therefore, since foreign cars tend to have a good reputation for dependability, I suspected that was what she drove. In other words, she told me what I needed to know. I just had to listen with my eyes instead of my ears.

I went on to explain that just as I could describe her in this way based on her appearance, I could do something similar by looking at her bedroom or her office. She couldn't help but leave clues for me in these places about who she is. Investigation of a homicide works the same way. As I review a crime scene, I am looking for information to point in the direction of a perpetrator. I always tell detectives in our first meeting that I have never been able to give investigators a name and address. The best I can hope to do for them is to provide potential suspects that they may not have considered and to point them in the right direction to continue their investigation.

I analyze the day, time, condition of the location of the murder, choice of weapon, position of the body, and so forth, and I allow this information to tell me who the murderer is likely to be as well as who it is unlikely to be. I listen with my eyes.

CASE STUDY

In most of the homicide cases I have been involved with, I have been an unofficial participant. Law enforcement agencies are very possessive about their investigations, and when they seek help, it is usually from within the law enforcement community. For example, most small police departments do not have the manpower, experience, or financing to investigate a homicide. Therefore, it is common practice for local agencies to hand the investigation of the scene over to state bureaus of investigation. Even if the agency does its own crime scene analysis, if investigators find themselves at a dead end, they may seek assistance from state bureaus of investigation (many have their own profiling experts, just like the FBI) or from the FBI.

Participation in investigations by non–law enforcement personnel may compromise the case by contaminating the evidence or investigation, and law enforcement officers fear that outside participants might divulge classified information to the press. I was once invited to participate in the follow-up investigation of a school shooting. After I had spent several hours at the scene, the ranking agent in charge changed his mind about my participation and asked me to leave the scene. His sole concern was not that I was unqualified, but rather that I was not a member of law enforcement. It was very disappointing.

Likewise, I was once called upon by a detective who was investigating a murder that was nearly a year old. He had run out of leads, had no clear idea of motive, and was stumped. I agreed to participate, but then I heard nothing from the detective for many months. Almost a year later, I was called again about the same case. As it turned out, the detective and his supervisors had wanted me to participate in the investigation, but when the commanding officer was consulted, he denied permission for me to have access to the case. Nearly two years after the murder I was called again. The commander had retired and the new commander was open to outside help, and so I worked on the case.

Several years ago, while I was lecturing on assessing risk for violent behavior at the FBI's National Academy at Quantico, Virginia, one of my students sat with a skeptical expression on his face throughout my lecture. National Academy students are officials from law enforcement agencies around the world who enroll in the 11-week program at Quantico to learn the latest in investigation techniques, management techniques, profiling, firearms, and other subjects related to law enforcement. This student confronted me in the dining hall later that evening while the two of us were alone. He expressed his skepticism about my lecture and, as he probed, it became obvious that he didn't think the process worked. He decided to test me and told me about a case he had worked on in his home jurisdiction.

In this murder case, he told me, investigators came to a rural farmhouse to find the front door standing open. Just inside the door, a deceased adult male lay face up in a pool of blood. He had an injury to the chest by what appeared to be a single, close-range shotgun blast. There was no other indication of any gunfire inside or outside of the residence. Upstairs the police found a young male, approximately two years old, hiding in a closet, shaken, but otherwise unharmed. I was told that the man was the boy's father and that the mother was nowhere to be found. There were signs of a minor struggle inside the home (an overturned chair, papers knocked off tables, etc.).

The house lay several hundred feet off a highway in a very rural area. An unpaved, dirt driveway led to the home. No tire tracks were found in the driveway except for those matching the family's vehicle, but numerous footprints were noted in the dirt driveway. Two parallel grooves in the dirt ran from the walk in front of the house, down the driveway, ending at the pavement of the highway.

At this point, novice investigators might suspect the wife of killing her husband and then fleeing the scene. Most murders have a connection either with some crime (robbery, drugs, prostitution) or some domestic situation. Family members are almost always suspects. Several clues, however, told me the wife did not commit this murder. My first clue was the position of the body, which implied that the victim had been opening the front door or standing in the doorway of the open front door. He was shot in the entry hall, not in the living room, the bedroom, the garage, or the front yard. He had apparently answered the door and someone shot him. Why would his wife knock on the front door? That made no sense to me. This shooting was committed by someone who would use the front door, not the back or side door. Therefore, I supposed it was someone who was not totally familiar with this family. In other words, it was a stranger or someone known only casually to the household. Yet I knew that this was probably someone who was known to the family. If you open the

211

door and someone is standing there with a shotgun, you will not leave the door open for very long. I speculated that the victim and the perpetrator had at least a brief conversation before the shooting because there was no evidence that the door was forced open or that the victim had tried to force the door shut.

It was possible that the woman had hired someone to kill her husband. That would explain why he was shot as he opened the door. The death of the husband was the purpose. Yet if she had hired someone to kill him, she most likely would have remained on the scene, playing the part of grieving spouse, rather than leaving, making herself a suspect.

My second clue that the mother was not the perpetrator was the child in the closet. I found it unlikely that a mother would abandon a young child and leave him in the home with his father's bleeding corpse. In some cases, parents have done just that, but it is relatively rare and often involves perpetrators living on the edge of life rather than middle-class homemakers.

A third clue was the disrupted living space. If the woman had killed her husband in the doorway before she entered the house, why would she then run about the house knocking things over? One might initially think that she was chasing the child or that the child caused the damage as he ran to hide. However, again, I found it unlikely that a mother would have been unable to catch this child if she wanted to. If she had been chasing him, she would have caught him and either killed him or taken him with her. Otherwise, there would have been no cause to give chase. Finally, if she had intended to kill her husband, but not the child, she would have had the child wait for her in the car or she would have left him with a friend or relative that night.

A final clue involved her escape. If the mother had committed this crime, how did she get away? The family car was in the garage and all of the tire tracks in the drive matched that vehicle. Did she walk or run away? In such a remote area as this it was unlikely.

For all of these reasons, I was certain the mother did not commit this crime. If it was not her, then who did it and where was the mother? My first clue was the location of the home. It was in a very rural area. Even though drifters and homeless people commit homicides, simple probability tells me that it would be unlikely that a person was walking down the highway with a shotgun, randomly selected this home out in the middle of nowhere, came down the driveway, shot the father, and left with the mother. A more likely motive would be some connection with the family. Since there was no known connection to any criminal behavior by any of the members of this family, I suspected either a sexual crime against the mother or a personal issue like a jealous lover of either the man or his wife.

Another clue, though, ruled out a jealous lover. How would she/he have gotten to the home? Remember, there were no tire tracks in the dirt driveway other than from the family's own vehicle. How would the perpetrator have gotten to and from the house? A quick supposition would be that he/she parked a vehicle on the road and walked to the home, but I dismissed that idea. If you were a jealous lover and you had intentions of threatening, harming, or killing someone, would you be more likely to park your getaway vehicle on a highway or well off the road in the driveway of the victim's home? I supposed the latter, yet there were no tire tracks. That implied to me that the perpetrator walked to and from the home.

I doubted that the motive for the crime was sexual assault. A shotgun is an unwieldy weapon for rape. Rape is a crime of control as well as power. Therefore, a rapist would more likely use rope, a knife, or a handgun. A rifle or shotgun is not a very convenient close-range weapon.

The parallel grooves in the driveway were important to me. As I questioned the officer, he told me that they were consistent in depth and ranged from approximately four to twelve inches apart as they went down the driveway. I was sure from this description that the woman had been incapacitated, probably unconscious, and dragged down the driveway, her heels creating the grooves as they went.

By this point, I hope you are beginning to see some potential suspects. Who would be the most likely person to walk to a rural home, shoot a person, and then leave with the victim's spouse in tow? This had to be a male or a very strong female. I tentatively suspected that it would have been a male. The individual would have had to live close by or be familiar with the area. He most likely would have been an adult. An adolescent would be more likely to use a handgun rather than a shotgun. A very young perpetrator carrying a shotgun would have generated attention.

The perpetrator's problem-solving skills were not very effective. This is evident in his confrontation. He chose to deal with his desires and/or frustrations with a shotgun. He killed the man without considering what to do with the woman or child. If he had been hired to kill the man, he probably would have shot the woman as well simply because she was there. Instead, after shooting him, he had to chase her around and then try to figure out what to do with her. Because his problem-solving skills would have been minimal, I assumed he was probably a laborer, a factory worker, or in some other blue-collar trade. One's personality tends to show up in choice of career. These careers do not require a great deal of foresight, planning, or problem-solving.

Since I believed that this perpetrator knew the family, at least minimally, I presumed that he would have known they had a small child. He apparently made no attempt to find the child or to silence him. After subduing the woman, he apparently had no plan other than to take her with him. I believed that he simply was making up his plan as he went. The perpetrator was a man who acted before he thought, and even then, he didn't solve problems very well. He probably had not committed a murder before. If he had, he would surely have been caught.

At this point in our conversation, the officer told me that a neighbor had reported his truck stolen around midnight that night. I asked if the neighbor was a male, living alone, between the ages of 35 and 50. He affirmed that the man was 45 and divorced. I now thought I knew who the prime suspect should be. You might suppose that the perpetrator had stolen the neighbor's truck, but that would make no sense. How did the murderer get there in the first place? The coincidence of the neighbor's truck being stolen at the same time as the murder in conjunction with the fact that I could see no logical way a perpetrator could have arrived on and then left the scene, was too extraordinary.

I told my skeptical student what I believed happened. I said that the woman was found dead within just a few miles of the house and that the neighbor's truck was also found within five miles or so of his home. He confirmed my hunch. The woman was found in a ditch along the highway about three miles away, dead from a shotgun wound, and the truck was found (albeit the next spring) about seven miles from the neighbor's home.

I believed that the neighbor was angry with the victim or his family and had come to their home intent on "settling" some issue. I found it plausible that his intent was to scare the victim with the weapon, but he probably did not intend to kill him. I also suspected that he was intoxicated at the time. He clearly did not plan for the child or the woman and seemingly had no plan other than to settle things. He left the door standing open and made no attempt to cover up the crime. He left a live potential witness in the house, but took another witness with him. He did not kill the woman, so he undoubtedly had no plan for what to do if he shot the man. Either he had extremely poor cognitive skills or his thinking was impaired. I supposed alcohol had impaired his thinking.

Chances are he sat at home drinking, fuming about some conflict he had with his neighbor. Maybe their dog defecated on his property or dug up his garden. Perhaps he wanted to buy their property and they refused to sell. Whatever the cause of his anger, as his ire grew and the results of the alcohol wore down his inhibitions, he grabbed his shotgun and stomped across the highway and down the neighbor's driveway. As the neighbor answered the door, they argued briefly. The neighbor left the door open even though he saw the shotgun. He undoubtedly didn't believe that the man would shoot him. As they argued, the wife came to the adjoining room to see what was going on. When the perpetrator shot the victim in the chest, she tried to flee through the adjoining room, but the man quickly caught her and rendered her unconscious. The child, hearing the gunfire and screaming, hid in the closet upstairs.

The perpetrator found himself with one body, one child (whom he probably didn't even think about), and a live witness. He bound the woman and dragged her out of the house and down the driveway. I believe she was unconscious because the ridges in the driveway made by her heels were consistent. In other words, she was not struggling.

I knew the man probably lived alone because he was bringing an abducted woman to his home. If he had a roommate or spouse, he would have had to explain the abducted woman. His roommate or spouse would have had to have been abetting the crime. I found this to be implausible. He loaded the woman in his truck and drove away, trying to decide what to do with her. As they drove down the road, the woman regained consciousness and struggled fiercely. Not knowing what else to do, he shot the woman and pushed her body out of the truck into a ditch where she was later found. Tissue from the woman was found inside the cab of the truck when it was discovered the next spring. The man abandoned the truck and walked home. He would have had to leave the vehicle close enough that he could walk home. Otherwise he would have had to call a cab, hitchhike, or find transportation in some other way that would have provided a witness to his whereabouts.

The police were able to charge the neighbor, who was eventually convicted of the crime. I concede that this murder was not the most challenging case to solve. In fact, the agency investigating the murder solved it expeditiously. However, it still makes a good example for describing the process. My student agreed that perhaps the subject I was teaching had some validity after all. I derived the information communicated above simply through his telling me the facts. In a more complicated case, he may not have remembered or even picked up on a clue that would matter to me—a clue that might tell me something about the perpetrator. Therefore, photographs and reports are minimal needs when I approach a case.

Many more issues are involved in profiling rape, homicide, serial homicide, or serial sexual crimes. For example, the skilled profiler will consider the organization or disorganization of a crime scene. Someone who tries to cover his or her tracks is considered an *organized* perpetrator. By attempting to hide their crime, these perpetrators demonstrate that they know what they are doing is wrong, making any future insanity plea unlikely. *Disorganized* perpetrators leave multiple clues at the scene and do not attempt to hide their crimes. They may stage their victims, arranging the scene in order to communicate a message, and a future insanity defense is more likely. Disorganized perpetrators are more likely to suffer from mental illness that impairs their thinking and functioning. Profiling is an art that requires training, experience, and analytical skill. It is the result of good deductive reasoning and sound psychological assessment.

CONCLUDING REMARKS

A murderer can't help but leave clues. Serial killers and serial rapists, for example, leave what is called signature when they commit their crimes. Robert Keppel distinguishes between signature and *modus operandi* (MO). The MO may change from crime to crime based on availability of weapon and victim, conditions, and so forth. The signature, however, never changes. The signature is the *meaning* of the crime to the perpetrator. The perpetrator cannot avoid leaving the signature, although it may be subtle. If he could leave a differing signature, that would change his circumstances and the motivation to commit the crime in the first place. Therefore, signature does not change.

Signature becomes more evident in serial crime simply because there is more evidence to use in developing and testing theory. It is more difficult to identify signature in single events because there may be little evidence available. I find it interesting that, while serial criminals may be more polished and better at their crimes, they also leave more evidence concerning their signature. However, inexperienced criminals like the perpetrator in the example above may only provide one incident, but in their inexperience, they leave many clues.

Profiling is a combination of statistics, probability, common sense, and experience. Accurately perceiving and interpreting the clues a perpetrator leaves at a scene requires that one understand the language of violence. Unfortunately, this language will always be with us, and there will always be a need for interpreters.

NOTES

1. Maria Elena Fernandez, "Hardwick pleads guilty: 'I struck my daughter . . . ,' " *Atlanta Journal/Constitution*, September 7, 1994, p. A01.

2. Craig Schneider, "JonBenet: Six months later, slaying probe mired in doubt," *Atlanta Journal/Constitution*, June 27, 1997, p. C06.

3. "First detective on Ramsey scene resigns from police," *Atlanta Journal/Constitution*, March 19, 1999, p. A8.

4. Patrick O'Driscoll, "Case was botched start-to-finish, some say JonBenet jury result seen as police failure," *USA Today*, October 14, 1999, p. A3.

5. Craig Schneider, "Book puts JonBenet Ramsey case back in spotlight," *Atlanta Journal/Constitution*, February 22, 1999, p. B3.

6. Craig Schneider, "JonBenet: Six months later, slaying probe mired in doubt," *Atlanta Journal/Constitution*, June 27, 1997, p. C06.

CHAPTER **12**

PAST, PRESENT, AND FUTURE:
CONCLUSION

Every man takes the limits of his own field of vision as the limits of the
world.

—Arthur Schopenhauer

Many of the cases I have reviewed in this book seem inexplicable. Theologians
might readily explain these behaviors as the work of some evil entity. I have no
doubt that something exists that we might call evil, but while placing the
blame on a single source may be convenient, I do not believe that such an over-
simplified explanation of all of the behaviors addressed in this book would be
prudent. Many people fear looking too deeply into the causes of *evil* behavior
because they fear that understanding behavior may lead to excusing it. There
must be a balance between understanding and failure to require some appropriate level of responsibility of our citizenry.

Yet understanding the causes of violence, as complicated as they are, need
not lead us to excuse them or remove the ultimate responsibility for the actions
from the perpetrator. Quite the contrary. Understanding violence may not
only help us require more responsibility from violent people, but it may also
help us prevent violence by adjusting social systems and by providing interventions that make a potentially violent person less likely to act aggressively.

This book and my earlier book, *Blind-Sided*, have provided a way to organize and explain evil behavior. Yet the field of forensic psychology is embryonic.
There is much to learn, and committed researchers are the key to chipping away

at the questions we cannot yet answer. I once reviewed a book proposal for a publisher from an individual who wished to write about violent behavior. Even though my critique of his proposal was less than complimentary, I sincerely wanted the publisher to encourage the writer to stay in the field. While he wasn't yet ready for book writing, he was interested in the field and wanted to contribute. Law enforcement agencies frustrate me because of their fraternal approach to information. If you are not "one of them" you have a difficult time getting help. The field of forensic psychology is not fraternal. It is an association that is open to all interested and qualified members. The more qualified people we have pursuing the subject, the more questions we can answer. Many times over the years I have spoken at conferences and afterward been confronted by young minds who were interested in following in my footsteps. I delight in knowing I may have inspired the world's next brilliant forensic analyst. I seek disciples whom I can teach and from whom I can learn.

AN IMPERFECT PROCESS

Despite what we know, the processes that I both write about and practice are not without flaws. Perfection will always be elusive. For example, books about behavior analysis and profiling have entertained many of us. The writings of John Douglas, Robert Ressler, and Robert Keppel provide a fascinating look into the lives and careers of the men and women who have been involved in pursuing and catching some of the world's most frightening killers. These works amaze us as we see how psychological profiling has led to the capture of violent criminals. While they are entertaining, many of these books fail to acknowledge the fallibility of the process. I do not recall ever reading any book on the subject in which the writer goes out of his way to examine a case where he had compiled a profile of a subject and then was shown to be dead wrong. I'll risk losing your confidence and do that for you here.

In 1996 the Centennial Olympic Games were held in the city of Atlanta, Georgia, my home. Along with my wife and thousands of other metro area residents, I participated as a volunteer for the Games, hosting our foreign and domestic visitors. It was a thrilling two-week event that I am glad I did not miss. The center of activity for the Games was Centennial Olympic Park in the heart of downtown Atlanta. Millions of people passed through this venue enjoying street performers, buying souvenirs, playing in the fountains, and watching live performances on a huge stage at the north end of the park. One week into the Games, on July 27, just before 1 A.M., a security guard noticed an unattended backpack under a bench near the stage and at the foot of a production tower. About that same time, a 911 operator received an anonymous telephone call warning that there was a bomb in the park. The caller informed the operator that the bomb would detonate in 30 minutes. Unfortunately, because of confusion about the street address of Centennial Olympic Park, it would take more than ten minutes for the dispatcher to contact a police unit.

In the meantime, bomb experts had arrived on the scene to examine the discovered backpack. They found it to be suspicious, and by 1:08 A.M. they decided that they should begin an evacuation of the area. Unfortunately, the bomb detonated earlier than the caller had said it would, exploding just 12 minutes after the evacuation had begun. The explosion killed 44-year-old Alice Hawthorne and injured 111 others. Many more visitors and staff might have been killed if park security and police had not begun the evacuation when they did. A 34-year-old security guard named Richard Jewell was credited with saving many lives because of his actions in spotting the backpack and later for helping with the evacuation. The news media around the world heralded Jewell as a hero.

For days, investigators combed the area on their hands and knees, sifting the debris for clues. Sadly for Jewell, just three short days after he was identified as a hero, he became a prime suspect, beginning three months of intense scrutiny by authorities, the media, and the general public. As images of Jewell pervaded the news at the end of July, NBC correspondent Tom Brokaw announced in a report on the investigation that "'there's probably enough to arrest him, there's probably enough to prosecute him."[1] Brokaw reportedly closed his comments that day by saying, "Everyone, please understand absolutely he is only the focus of this investigation—he is not even a suspect yet."[2] This brief comment, however, was more than an understatement considering the massive network and independent media attention that portrayed Jewell as a potential suspect.

Jewell drew the attention of investigators when they received information from a north Georgia college where he had once been a campus policeman. It was reported that Jewell had that job until May 1996, when he had been "asked to resign for an 'overzealous attitude.'"[3] Investigators hounded Jewell, even attempting to deceive him into being an unwilling participant in his own interrogation. FBI agents told Jewell that they wanted him to participate in a training video. In order to make the video seem real, they said, they had to read him his Miranda rights. In reality, the "training tape" was a sham set up in an attempt to get Jewell to waive his right to remain silent and his right to an attorney and to give agents the freedom, on videotape, to interrogate him.[4] Apparently, Jewell was not fooled by the trick and asked for his attorney.[5]

In the coming days, federal agents acquired a search warrant and scoured his home, a storage building, and his vehicle. They took "pieces of metal pipe, batteries, nails, guns, bullets and other items from the Atlanta home of Richard Jewell. Agents even snipped wires to the fog lights on his pickup, looking for possible clues."[6] They also took Walt Disney videotapes, and even some of his mother's Tupperware. They examined his credit card records and receipts, and Jewell later said on *Larry King Live* that investigators destroyed family photographs during their 12-hour search.[7] Leaving little of his past unscrutinized, they traveled to the small north Georgia college where he had once worked in order to examine computers, looking for evidence that Jewell used them to acquire information on bomb-making.[8]

Throngs of media personnel set up camp outside his apartment, photographing his every move. For days, Atlanta local news showed images of Jewell as he walked to his car or as he sat in a stairwell while agents searched his apartment. Agents followed him everywhere he went, including an Atlanta Braves baseball game.[9]

Considering the personality profile that I would have developed on the bomber, Jewell was a perfect suspect. Likewise, the circumstantial evidence that someone like Jewell had committed this bombing was substantial. A government memorandum filed with a U.S. district court showed several reasons why the government considered him a suspect.[10] Jewell had a backpack resembling the one used in the bombing that was unaccounted for.[11] Also, a neighbor of Jewell's once reported an explosion and later saw Jewell in the area and just two days before the explosion, Jewell allegedly told Centennial Park employees, "You better take a picture of me now because I'm going to be famous."[12] The memo indicated that Jewell never took long breaks from his post as a Centennial Park guard, but on the night of the bombing, he was said to have been away for 15–20 minutes.[13] He was going to be reassigned to another area of the park, but he argued to keep his assignment near the tower.[14] Jewell raised the curiosity of some when "4–6 weeks before the bombing, during the construction of one of the towers in the park, Jewell inexplicably asked whether the tower would stand up to an explosion."[15] Finally, the memo indicated that Jewell was said to have expressed interest in bomb-making.[16]

Other information added evidence that a man like Jewell could have been the perpetrator of the explosion. His reportedly "overzealous" behavior in writing traffic citations at the north Georgia college is consistent with the profile agents developed on this suspect, and he was said to have received bomb training while a deputy sheriff in Habersham County, Georgia.[17]

Around this time, a colleague asked me what I thought about Jewell and his potential involvement in the bombing. I explained the general process of profiling and outlined the many coincidences that would have been necessary to bring all of these things together in one man. In my opinion, and based on what I knew, I told my friend that Jewell fit the profile of such a perpetrator. I found it more than coincidence that it would have been Jewel who would find the backpack in that very dark area, recognize it as a threat, and take action to clear the area. These facts, along with the information provided by his former employer led me to believe that Jewell was the type of individual who would perpetrate such a crime in order to gain recognition as a hero—as happened. At the time I believed that Jewel built the bombs, placed them in the park himself, "found" them himself, and cleared the area to save lives because he knew what the backpack contained. I did not believe that Jewell intended for the bombs to explode, and I did not believe he intended to harm anyone, but I was certain he was either solely responsible, or at least involved.

My friend was unconvinced that the process worked and he asked me how I could say the man did it just based on a profile. I remember my words as clearly, as if it were yesterday. "I don't know for certain that it was him, but based on what I know, I'd bet my reputation on it." I'm glad I did not have to pay off the bet because, as we now know, the evidence is clear that Jewell did not commit this act. The FBI made serious mistakes in the process, and other investigators erred, as did the media and the public. More important for you as a reader, though, is the fact that *I* was completely wrong. The evidence that pointed to Richard Jewell as the perpetrator was indeed simply coincidence. I adhered to the profile and to the fact that Jewell fit the profile as closely as could reasonably be expected, but he was not the perpetrator. Recent facts, however, have pointed to an entirely different motive.

The major mistake that I made in this case was placing too much emphasis on the profile to the exclusion of facts that exonerated Jewell. There was evidence that Jewell was not the bomber. He passed a privately administered polygraph test.[18] Even though he was away from his post for several minutes during the evening of the bombing, Jewell said he had gone to the restroom. Even if he did not ordinarily stay away from his post, many things could account for such a trip to the restroom. How many patrons of the Games had perfectly routine bathroom habits? Further, the 911 phone call was made from a pay phone near the park. It would have been difficult, if not impossible, for him to have gotten to the pay phone where the call was made, phoned in the warning, and returned to the park in the amount of time he was away from his post. Finally, voice analysis of the 911 tape showed "no similarities between Jewell's voice and that of the caller."[19]

As for his interest in explosives and the training he received as a deputy sheriff, it is not unusual for law enforcement personnel to receive training in a wide variety of areas, including explosives. Further, his interest in whether the tower could withstand an explosion could simply have been a result of his explosives training. He was, after all, retained as a security guard whose job it was to secure the site to the best of his ability. Why wouldn't he call on his training and ask such a question? In fact, when I am asked to address a business on workplace homicide and safety, I occasionally will volunteer information about weaknesses I see on their sites. As noted in chapter 7, at a meeting with a manufacturing company a few years ago I did not have to pass through the security checkpoint to park in the visitors' parking area, but I had to drive right next to the guard shack. The security guard did not even look up at me as I drove into the parking area, and I made suggestions for correcting this problem. I hope that making these suggestions doesn't make me a potential suspect if someone does just such a thing at that business.

As for his overzealous behavior as a campus cop, the same could be said of many law enforcement officers. I work with law enforcement at all levels, city, county, state, and federal. Many men and women in this career are professional and kind individuals, but there are also many who could easily be described as overzealous. Concerning the neighbor's comment that she had heard an explosion and then later saw Jewell in the area, to my knowledge, no evidence existed that Jewell constructed or detonated any such device. As for his comments that he would be "famous," many news organizations had their headquarters at Centennial Olympic Park where Jewel was posted. It would have been quite possible that he would be seen on TV or in the news during the course of his daily job as a security officer. As for his reassignment, maybe he simply liked his job where he was. As I have said, I was a volunteer for the Olympic Games, and after several days of work and getting to know my fellow volunteers and my site, I would not have wanted to be reassigned either.

Eventually, the facts showed that Jewell had nothing to do with the bombing and he had, indeed, been the hero. In an interesting twist of fate, I had visited the park between midnight and 1 A.M. as I left my volunteer position with the Games every night. I routinely stood in the very spot where the explosion occurred because it was close to the stage, but away from the heavy flow of pedestrian traffic in the park. I was not working the night of the blast, so I was at home in bed that night. If I had worked that night, I might have been personally indebted to Jewell for saving my own life.

Eighty-eight days after Jewell came under scrutiny of authorities, U.S. Attorney Kent Alexander notified Jewell's attorneys that he was officially no longer a suspect.[20] The FBI director at that time, Louis Freeh, admitted in testimony to Congress that agents had made a "major error in judgment" in the way they handled the interview with Jewell (referring to the supposed training videotape).[21] In the end, three agents were disciplined for their actions in regard to this event. Jewell sued the *New York Post*, NBC, CNN, Cox Enterprises, owners of the *Atlanta Journal/Constitution*, and the college where he had once been a security guard.[22] He eventually settled the suit with NBC for over $500,000.[23] Ironically, Jewell himself was named in a lawsuit filed by a woman injured in the blast. She claimed that Jewell and other park security were too slow in evacuating the area after the device was found.[24]

In summary, no process is without imperfection. Jewell was a logical suspect. Based on the evidence, the FBI profile of the suspect as "a former law enforcement officer seeking the spotlight as a hero" was not unreasonable.[25] This case remains unsolved, but I suspect that if anyone is ever successfully prosecuted for this crime, the profile may still fit.

Our choice of dress, words, behaviors, and even our careers says something about who we are. I often have to remind my students to consider context, though. For example, on the one hand, even though Richard Jewell received special training in explosives, that makes sense given his career. Yet, on the other hand, one might ask the question, why did he pick this career? In every National Academy class to whom I lecture, there are members of the military police or Special Weapons and Tactics (SWAT) officers. I would suppose that people in these careers would be interested in explosives and weapons and that they would be trained on a broad range of topics that might seem unusual for the average citizen. Most of us do not need to know much about machineguns, various kinds of explosive devices, their effects, and so forth. Yet if that is one's career, it would be necessary to be well versed in such subjects.

The question arises, then, as to which came first, the interest in the subject or the career. I would argue that a fine line exists between these two issues. Most law enforcement agencies have a screening process whose purpose is to weed out "overzealous" types and to admit mentally stable and highly functioning professionals. Yet the two are somewhat confounded. I suggest that we pick careers that fit our interests. I would hope that most of the men and women who choose careers in which they spend their days with explosives and firearms are mentally healthy.

THE LEGAL SYSTEM

I wish that the many arms of law enforcement, social agencies for prevention, and the legal system could work together. However, they do not. Each acts as a separate entity and is vulnerable to its own flaws. For example, I am somewhat cynical about the jury system as it operates today. Smooth talking and high priced defense attorneys can direct attention away from the facts of a case and sway a jury by stressing details and information that may have no logical connection to the case whatsoever. In the O.J. Simpson trial, defense attorneys alleged conspiracies in the police department that supposedly sought to frame Simpson, but they were never required to produce any concrete evidence of a conspiracy.

In Missouri, a man was convicted in his first trial of killing his wife in cold blood for insurance money. A subsequent retrial ended in a hung jury, and the third trial resulted in his acquittal. Jurors in the third trial, eleven women and one man, were interviewed and asked about the facts of the case that led to their decision to acquit. The majority of the jurors said they believed the man had either directly or indirectly contributed to the premeditated death of his wife, yet they still acquitted him. One juror did not understand the technical issues revolving around the alarm system in the man's home, so she ignored that evidence—evidence that the prosecutor in the first trial considered the most important detail of all. Other jurors acquitted the man because they were swayed by the fact that the accused man's mother-in-law still liked him. They looked beyond an enormous amount of physical evidence and placed great significance on one person's personal opinion of the accused.

Most disturbing to me was the fact that the jurors allowed the defense attorney to persuade them to put the investigators on trial instead of the accused. He called into question the conduct of the officers who investigated the crime. This culminated with the introduction of a photograph that showed the sheriff of the county holding the deceased woman's breast at the hospital morgue. As cold-hearted as this was, it has nothing to do with the husband's guilt or innocence. I understand that these jurors felt that the sheriff had desecrated her body, showing no reverence for the deceased. Yet they did not understand the psychology of homicide investigation. The way one deals with death, bodies, and the mutilation associated with homicide is to depersonalize the victim. When I began my training in psychology and was attending my first brain autopsy, I consciously forced myself to view the deceased as "tissue" rather than as a person with a name. I can do that rather easily now. Touching the deceased woman in this case, even in this crude way, was undoubtedly not much different for this sheriff than making a joke with a chicken or a piece of steak that one is preparing for dinner. This says nothing about his competence in law enforcement—only something about his social judgment, allowing himself to be photographed, and the way he views a dead body. Hence, it is my opinion that this jury let a murderer go free because they didn't like the way the police behaved, even though the majority of them believed the man was guilty. Given these two examples, the Missouri case and the Simpson case, it seems evident that our jury system, as it is, is often less about justice and more about the economics—who can afford the most expensive and experienced lawyer—and the rhetoric of the legal profession.

When perpetrators face trial and are convicted, society expects stiff penalties, especially for people who commit violent crimes. Grace is a part of neither our legal system nor our social system. As we drive down the interstate ten miles an hour over the speed limit, we may feel a sense of satisfaction when other drivers are caught speeding. Yet if we were stopped for speeding, we would readily give the officer a reason why it was excusable for us to speed and why we don't deserve a ticket. We might wonder why the state trooper wasn't out catching "real" criminals. We are an unforgiving people when it comes to simple violations of the law like speeding. How much more so is this true when the crime is molestation, rape, murder, or mass murder.

It seems self-evident that violence is a part of our culture, and there is no reason to suppose it will go away any time soon. How, then, can we deal with the potential for violence that haunts us? Proponents of the death penalty argue that the fear of execution will lead to a reduction in homicide in the United States. These advocates point to other countries that have very harsh penalties and very low homicide rates. This is not a fair comparison, however. First of all, as I often explain to my students at the FBI National Academy, comparing one culture to another is like comparing apples and oranges. Such an argument presupposes that the homicide rate is low because of harsh penalties. The problem with this idea is that a relationship between two variables (homicide rate and severity of penalty) does not in any way demonstrate that one variable is the *cause* of the other. Based on the same logic, one could also say that these countries have harsh penalties because the homicide rate is low—the reverse argument. That, of course, makes no sense. A second problem with this argument is the assumption that the homicide rate is low because of one single variable. Suppose for the sake of argument that harsh penalties for violent behavior do, in fact, have some effect on its frequency. Can we say that this is the only variable that contributes to the low rate of violence? Of course not. Humans are much too complex for such reductionist ideas.

A third major problem with the supposition that harsher penalty will lower the crime rate is the assumption that the perpetrator even thinks about consequences before committing a violent crime. As I have demonstrated in the previous chapters, this is not a reasonable assumption. Yet with these criticisms stated, I must also concede that prisons are necessary. Every time I leave a prison I am very relieved that the door locks behind me. Some people refuse to be rehabilitated and must be isolated from the society at large. Other people commit crimes so atrocious that society cannot risk the person ever being free again.

What about rehabilitation? Can we retrain the violent individual and have confidence that he or she can reenter society without posing a threat? Some individuals can be successfully treated in prison and change their lives. There are many stories of successful rehabilitation. However, the way our prison systems work right now, prison is much better at training inmates to be better criminals than at training people to be better citizens. Overcrowded prisons, overworked counselors, and over burdened probation officers make true rehabilitation of the majority of convicts unlikely. In order to change, the convict must want to change and must take initiative to change. Even when he or she wants to change, every area of his or her life must be adjusted to prevent relapse. The person can no longer live in the same place he once lived. He cannot associate with the people with whom he once associated. He would be better off not working at the same place he once worked. In essence, his life must start over. When one is released from prison, halfway houses attempt to make this adjustment, but the comfort of familiar friends and surroundings is very powerful to us all, especially when we are down on our luck. This kind of dramatic change takes great internal will and determination.

I am impressed when I hear of a person who truly wants to make a change. Their resolve for something better is motivating. Many years ago, I listened to the news as a professional baseball player was being interviewed. He had been suspended for drug use, and the interview was taking place several months later as he prepared to make his return to the sport. The interviewer asked the athlete about his plans for his life on the ball team and how he would keep from falling back into drug use. The man replied, "I cannot associate with my friends anymore. I go home after the game instead of hanging out with the guys. I can't go the places I used to go." He went on to describe a total change of life. This kind of commitment has to come from within. Many criminals do not want to change or have no motivation to do so. When that is true, no prison, counselor, or social worker can keep the person from returning to his chosen path.

In Michigan in 1978, long before anyone used the term "postal" to refer to mass murder, and many years before "school shootings" and Columbine became a part of our vocabulary, a 15-year-old boy shot and killed a classmate and wounded a second in the halls of his high school. In our jaded view of school violence these days, the reader might be thinking, "So what? It has happened many times." Yet this is unlike any other story you might hear. This young man provides an exciting case for possibilities. You see, unlike the many other perpetrators of school shootings around the nation, this man is an adult now. He is nearly 40 years old, but he is not in prison. He served several years in a youth detention facility. During that time he earned his high school diploma and began work on a college degree. Four years after the shooting, he was released, and by 1984 he had earned his college degree. He went on to pursue graduate studies, and in 1992 he earned his Ph.D. in mathematics. This young man, so troubled at one time, went on to become a college teacher. By today's standards, society would have been screaming for this young man to be sentenced to life in prison. Fortunately, this boy committed his crime at a time in history when society at least considered the possibility of rehabilitation.

One might suppose that he must not have been that bad of a kid to start with. Yet his background and behaviors were eerily similar to those of other perpetrators of school shootings and even some serial killers. He was obsessed with Hitler and Nazism and he was a loner. His father was cruel to his mother during his early years, and they divorced when he was five. He lived in several homes during his early years and most likely had little stability at home. He brought the gun to school for the specific purpose of shooting one of the two boys who were his victims. After the shooting, his mother cut off contact with him. Somehow, though, this young man, determined by the court to be mentally troubled, rose above his circumstances and has become a productive member of society. This man has proven to me that dramatic change is possible.

Is prison the answer? One possibility I see that may lower recidivism among convicts is creating a more difficult prison life. For the average American, the thought of going to prison is among the worst things that could happen. At the very least, a prison sentence would be a significant embarrassment. For many people in our culture, however, except for the loss of freedom, going to prison is actually a step up on the socioeconomic ladder.

I used to take my students to a state prison in the Atlanta metro area for a tour each year. We toured the clean hallways, saw the library, which was superior to the one on our own campus, and traveled through the recreational facility. My students learned that inmates had regular health care, free meals, and TVs in their cells. These inmates could earn not only a bachelor's degree, but also a master's degree from a nationally known university in Georgia, both fully paid for by state taxpayers. After this tour, I could always count on some student saying, "How do I get in on this plan?" These college students borrowed thousands of dollars and worked very hard to get through college. Many of them didn't have adequate insurance or TVs in their dormitory rooms. Yet these inmates had all these things and could earn both a bachelor's and master's degree for free. Needless to say, some of my students deeply resented this perk of incarceration.

Don't get me wrong. None of my students would have traded their freedom for these perks, and there are certainly many disadvantages to being in prison. The point I am trying to make is that the idea of prison is not an equal deterrent across the culture. For people who come from environments where they cannot, or will not, keep a job and have little to live on, no health care, and no prospects for a better future, this particular prison was not such a bad place to be.

We have come a long way, especially in the South, from the chain gangs of the early 20th century. I would not recommend that we go back to the days where prisoners were treated worse than animals. But there must be something punitive about incarceration. Many states have experimented with boot camps for juveniles rather than sending them to traditional juvenile detention centers, and the results are encouraging. In Arizona, one governor resolved the adult prison overcrowding problem by erecting tent cities for inmates. Their basic needs were met and no cruel living conditions existed. Yet these incarceration camps were constructed and operated at a fraction of the cost of building traditional prisons. Plus, it was not a place to which anyone would want to return. Another state governor removed recreational equipment from the prisons, arguing that they were not supposed to be recreational facilities.

These are all honest attempts, but by far the most promising solution is prevention. As I observed in *Blind-Sided*, poor coping skills and weak social skills contribute to aggressive behavior. I suggest that the best solution to our violent culture is to teach children while they are still young how to deal with life's problems and challenges. Programs that teach children how to problem-solve can be a first step in the prevention of violence.

ENCOURAGEMENT AND SURVIVAL

The story of one victim named Tammy is one of horror, but also one of surviving and overcoming. In 1987 Tammy was minding her own business, on her way to a party where she was supposed to meet her boyfriend for supper. She stopped by a grocery store to buy a dessert that she needed to take to the party. As she parked her car a man approached and said the battery in his car had died and he needed a jump. She attempted to help the man, but he presented a knife and forced her into her vehicle. The man crouched on the floor and forced Tammy to drive to a secluded area, where he robbed her. He then forced her down an embankment near a creek, violently dragging her through the bushes, where he repeatedly raped and sodomized the 20-year-old woman. Tammy tried to escape, but she fell and the perpetrator caught her. She fought back, he stabbed the young woman, and the two struggled for control of the knife. The perpetrator then bit Tammy's hand to gain control of the knife and stabbed her repeatedly, twice slashing her neck. Tammy lay motionless on the ground and the perpetrator thought that she was dead, but then he saw her stir. In his own words later, he said he tried to "put her out of her misery" by strangling her with his belt. When Tammy lost consciousness, he left her for dead and fled. Tammy was not to be defeated. Although seriously wounded, she regained consciousness and stumbled to a nearby road where she flagged down two passersby on motorcycles. She was taken to the hospital, where she underwent surgery for her injuries and was eventually interviewed by authorities.

A composite drawing was constructed based on her description of the assailant. In the meantime, authorities had retrieved a clear handprint from her vehicle that they believed the perpetrator had left as he leaned on her car when he asked her for help. When the composite sketch aired on the news a few days later, a co-worker of the perpetrator realized the man could be the suspect because he had quit his job, changed his appearance, and disappeared. Three weeks after the attack, the perpetrator was arrested in another state and extradited to the state where Tammy lived.

Initially he pleaded not guilty to charges of rape, kidnapping, aggravated battery, and robbery, but after his psychiatric evaluation demonstrated that he was aware of his actions at the time of the crime, the man changed his plea to guilty. At his sentencing, his attorney asked the court for leniency, saying that the man was not the "beast that the victim and her family described him as." I can't imagine what else one has to do in order to be described as a "beast." Fortunately the judge was not swayed by this rhetoric, and just six months after the attack that nearly took Tammy's life, the man was given two life sentences in prison plus 20 years. He was also required to pay several thousand dollars in restitution.

Tammy's story is the substance of one's worst nightmares, only for her it was real. But as horrifying as this story is, one can be encouraged to know that the will to survive is stronger than any perpetrator's hate or weapon. The best part of Tammy's story is that she married the man she was on her way to meet for dinner that evening in 1987 and is now a mother, a wife, and a middle school teacher. I sat and talked with Tammy and, over a glass of iced tea, we laughed and she told me stories about her middle school students, her family, and her children. She also told me about her experience and how she coped with her fear, anger, guilt, and other emotions that are very common in victims of violent crime. The physical wounds have long since healed, but the emotional wounds are still present. Even so, Tammy survived and has refused to allow her experience to control her existence. "Every day I win," she said. "Every day I wake up, I don't necessarily think about it, but I win and he loses. He is in prison." Survivors like Tammy encourage me and convince me of the resilience of the human race.

The many stories in both this book and my first book are more than entertainment. My goal always has been to improve lives and I hope, to save lives. As we discussed how hard it was to measure the impact of my work, one of my FBI Academy friends once told me that there is no way to know how many lives I may have saved through my seminars, speeches, articles, and books. I am confident, just as I know my work as a therapist can help people move toward a more productive life, that my words in these books can be helpful, too. A woman who had read my first book e-mailed me and told me an encouraging story. Her boyfriend exhibited all but one of the symptoms I discussed in *Blind-Sided* that put one at high risk for violent behavior. She told me that in a six-month period he had been the aggressor in two road rage incidents, using mace in one and his fists in another. According to this woman, she had never been able to reach him emotionally and she could not get him to deal with his aggression. I was greatly encouraged with the end of this story. After showing her boyfriend my book and demonstrating through its case studies what could become of such individuals, he was willing to get help. Now in counseling for the first time, he is no longer living in denial of his mental problems and is on his way to a more productive and safer life. My vision of the world is limitless, and my hope for a better world for my children's future is enduring.

CONCLUDING REMARKS

I never like to close a speech, article, or book without providing some sense of hope. The topic of this book is depressing, and when we look at all of the terrifying things going on around the world today, it would be easy to get discouraged. However, the fact is we are surrounded by many more people who are our allies than who threaten us. These people make us laugh, they celebrate with us when we have successes, and they support us when we are struggling. Every day, strangers sit side-by-side on subways, airplanes, and buses. They share roadways and office space. At the very least, most of these people are indifferent to those around them, but I believe that most of us care more than we show. When crises arise, we set aside our differences and rise to the aid of one another.

NOTES

1. " 'I am not the Olympic Park bomber,'" *CNN Online*, *www.cnn.com/US/ 9610/28/jewell.presser/index.html*, October 28, 1996.

2. "Report: Richard Jewell to get more than $500,000 from NBC," *CNN Online*, *www.cnn.com/US/9701/03/olympic.bombing/index.html*, January 3, 1997.

3. " 'I am not the Olympic Park bomber,' " *CNN Online*, *www.cnn.com/US/ 9610/28/jewell.presser/index.html*, October 28, 1996.

4. "FBI chief: 'Major error of judgment' in bombing interview," *CNN Online*, *www.cnn.com/US/9707/28/fbi.olympic.park/*, July 28, 1997.

5. "FBI chief: 'Major error of judgment' in bombing interview," *CNN Online*, *www.cnn.com/US/9707/28/fbi.olympic.park/*, July 28, 1997.

6. "FBI examines evidence found in security guard's home," *CNN Online*, *www.cnn.com/US/9608/02/jewell.search/index.html*, August 3, 1996.

7. "Jewell: 'My name is ruined forever,' " *CNN Online*, *www.cnn.com/US/ 9701/08/jewell.lkl/index.html*, January 8, 1997.

8. "FBI examines evidence found in security guard's home," *CNN Online*, *www. cnn.com/US/9608/02/jewell.search/index.html*, August 3, 1996.

9. "Search warrant turned over to Olympic bombing suspect," *CNN Online*, *www.cnn.com/US/9609/25/olympic.park.bombing/index.html*, September 25, 1996.

10. "Why the government considered Jewell a suspect," *CNN Online*, *www.cnn. com/US/9610/28/jewell.suspect/index.html*, October 28, 1996.

11. "Why the government considered Jewell a suspect," *CNN Online*, *www.cnn. com/US/9610/28/jewell.suspect/index.html*, October 28, 1996.

12. "Why the government considered Jewell a suspect," *CNN Online*, *www.cnn. com/US/9610/28/jewell.suspect/index.html*, October 28, 1996.

13. "Why the government considered Jewell a suspect," *CNN Online, www.cnn.com/US/9610/28/jewell.suspect/index.html,* October 28, 1996.

14. "Why the government considered Jewell a suspect," *CNN Online, www.cnn.com/US/9610/28/jewell.suspect/index.html,* October 28, 1996.

15. "Why the government considered Jewell a suspect," *CNN Online, www.cnn.com/US/9610/28/jewell.suspect/index.html,* October 28, 1996.

16. "Why the government considered Jewell a suspect," *CNN Online, www.cnn.com/US/9610/28/jewell.suspect/index.html,* October 28, 1996.

17. "Friends, former co-workers aroused FBI suspicions of Jewell," *CNN Online, www.cnn.com/US/9610/28/fbi.affidavit/index.html,* October 28, 1996.

18. "Richard Jewell faces cloudy future," *CNN Interactive, www.cnn.com/US/9707/olympic.park.bombing/wrong.man/,* July 1997.

19. "FBI examines evidence found in security guard's home," *CNN Online, www.cnn.com/US/9608/02/jewell.search/index.html,* August 3, 1996.

20. "Richard Jewell faces cloudy future," *CNN Interactive, www.cnn.com/US/9707/olympic.park.bombing/wrong.man/,* July 1997.

21. "FBI chief: 'Major error of judgment' in bombing interview," *CNN Online, www.cnn.com/US/9707/28/fbi.olympic.park/,* July 28, 1997.

22. "Jewell sues New York Post for libel," *CNN Online, www.cnn.com/US/9707/24/briefs/jewell.lawsuit/index.html,* July 24, 1997.

23. "Report: Richard Jewell to get more than $500,000 from NBC," *CNN Online, www.cnn.com/US/9701/03/olympic.bombing/index.html,* January 3, 1997.

24. "FBI examines evidence found in security guard's home," *CNN Online, www.cnn.com/US/9608/02/jewell.search/index.html,* August 3, 1996.

25. " 'I am not the Olympic Park bomber,' " *CNN Online, www.cnn.com/US/9610/28/jewell.presser/index.html,* October 28, 1996.

BIBLIOGRAPHY

Adler, Jerry, and Theodore Gideonse. "'Road rage': We're driven to destruction." *Newsweek* (Internet edition), June 2, 1997.

"Aggressive driver self-test." National Highway Traffic Safety Administration, *www. nhtsa.dot.gov/people/outreach/employer/nets98/pdf_2/Agdriv.pdf*, 1998.

"Aggressive Driving and the Law. A Symposium." National Highway Traffic Safety Administration, *www.nhtsa.dot.gov/search97cgi/s97_cgi.exe*, January 22–23, 1999.

"Aggressive driving fact-tip sheet with talking points." National Highway Traffic Safety Administration, *www.nhtsa.dot.gov/search97/cgi/s97_cgi.exe*, 1998.

" 'Aggressive driving' law is nation's first." *American City & Country,* 114, p. 76, April 1999.

"Air rage." *Reader's Digest*, March 2000, p. 115.

Alter, Jonathan, John McCormick, Mark Miller, and Kevin Peraino. "The death penalty on trial." *Newsweek* (On-line edition), June 12, 2000.

American Psychiatric Association. *Diagnostic and Statistical Manual of Mental Disorders, Fourth Edition Text Revision.* Washington, DC: American Psychiatric Press, 2000.

Anderson, Kevin. "Getting a handle on road rage." *Black Enterprise* (Internet Edition), January 1999.

Bardsley, Marilyn. "Jeffrey Dahmer: Exposed." *www.crimelibrary.com/dahmer/dahmer xposed.htm*. 2001.

Bardsley, Marilyn. "Jeffrey Dahmer: Runaway trail." *www.crimelibrary.com/dahmer/ dahmerevil.htm*. 2001.

Bardsley, Marilyn. "Jeffrey Dahmer: Why." *www.crimelibrary.com/dahmer/dahmer why.htm*. 2001.

BIBLIOGRAPHY

Beck, Melinda. "The sad case of Polly Klaas." *Newsweek*, December 13, 1993.

Bing, Leon. "Homegirls." *Rolling Stone*, April 12, 2001, pp. 76–86.

Cannon, Angie. "In the name of the son." *U.S. News & World Report* (On-line edition), November 15, 1999.

Capozzoli, Thomas K., and R. Steve McVey. *Kids Killing Kids: Managing Violence and Gangs in Schools*. New York: St. Lucie Press, 2000.

Chidley, Joe. "Uncivil aviation." *Canadian Business* (Internet edition), February 21, 2000.

"Children and domestic violence." Family Violence Prevention Fund, *www.fvpf. org/kids/*, 2001.

"Children and family violence: The unnoticed victims." Minnesota Center Against Violence and Abuse, *www.minicava.umn.edu/papers/nzreport.htm*, May 1994.

"Domestic violence and children." Famvi.com, *www.famvi.com/othersts.htm.* 2001.

Douglas, John, and Mark Olshaker. *Mindhunter*. New York: Pocket Books, 1995.

Elder, Larry. "When the bad guy is black." *Human Events* (On-line edition), March 31, 2000.

Emmerman, Michael. "Air travel." *Esquire*, September 1989, pp. 141–142.

"Facts and myths." *Unite for Kids: Helping Kids and Teens Exposed to Violence. www. bmcstage.tvisions.com/understand/facts.html*, 2001.

Fantuzzo, John W., and Wanda K. Mohr. "Prevelance and effects of child exposure to domestic violence." *The Future of Children Journal* 9, no. 3 (1999): 21–32.

Fick, Ana C., John D. Osofsky, and Marva L. Lewis. "Perceptions of violence: Children, parents, and police officers." In *Children in a Violent Society*, ed. Joy D. Osofsky, pp. 261–276. New York: Guilford Press, 1997.

Frankel, Bruce, Alex Tresniowski, Karen Grigsby Bates, Matt Birkbeck, Susan Gray, Margery Sellinger, and Ellen Tumposky. "Stormy skies." *People* (Internet edition), July 31, 2000.

Free, Cathy. "Make their day." *People Weekly* (Internet edition), September 1, 1997.

"Gang members arrested in shooting." *Creative Loafing* (Online edition), *www.creative loafing.com/gwinnett/newsstand/current/n_report.htm*, November 11, 2000.

Garbarino, James, and Kathleen Kostelny. "What children can tell us about living in a war zone." In *Children in a Violent Society*, ed. Joy D. Osofsky, pp. 32–41. New York: Guilford Press, 1997.

"God Hates Fags." *www.godhatesfags.com/main/index.html*, May 3, 2001.

Goldberg, Carl. *Speaking with The Devil: Exploring Senseless Acts of Evil*. New York: Penguin Books, 1996.

Golding, William. *Lord of the Flies*. New York: Perigee Books, 1959.

Goodell, Jeff. "Nathaniel Brazill's last day of school." *Rolling Stone* (On-line edition), October 10, 2000.

Grann, David. "Crimetown USA." *New Republic*, July 10, 2000, pp. 23–31.

Hammer, Joshua. "The 'gay-panic' defense." *Newsweek* (On-line edition), November 8, 1999.

Harrop, Froma. "Abusive parents ruining children's sports." *Providence Journal* (Internet edition), *www.thehollandsentinel.net/stories/071800/opi_ruining.html*, July 18, 2000.

Hayden, Torey. *Murphy's Boy*. New York: Avon Books, 1983.

Hewitt, Bill, Champ Clark, and Amy Mindell. "A life in the balance." *People Weekly*, November 22, 1999, pp. 197–201.

"History and description of Big Brothers, Big Sisters of America." Center for the Study of Violence Prevention, *www.colorado.edu/cspv/blueprints/model/chapt/BBBSAExec.htm*. 1998.

Hood, Ralph, Jr., Bernard Spilka, Bruce Hunsberger, and Richard Gorsuch, *The Psychology of Religion: An Empirical Approach*. 2nd ed. New York: Guilford Press, 1996.

Hornblower, Margot. "The Spokane murders." *Time*, July 17, 2000, pp. 42–44.

"Investing in girls: A 21st century strategy." Office of Juvenile Justice and Prevention, *www.ncjrs.org/html/ojjdp/jjjournal1099/invest2.html*, October 1999.

James, Leon. "Aggressive driving and road rage: Dealing with emotionally impaired drivers." *www.aloha.net/~dyc/testimony.html*, 2001.

James, Leon. "Facts and statistics by Dr. Driving." *www.aloha.net/~dyc/facts.html*, 2001.

James, Leon, and Diane Nahl. "Road Rage and aggressive driving." *www.aloha.net/~dyc/booktoc.html*, 2001.

Jenish, D'Arcy. "Unparalleled evil." *Maclean's* (Internet edition), December 6, 1993.

Johnson, Terry E., and Daniel Shapiro. "A mass murder in Arkansas." *Newsweek*, January 11, 1988, p. 20.

"Judge spares 13-year-old murderer life prison term; sentences him to youth detention until age 21." *Jet* (Internet edition), January 31, 2000.

Keppel, Robert. *Signature Killers*. New York: Pocket Books, 1997.

Kimes, Kent. "Girls in the gang." *Creative Loafing* (On-line edition), *www.atlanta.creativeloafing.com/2000-11-18/cover2.html*, November 18, 2000.

"Kitsch Report." *www.time.com/time/asia/asia/travel_watch/980907/kitsch_report.html*, September 7, 1998.

KlaasKids Foundation. "The Polly Klaas story." *www.klaaskids.org/pg-stry.htm*. 1996.

Lafferty, Elaine. "Final outrage." *Time*, October 7, 1996, p. 64.

Leo, John. "The top ten victims." *U.S. News & World Report*, January 31, 2000, p. 16.

Meyer, Michael. "Flying wildly out of control." *Newsweek* (Internet edition), November 29, 1999.

Miedzian, Myriam. *Boys Will Be Boys: Breaking the Link Between Masculinity and Violence*. New York: Anchor, 1991.

Milgram, Stanley. "Behavioral study of obedience." *Journal of Abnormal and Social Psychology* 67 (1963): 371–378.

Moffatt, Gregory K. *Blind-Sided: Homicide Where It Is Least Expected*. Westport, CT: Praeger, 2000.

Morgan, Len. "Deplorable air rage." *Flying* (Internet edition), September 1998.

BIBLIOGRAPHY

Nack, William, and Lester Munson. "Out of control." *Sports Illustrated* (Internet edition), July 24, 2000.

National Association of Sports Officials, *www.naso.org/benefits/sos.htm#Assault ProtectionProgram.* 2000.

National Institute of Justice. "Crime in the United States 1999," Washington, DC: Government Printing Office, 1999.

Norris, Joel. *Serial Killers.* New York: Anchor Books, 1988.

Osofsky, Joy D. "The impact of violence on children." *The Future of Children Journal* 9, no. 3 (1999): 33–49.

"Overview of Big Brothers, Big Sisters of America," Center for the Study of Violence Prevention, *www.colorado.edu/cspv/blueprints/model/ten_Big.htm.* 1998.

"Psychiatric effects of media violence." American Psychiatric Association, *www.psych. org/public_info/media_violence.htm,* October 1998.

"Put the brakes on aggressive driving." National Highway Traffic Safety Administration, *www.nhtsa.dot.gov/search97/cgi/s97_cgi.exe.* 2001.

Ressler, Robert K., and Tom Shachtman. *I Have Lived in the Monster: Inside the Minds of the World's Most Notorious Serial Killers.* New York: St. Martin's Press, 1997.

Ripley, Amanda, and Helen Gibson. "When killer boys grow up," *Time* (Internet edition), January 22, 2001.

Robinson, Thomas N., Marta L. Wilde, Lisa C. Navrocruz, K. Farish Haydel, and Ann Varady. "Effects of reducing children's television and video game use on aggressive behavior." *Archives of Pediatrics and Adolescent Medicine,* 2001, 155, pp. 17–23.

Scott, Shirley Lynn. "The death of James Bulger: Tragic child abduction caught on tape: Jon Venables." *www.crimelibrary.com/classics3/bulger/8.htm.* 2000.

Scott, Shirley Lynn. "Ten-year-old suspects." *www.crimelibrary.com/classics3/bulger/4.htm.* 2000.

"Seeing red over air rage." *Consumer Reports Travel Letter* (Internet edition), February 1999.

"Signposts pointed to possible bloodshed at U of WA; colleagues afraid of doctor." *In the Line of Duty, www.lineofduty.com/blotter/july00/jul-1-7/7100-9.htm,* July 2000.

Silverstein, Marilyn. "Pair of alleged 'hit men' confess to slaying rabbi's wife." *Jewish Bulletin News* (Online Edition), *www.jewishsf.com/bk000505/ushitmen. shtml,* May 5, 2000.

Simon, Robert. *Bad Men Do What Good Men Dream.* Washington, DC: American Psychiatric Press, 1996.

Smithson, Carla. "When passengers explode." *Report/Newsmagazine (Alberta Edition)* (Internet edition), February 7, 2000.

"Taken in the night." *People Weekly* (Internet edition), October 25, 1993.

Tjaden, Patricia, and Nancy Thoennes. "Prevalence, incidence, and consequences of violence against women: Findings from the national violence against women survey." Washington, DC: U.S. Department of Justice, November 1998.

"Traffic Safety Facts." Washington, DC: U.S. Department of Transportation/National Highway Traffic Safety Administration, 1994.

Underwood, Nora. "Murder in America." *Maclean's*, January 11, 1988, p. 27.

U.S. Department of Justice. *Uniform Crime Reports*, Washington, DC: Government Printing Office, 1997.

Vest, Jason, Warren Cohen, and Mike Tharp. "Road rage." *U.S. News & World Report* (Internet edition), June 2, 1997.

"What Is domestic violence" Centers for Disease Control and Prevention, *www.cdc.gov/ncipc/dvp/fivpt/spotlite/home.htm*. February 2001.

"Who killed Matthew Shepard?" *Christianity Today* (On-line edition), December 7, 1998.

INDEX

abandonment, 24, 25, 32
abduction, 40, 44, 45, 46, 47, 48, 112, 204
abnormal behavior, 83, 116, 142
abortion, 174, 175, 177, 187, 190, 195
Abraham, Nathaniel, xi, 24–35, 59
abstract reasoning, 51, 52, 55, 57, 58
abuse, vii, viii, 12, 13, 20, 28, 29, 41, 42, 49, 59, 79, 81, 82, 83, 84, 85, 86, 87, 88, 89, 90, 91, 92, 93, 94, 102, 106, 108, 115, 116, 127, 149, 204
acculturated behavior, 154
acid, 108, 110, 111
acquittal, 31, 114, 181, 198, 223, 224
acting inward, 88
acute mental disorders, 127
Adams, Cherica, 174–182
addict, 32, 106
Attention Deficit Hyperactivity Disorder (ADHD), 33
affair, sexual, 1, 14, 166, 170, 175, 188
affiliation, 25, 32, 66, 67, 68, 72, 73, 74, 75, 188, 192

African-American gangs, 68
aggravated robbery, 198
aggression, vii, viii, ix, 1, 2, 3, 4, 5, 6, 7, 8, 11, 12, 13, 16, 17, 21, 22, 23, 27, 32, 48, 49, 52, 58, 59, 79, 85, 87, 88, 91, 93, 98, 100, 141, 142, 145, 147, 149, 154, 159, 160, 161, 168, 176, 187, 193, 200, 229. *See also* aggressive behavior
aggressive behavior, 4, 5, 6, 7, 8, 13, 14, 16, 21, 23, 30, 39, 41, 42, 48, 49, 50, 54, 63, 84, 88, 101, 143, 146, 153, 228. *See also* analysis of aggressive behavior
aggressive driving, 151–157; self-test for, 157
aggressive thinking, viii
AIDS virus, 195
air rage, 23, 141–149
Alaska Airlines, 144, 145
alcohol, 8, 27, 33, 75, 82, 84, 90, 101, 108, 113, 115, 143, 145, 146, 149, 214
alcoholism, 5, 29, 41, 85, 108, 158

INDEX

Allport, Gordon, 194
Alomar, Roberto, 21
altercations, 86, 87, 89, 151, 152, 155
Alzheimer's Disease, 12
Amalekites, 195
American Airlines, 144
Amnesty International, 31
amphetamines, 8
analysis of aggressive behavior, 5, 16, 24, 40, 208, 210, 215, 218, 221
anonymity, 45, 48, 153, 154, 218
antidepressant, 130
anti-Semitic, 194, 198, 199
antisocial behavior, 11
apathy, 89, 107
Archer, Crystal Gail, 1–2
arson, 27, 41, 136
Asian, 22, 64, 68, 107, 128, 143, 199
assassination, 177, 182
athletes, 75, 158, 173
Atlanta Project, 74
attachment disorder, 48–49
Auschwitz, 189
autonomy, 88, 90, 153
autopsy, 7, 40, 44, 159, 191, 208, 224
ax, 83, 98

Barton, Mark, 101, 131
Batcho, Mark, 172
battered women, 93
Baumhammers, Richard, 199
beat/beating, 1, 3, 20, 26, 44, 46, 64, 69, 72, 80, 82, 85, 88, 158, 159, 167, 171, 193, 194, 196, 197
beating in, 67, 69, 72
bed-wetting, 49, 88
Bianchi, Kenneth, 100
Bible, 9, 193, 195
Big Brothers/Big Sisters of America (BBBSA), 75
biological theories, 4–8
bipolar disorder, 136
blame, 9, 33, 34, 46, 81, 93, 115, 123, 124, 127, 147, 188, 217

Bloodettes, 76
Bloods, 64, 69, 76
body piercing, 67
Bonaparte, Napoleon, 180
boot camps, 227
Bootle Strand, 42
Bosnia, 70
Boy Scouts of America, 65
brain, 5, 6, 7, 12, 110, 116, 151, 159, 224
Branch Davidian, 191
Brazill, Nathaniel, 51–60
British Airways, 148
Brokaw, Tom, 219
Bruce, John David, 98–99
brutality, 40, 101, 191, 193, 196
Buddhist, 133
Bulger, James, 42–48
Bullock, Eric, 171
bully, 26, 42, 48, 73
Bundy, Ted, 98, 100, 101, 102, 103, 115, 159
burglary, 27, 66, 102, 113, 135
Bush, George W., 83–84

California Highway Patrol, 113
cannibalism, 12, 107, 110, 115, 116
Capitol, U.S., killings in, 12, 115
carjacking, 167
Carolina Panthers, 174, 178, 179
Carpenter, John, 98
Carruth, Rae, 173–182
Caucasian, 72, 87, 105
cause-effect relationship, 4, 58, 97
Centennial Olympic Games, bombing, 195, 218–219, 222
Center for Disease Control and Prevention (CDC), 86
Center for the Study and Prevention of Violence, 75
Center on Juvenile and Criminal Justice, 32
Chen, Jian, 127–129
child molestation, 109, 110

Children Against Road Rage (CARR), 157

choking, 41, 48

Christian Identity movement, 195

civil orders, 93

civil rights 31, 198

Civil War, 68

Clinton, Bill, 21

cognitive function, 23, 33, 34, 35, 45, 59, 88, 214

collectivism, 22

Columbine, 40, 57, 100, 226

comorbidity, 93

competition, 22, 69, 146, 158, 206

concentration camp, 189

congestion, traffic, 153, 155

conjugal violence. *See* domestic violence

conscience, 47, 101, 114, 115, 197

consequences, 11, 28, 50, 155, 225

conspiracies, 223

contamination, 207, 210

contempt, 21, 23, 106, 114, 182

Continental Airlines, 144

control, 4, 5, 6, 14, 45, 67, 70, 79, 80, 88, 89, 99, 107, 124, 142, 143, 144, 147, 150, 151, 160, 180, 189, 206, 207, 213, 228, 229

Cooper, Desiree, xi, 34

cope/coping skills, 8, 12, 13, 17, 49, 50, 52, 55, 87, 90, 92, 126, 127, 130, 142, 143, 148, 149, 160, 161, 183, 188, 189, 228

corruption, 171

Costin, Michael, 158–159

counseling, vii, viii, 14, 21, 26, 60, 80, 81, 128, 132, 157, 229

counselors, 26, 48, 53, 72, 75, 89, 225, 226

criminal justice system, 28

Crips, 64, 69

cross-bow, 152

Cruz, Kevin William, 134–135

culture, vii, 7, 8, 9, 10, 11, 12, 13, 19, 20, 21, 22, 23, 34, 35, 59, 63, 64, 69, 74, 75, 76, 99, 114, 128, 143, 153, 154, 160, 201, 225, 227, 228

Cunanan, Andrew, 100–101

Dachau, 189

Dahmer, Jeffrey, ix, 2, 100, 114–117

Davila, Jose and Josefa, 20

Davis, Richard Allen, 111–117

deception, 21, 179, 203

defensive driving, 149, 155–156, 157

dehumanizing, 46, 109

Deitz, Parker, 133

delays, 49, 50, 143, 145, 146, 147, 148, 149

delinquency, 24, 25, 26, 28, 29, 64, 89, 90

Delta Airlines, 124, 145

delusions, 12, 115, 132, 133, 192, 193

dementia, 12

denial, 46, 94, 142, 143, 149, 230

depersonalization, 40, 188, 190, 224

depression, 6, 33, 70, 88, 90, 91, 128, 130, 230

deprivation, ix, 34

desensitization, 11, 40, 46, 71, 101, 115, 188, 191

Desert Storm, 196

discrimination, 194

disease, 12, 13, 90, 141

disgruntled, as factor in aggression, 121, 127

disguise, 135

dismember, 107, 108, 109, 110

displacing, 48, 190

disruptive passenger, 145, 149

dissatisfaction, 127, 149

distress, 14, 89, 90, 191, 196

disturbed, vii, 41, 115, 192

diversion, 144, 145, 149

DNA, 83, 104, 105, 135, 207; and genetics, 5

doctrines, 192

doli incapax, 39, 40, 45

domestic violence, 70, 79–94, 135, 136
Douglas, John, 86, 218, 208
drive-by shootings, 67, 69, 71
Drug Enforcement Administration (DEA), 167
drug proliferation, 70
Diagnostic and Statistical Manual of Mental Disorders, Fourth Edition Text Revision (DSM IV-TR), 49, 101, 123
DUI, 113
dysfunction, 7, 9, 50, 79, 86, 101, 102, 115, 116, 126, 133, 192
dysfunctional behavior, 32, 35, 116; dysfunctional thinking, 12, 17

efficacy, 76, 90
egocentric, 23, 35, 49, 50, 52, 55, 182
Emmerman, Michael, 146
empathy, 50, 51, 75, 89, 115, 142, 195
empowerment, 32, 75
epileptic seizures, 6
ethnically diverse gangs, 65
evil, 23, 35, 40, 52, 59, 85, 99, 111, 192, 217. *See also* malevolence
expectations, 14–16
explosion, 6, 219, 220, 221, 222
extermination camps, 189
externalize, 8, 22, 23, 88, 91

"failure to bond," 49
Family and Children's Services (DFACS), 93, 193
FBI National Academy, 121, 211, 223, 225
Federal Aviation Association (FAA), 145
Federal Bureau of Investigation (FBI), 97, 99, 100, 107, 110, 122, 150, 168, 171, 171, 176, 194, 196, 201, 208, 210, 219, 221, 222, 223
Federal Highway Association (FHA), 155

female gang, 66–67
Ferguson Enterprises, 130
Field Investigative Team, 14
"fight-or-flight" behavior, 5
fines, 148, 149
firearms, 11, 16, 24, 27, 31, 58, 67, 71, 107, 154, 211, 223
firefighters, 135, 136
flight attendant, 143, 144, 145, 148, 160
Folk Nation (gang), 65
forensic psychology, 116, 178, 218
Free Market Party, 199
Freeh, Louis, 222
Freud, Sigmund, viii, 63
frontal lobe, 6
frustration, viii, 8, 13, 20, 46, 50, 55, 56, 126, 142, 148, 153, 154, 160, 170, 172
frustration-aggression hypothesis, 13
fundamentalist, 194
Furrow, Bufford, 198–199

Gacy, John Wayne, 85, 100
Gage, Phineas, 5–6
Gains, Paul, 171–172
"gangsta-lettes," 67
Garcia-Bonilla, Raul, 73
gays, 109, 195, 196, 197; bashing, 65, 196; panic, 197, 198
genetics, 5; and DNA, 83, 104, 105, 135, 207
Georgia Bureau of Investigation (GBI), 169
Girls Scouts of America, 65
Goldberg, Carl, 19, 23, 116, 191
Golding, William, 39, 40, 59
Goodman, April, 168–169
graffiti, 64, 67, 68, 74, 199
Grand Inquisition, 195
Green River killer, 104
Greene, Ronnie, 24, 27–34
grievances, 122, 125
Grunow, Barry, 53–60

guns: BB, 26; 9mm, 15, 132, 134; 12–gauge shotgun, 136; .22 caliber, 27, 28, 29, 31, 200; .25 caliber, 54; .38 caliber, 172

Haggitt, Rodger, 128–129
Hamilton, Thomas, 100, 123
hand signs, 69, 74
handguns, 71, 134, 197, 213
Hardwick, Kenneth, 204–205
hedonism, 111, 114, 141, 143, 161
hedonistic, 23, 35, 100, 102, 142, 146
Hegel, Georg, 23
Hell's Angels, 65
helplessness, 49, 88, 89, 126, 145, 147, 148
Henderson, Russell, 196–198
Hills, John, 158
Hirschbeck, John, 21
Hispanic, 65, 68, 73, 75, 91, 154. *See also* Latino
Hitler, Adolf, 226
Holocaust, 189
holy war, 187
Home Safe Project, 75
homophobia, 196
homosexual, 85, 87, 110, 195, 196, 197, 198
hopelessness, 22, 40, 46, 63, 64
hormones, 7
hostages, 71, 200
House of Lords, 46
humiliate, 50, 88, 89, 107
hypoglycemia, 8
hypothalamus, 7

identity, 19, 20, 48, 64, 65, 75, 106, 135
ideology, 195
immaturity, 26, 90, 155, 173
immigration law, 199
impairment, 33
impeachment, 20
impediments, 153, 156, 157

impersonal, 154
incapacitated, 87, 110, 213
individualism, 22, 23, 143, 161
inhibitions, 8, 145, 214
initiation, 65, 66, 67, 69, 73
innate, 5
intellectual deficits. *See* cognitive function
intelligence, 102. *See also* congitive function
interference, 90, 143, 144, 195, 198
internalize, 8, 22, 88, 91
International Transport Worker's Federation, 145
internet, 58, 165, 166, 188
interpret/interpretations, viii, 14, 16, 43, 49, 179, 193, 203, 208, 209, 216
intervene/intervention, 23, 24, 26, 27, 28, 29, 32, 33, 34, 41, 43, 73, 74, 75, 76, 87, 88, 92, 93, 94, 100, 108, 132, 149,.217
invincibility, 101, 110, 153, 174, 180
IQ, 26, 33, 34
Irish, 68
irresponsible, 9, 32, 147
irritability, 6, 90, 145, 188
Italian, 68

Jackson, Danny, 15
Jacob, Courtney Duvall, 169
James, Jesse, 100
James, Leon, 153, 157
Japan, 12, 22, 98, 148
jealous/jealousy, 58, 81, 82, 177, 180, 208, 212
Jewell, Richard, 219–223
Jews/Jewish, 10, 68, 189, 190, 191, 194, 198, 199, 200, 201
Johns Manville, 124
Joseph, Jennifer, 104, 105
Junta, Thomas, 158–159
justification/justify, 10, 11, 12, 16, 23, 88, 107, 122, 123, 124, 134, 136,

147, 154, 188, 189, 190, 193, 194, 195
juvenile: court, 9, 33; crime, 9, 66; detention, 1, 33, 60, 227; facility, 48; prison, 168

Kaiser Aluminum Corporation, 103, 104
Kemper, Edmund, 2, 86, 100
Keppel, Robert, 216, 218
kidnapping, 113, 114, 165, 198, 204, 229
Klaas, Polly, 111–114
knife, 2, 7, 69, 72, 86, 112, 213, 228
Krakow, 191, 201
Kroner, Robert, 172
Ku Klux Klan, 65, 68

Lake, Leonard, 100
Laotian, 109, 110
latent exposure, 93
Latino, 72. See also Hispanic
layoff, 114, 126
Lee, Henry, 178
Lewinsky, Monica, 21
Liverpool, 41, 42; "Liverpool 38," 46
lobotomy, 6
loners, 192, 195, 226
Lucas, Henry Lee, 85

magical thinking, 51, 55, 58
maladjustment, 89
malevolence, 23, 24, 111, 114, 115, 116. See also evil
management, 93, 125, 132, 173, 211
managers, 124, 125, 126, 133, 134, 135, 144, 160
manipulate, viii, 49, 75, 80, 102, 111, 190
Mannington Carpets, 124
Manson, Charles, 137
marijuana, 144, 178
Martinez, Ramiro, 7
Martinez, Richardo, 154
mass murder, ix, 8, 100, 101, 121–137

masturbation, 108, 110
McBurnett, Sara, 152
McDonald's, 169, 200
McGinn, Ricky, 83–84
McKinney, Aaron, 196–198
McVeigh, Timothy, 122, 190, 191, 195–196
mental disorder, 5, 6, 17, 109, 111, 127, 133, 179, 199, 230
mental health, 12, 26, 117, 123, 131, 132, 133, 134, 197; illness, 6, 12, 13, 32, 45, 100, 101, 114, 116, 122, 123, 130, 133, 136, 169, 170, 178, 187, 192, 198, 200, 215, 227; instability, 167, 169
mental hospital, 179
mentally: condemning, 157; disabled, 27, 30, 32; stable, 223
mentoring, 75
methamphetamine, 197
Milgram, Stanley, 10–11, 190
Miller, Alan Eugene, 130–131
Miller, Kenneth, 129–130
minority, 72, 74, 87
Miranda rights, 30, 33, 219
misinterpret/misinterpreted, 12, 154, 177
mob, 76, 166, 171, 172
modus operandi (MO), 216
molestation, 84, 86, 109, 110, 113, 225;
Mothers Against Drunk Driving (MADD), 157
motivate/motivation, xi, 57, 74, 75, 89, 110, 111, 114, 115, 117, 123, 126, 149, 198; 216, 226
motives, 1, 17, 46, 57, 98, 101, 103, 107, 110, 113, 136, 153, 168, 173, 176, 177, 178, 178, 180, 182, 204, 206, 209, 210, 212, 213, 221
motorcycle: gangs, 65; shop, 15
MP-5 machine-gun, 150
Muhammad, Muhsin, 179
multitasking, 155

Murrah Federal Building, 122, 190, 195–196
My Lai, 194

NAACP, 31
Nahl, Diane, 153
National Association of Sports Officials, 160
National Guard, 103, 105
Navies, Hannibal, 178
Nazism, 65, 189, 190, 226
NBC, 219, 222
necrophile, 110
neo Nazi, 65
nervous breakdown, 8
neuropathology, 7
neurotransmitters, 8
National Highway Traffic Safety Administration (NHTSA), 151, 154, 156, 157
nicotine, 145
Niemoller, Martin, 189, 190
Nietzsche, Friedrich, 107
Nixon, Richard, 189
normalized, abnormal situations and behaviors, 69, 83,142, 188
nurturing, 48, 125, 126, 127, 141

Oakland County Children's Village, 28
Occupational Safety and Health Association (OSHA), 125, 133
Ohio State University, 108
organized crime, 167, 171
Orwell, George, 39
Osofsky, Joy, 90, 92

paranoid schizophrenia, 199, 200
parenting, 87, 88
passenger behavior, 143, 145
passive-aggressive, 142, 154, 195
pathology, 128
phencyclidine (PCP), 8
peer: group, 8, 19, 32, 64, 72, 73, 74, 75, 89, 90, 91; mediator, 52; trademarks, 67

Penn State University, 22
People Nation, 65
personal space, 148
personality, 3, 5, 6, 7, 101, 114, 208, 213
personality disorder, 101, 169
Phelps, Fred, 196
phobias, 88, 91
physical reactions, 88, 89
physiology, 19, 24, 33, 35, 146
Pickney, Waine, 14–16
pistol, 53, 54, 58, 129, 130, 150, 156, 172, 175. See also guns
pitchfork, 98
poison, 101, 136, 199
Post Airgas, 131
post office/postal worker, 13, 97, 100, 121, 135, 198, 226
postmortem, 107, 116
post-traumatic stress disorder (PTSD), 70, 88, 90, 91
power center, 110
powerlessness, 40, 56, 88, 153
predictability, 32, 48, 49, 63, 97, 99
pregnant, 9, 168, 170, 171, 174, 175, 176, 177, 179, 182
prejudice, 194
prevention, 13, 67, 74, 75, 76, 156, 223, 228
priests, 80
probability, 98, 212, 216
problem-solving, 49, 50, 55, 58, 88, 89, 127, 213
profilers/profiling, 99, 103, 107, 194, 205–208, 210, 211, 215, 216, 218, 220
profiles, 99, 102, 104, 166, 206, 218, 220, 221, 223
prostitute/prostitution, 26, 32, 98, 103, 104, 105, 106, 107, 117, 211
provocation, 5, 159
psychiatrists, 33, 34, 133, 169

psychological: contracts, 13, 14; defenses, 187, 188–192, 200; theories, 4, 12–14, 17
psychosociological need, 19

Quantico, Virginia, 211

rabbi, 9, 80, 179, 171, 194
racial gangs, 64–65
racism, 64, 65, 200
Rainey, Robin, 72–73
Ramsey, JonBenet, 206–207
rape, 2, 9, 73, 83, 84, 85, 102, 213, 215, 225, 228, 229
rapist, 104, 213, 216
rationalize, 23, 47, 48, 59, 122, 123, 142, 143, 149, 159, 188, 189–190, 192, 194, 196
reactive attachment disorder (RAD), 48–49
regression, 90
rehabilitation, 35, 72, 115, 225, 226
resentment, 13, 87, 125, 147
resilience 92, 229
respect, 19, 56, 64, 74, 75, 103, 125, 129
Ressler, Robert, 208, 218
retribution, 10, 154, 206
revenge, 132, 167, 169, 180
Revolutionary War, 68
Riddle, Jeffrey, 172
righteous, 187, 192, 193, 200
risk, 27, 57, 60, 64, 75, 84, 87, 89, 90, 92, 93, 99, 115, 122, 126, 127, 129, 145, 157, 166, 206, 211, 218, 225, 229; assessment, 121; taking, 88
road rage, 23, 141, 142, 149–157, 229
Reserve Officers Training Camp (ROTC), 75
Rowanda, 70
Ruby Ridge, 196
"ruby satellite," 12, 115
Rudolph, Robert Eric, 195

sanity, 133
Sauls, Willie, 14–16
schizophrenia, 12, 25, 115, 130, 133, 199, 200
school shootings, 11, 51, 52, 100, 210, 226
Secret Service, 38, 192
self-awareness, 149
self-blame, 88
self-control, 25, 91
self-destructive, 41
self-esteem, 88, 91, 160
self-examine, 19, 22, 23
self-image, 88
self-justification, 23, 154, 187–188, 189, 194, 200
self-perpetuating, 64
self-protection, 129, 171
self-reliance, 22
self-seeking, 49, 142
self-serving, 115
selfish, 35, 82, 141
semen, 84
serial killers/predators, ix, 47, 85, 86, 92, 94, 97–117, 122, 215, 216, 226
Seventh Day Adventist, 103
sex in, 67, 69
sexist, 122
sexual harassment, viii
Shackleford, Charles, 177, 179
shame, 22, 23, 46, 88, 128
Shepard, Matthew, 196–198
shipyard, 134, 135
shotgun, 27, 126, 135, 136, 211, 212, 213, 214
signature of crimes, 216
Simmons, Ronald, 84–85, 122
Simpson, O.J., 223, 224
skeletons, 108, 110
Skinheads, 65
sledge hammer, 193
sleep disturbances, 70, 90
smokers, 145
Smoll, Frank, 160

social gangs, 64

social skills, 5, 12, 13, 127, 192, 228

socialization, 192

sociological, 4, 17, 19, 22, 32, 68;theories, 8–12

sociopathology, 101, 102

sodomized, 85, 228

somatic complaints, 91

Spann, Gina Lynn, 170

speeding, 150, 151, 155, 156, 188, 224, 225

Spirit Airline, 144

sports rage, 157–160

sportsmanship, 158; training programs, 160;

spree killer, 85, 100, 101, 116, 122

stalkers, 13, 99

Stanford University, 21

steroids, 8

stress, 8, 70, 89, 94, 142, 127, 128, 146, 148, 156

suicide, 22, 58, 129, 136, 170, 187, 299

"suicide by cop," 134

supervisors, 125, 126, 128, 132, 210

"Sur 13," 72

swastikas, 65, 199

Special Weapons and Tactics (SWAT), 7, 130, 223

Swissair, 145, 146, 148

synagogue, 171, 199

tagger gangs, 64

tailgate, 151, 152, 154, 156, 157

Tate-LaBianca, 137

tattoos, 65, 67, 68, 72, 74

Taylor, Ronald, 199–200

Tennessee Safety and Health Council, 124

terminate, 35, 123

terrorism/terrorists, 136, 187, 188, 190, 191, 194, 195, 196, 200, 226

testosterone, 7, 8

therapists, vii, 40, 49, 80, 92, 93, 229

therapy, 40, 48, 80, 82, 93, 208

Thompson, Robert, 41–48, 59, 60

threaten, 2, 3, 4, 12, 27, 28, 58, 97, 124, 132, 136, 142, 143, 144, 175, 176, 177, 178, 180, 188, 213, 230

threats, 11, 56, 58, 59, 80, 85, 121, 129, 130, 132, 134, 143, 151, 172, 180, 188, 192, 220, 225

"three strikes" law, 114

torture, 9, 20, 40, 46, 80, 85, 107, 108, 111, 113, 115, 116, 193

totem, 109

trade unions, 66, 190

traffic congestion, 153, 155

trauma, vii, 91, 115, 151, 190

treatment, 6, 10, 22, 34, 92, 93, 125, 189

trigger, 33, 34, 55, 58, 72, 85, 154, 172, 200

triggerman, 176, 177

tumor, 7

turf, 63, 71, 74

undercover, 14, 15, 166, 168, 182

Uniform Crime Reports, 97

University of Mississippi, 128

University of Texas, 7

University of Washington, 138

University of Wyoming, 197

U.S. Advisory Board on Child Abuse and Neglect, 91

U.S. Airways, 124

U.S. Constitution, 35

U.S. Department of Justice, 97

U.S. Department of Transportation, 151

Uyesugi, Bryan, 131–134

vandalism, viii, 9, 70, 74

Vatos Locos 72–73

Venables, Jon, 41–48, 59–60

Versache, Gianni, 101

"veteranos," 65

video games, 21, 51, 170, 178

Viet Cong, 194
Viet Nam, 194
violence risk, 121
violent: behavior, ix, 6, 8, 10, 12, 14, 42, 63, 88, 98, 123, 159, 188, 191, 211, 218, 225, 229; crime, 8, 9, 16, 67, 91, 218, 224, 225, 229; culture, 228; fans, 160; gangs, 64, 65, 68, 69, 70; passengers, 148; reaction, 197

Waco, 191, 196
warning cards, 148
warning signs, 3, 137
Watergate, 180
Waterloo, 180
Watkins, Van Brett, 174–181
weapons, 7, 11, 12, 15, 16, 26, 27, 29, 30, 32, 33, 54, 56, 57, 63, 66, 67, 70, 71, 72, 74, 101, 124, 129, 130, 134, 135, 136, 150, 151, 154, 156, 157, 159, 198, 208, 210, 213, 214, 216, 229, 233
Westinghouse Corporation, 124
Weston, Russell, 12, 115
white supremacist, 65, 194, 198
Whitman, Charles, 7–8
Williams, Fred, 135–136
workplace shootings, 100
World War II, 10, 189, 190

Xerox Corporation, 131–134

Yale University, 10
Yates, Robert, 102–107, 117

Zaire, 70

About the Author

GREGORY K. MOFFATT has been a college professor for 17 years and in private practice as a therapist, specializing in children, since 1987. He has addressed hundreds of audiences, including law enforcement professionals, parenting groups, and schools on the topic of homicide risk assessment, and he regularly lectures at the FBI Academy at Quantico, Virginia. He is also a Diplomate with the American College of Forensic Examiners. He writes a regular column in a local newspaper addressing families and children, and he consults with businesses in regard to violence risk assessment and prevention.